30°   45°   60°   75°   90°   105°   120°   135°   150°   165°   180°   90°

75°

Arctic Circle

60°

RWAY

SWEDEN
FINLAND

Oslo
Stockholm   EST.

MARK   LAT.
LITH.
POLAND   BELARUS

GERMANY
CZ.REP.   SLVK.
AUS.   HUNG.   ROM.
ITZ.   CRO.   MOLD.
ITALY   YUGO.   BUL.
Rome   GEORGIA
GREECE   Istanbul
Athens   TURKEY   ARM.
lgiers   AZER.
TUNISIA

LIBYA

EGYPT

NIGER   CHAD

NIGERIA   CEN.
Lagos   CAMEROON   AFR. REP.

GABON   CONGO   ZAIRE

ANGOLA   ZAMBIA

ZIMBABWE

BOTSWANA   MOZAMBIQUE

NAMIBIA
Johannesburg

SOUTH
AFRICA

Cape Town

ANTARCTICA

RUSSIA

Moscow

UKRAINE

KAZAKHSTAN

UZBEKISTAN
TURKMENISTAN
SYRIA   Baghdad
ISRAEL   IRAQ   IRAN
Cairo   JORDAN
AFGHANISTAN

SAUDI
ARABIA   OMAN

PAKISTAN   Delhi   NEPAL

ERITREA   YEMEN

SUDAN

ETHIOPIA

SOMALIA

UGANDA   KENYA

TANZANIA

MADAGASCAR

KYRG.
TAJIK.

MONGOLIA

CHINA

Beijing   NORTH
KOREA
SOUTH

Bombay   INDIA

Calcutta

Tropic of Cancer

BURMA
(MYANMAR)

THAILAND
CAM-
BODIA   VIETNAM

SRI LANKA

MALAYSIA
Singapore

Jakarta   INDONESIA

Shanghai

TAIWAN

HONG
KONG

Manila

PHILIPPINES

Equator

JAPAN
Tokyo

75°

60°

45°

30°

15°

0°

15°

PAPUA
NEW GUINEA

AUSTRALIA

Tropic of Capricorn

Sydney

Melbourne   Auckland

NEW
ZEALAND

Antarctic Circle

75°

A-510000-279   4-4-6
©1992 Rand McNally & Co.

30°

45°

60°

15°

30°

45°

60°

75°

Kilometers   0   1000   2000   3000   Km.
Statute Miles   0   1000   2000   3000   Mi.

30°   45°   60°   75°   90°   105°   120°   135°   150°   165°   180°   90°

NATURAL WONDERS
OF THE WORLD

LONGMEADOW
PRESS

Writers: Dr John Baxter, Dr Peter Clarkson,
Dr Elizabeth Cruwys, Dr Beau Riffenburgh
Copy Editor: Virginia Langer

World locator maps © The Automobile Association
1995.
Reference maps and endpapers :
© 1995 Rand McNally & Company.
Mountain High Maps Image pages 6 and 7 copyright ©
Digital Wisdom Inc.

Published by Longmeadow Press, 201 High Ridge
Road, Stamford, CT 06904.

Published by AA Publishing (a trading name of
Automobile Association Developments Limited, whose
registered office is Norfolk House, Priestley Road,
Basingstoke, Hampshire RG24 9NY;
registered number 1878835).

ISBN 0-681-10496-1

First Longmeadow Press Edition

0 9 8 7 6 5 4 3 2 1

The contents of this book are believed correct at the
time of printing. Nevertheless, the publishers cannot be
held responsible for any errors or omissions or for
changes in the details given in this book or for the
consequences of any reliance on the information
provided in the same.

Colour separation by Fotographics Ltd
Printed and bound by Edicoes ASA, Portugal

CONTENTS

*Title page: Victoria Falls, Zimbabwe
(Tony Stone/Ian Murphy).*

*This page: the Mittens, Monument Valley, USA
(Bruce Coleman Ltd/Jules Cowan).*

*Next page: the Guillin Hills, China
(PowerStock).*

NATURAL WONDERS OF THE WORLD

THE Earth is one of nine planets that orbit the sun, just one of millions of stars in our galaxy, the Milky Way. There are, in turn, millions of galaxies in the universe. What, then, could possibly be special about our world?

Looking ever upwards and outwards, humankind has only just begun the great adventure into Space. In these times of rapid technological advance it is important that we do not lose sight of the fact that it is not long since whole continents on earth were more or less unexplored. In fact, much of the ocean floor is still a complete mystery to us. All one needs to do is turn through the pages of this book to see that aspects of the Earth are truly special, and that

there are places of exceptional beauty, majesty and splendour, and the life it supports can be extraordinary. From the Grand Canyon, the almost incomprehensibly vast gorge in the Arizona Desert scored more than a mile deep by the Colorado River, to the Ross Ice Shelf, the world's largest sheet of floating ice, or the aurorae, the glorious lights coming from collisions of particles in the outer atmosphere, the natural wonders of this planet are virtually limitless. Indeed, this book can show but a selected few of the wonders that surround us; there are many more, large and small, animal, vegetable and mineral, that have not been included, and new discoveries are made all the time.

Yet many of our natural wonders are in danger of disappearing or changing beyond recognition. Certainly, Nature dictates such changes – parts of the volcano Krakatoa disappeared utterly and for ever late last century, while the Hawaiian Islands continue to grow every year. While people may be powerless against the overwhelming forces of Nature – the drift of continents, the ravages of weather, and the natural extinction and evolution of species – humankind, by adapting its very environment, has the ability to hasten such change and to damage many of the wonderful places on the planet. The Amazonian rainforest – only one example of many endangered forests around the globe – is being felled and cleared at an alarming rate, and before many invertebrate species there have been identified. The ozone layer is being destroyed, at least in part by human-produced emissions, and the increased ultra-violet radiation is affecting plants, animals and even the polar ice-caps. Lake Bajkal, the deepest lake in the world, has become as remarkable for its pollution as for its natural beauty and rare animal forms.

Natural features that have been regarded as permanent for generations are now changing, and not always by direct actions. Some animal species, for example, are on the verge of extinction not because they have been hunted but because their habitats are being destroyed. Individuals, communities, nations and humankind as a whole must become more aware of the full consequences of actions affecting the natural world, not just for today but for the generations of the future.

Tourism has opened the eyes of millions to the wonders of this planet, drawing people to the very places celebrated here. With proper care, millions more will be able to appreciate this wonderful world and its magnificent sites. Natural Wonders of the World is a lavish tour of some of the most splendid natural marvels of our planet. For no matter how many planets there are in the depths of the heavens, Yosemite and the Galapagos and the Frasassi caves must be as remarkable and as beautiful as anywhere that can be found – in this world or another.

JOHN BAXTER
PETER CLARKSON
ELIZABETH CRUWYS
BEAU RIFFENBURGH

The Fossil Forest
of Axel Heiberg

Caribou

Lemmings and
the Arctic
Ecosystem

Greenland

SE[...]

The Burgess
Shale

Dinosaur Provincial
Park

Devil's Tower

Niagara
Falls

The Bay of
Fundy

Redwoods and
Giant Sequoias

Dinosaur National
Monument

The Grand
Canyon

Yosemite National
Park

Mojave and Sonoran
Deserts

The Petrified Forest

Horseshoe Crabs

Zion National
Park

Carlsbad Caverns

Meteor
Crater

The Sargasso
Sea

The Everglades

Kauai

The Hawaiian
Island Chain

The Great
Sahara

The Pitch Lake

The Orinoco Delta

Angel
Falls

Galapagos
Islands

The Amazon
Basin

The Atacama
Desert

Iguassu
Falls

ANTARCTICA

Bouvetøya

Blue Whale

Deception
Island

The Lambert
Glacier

The Ross
Ice Shelf

Mount
Erebus

Tierra del
Fuego

Not to scale

NATURAL WONDERS
OF THE WORLD

The urorae

Lena Delta

Lake Bajkal

The Tibetan Plateau

Yellow River

Mount Fuji

Forests of Sichuan

Geothermals of Beppu

The Himalayas

The Guilin Hills

Sundarbans

The Bay of Bengal

Mariana Trench

The East African Rift Valley

Ruwenzori Mountains

Lake Nakuru

The Zaire River

Mount Kilimanjaro

Ngorongoro Crater

Aldabra Atoll

Krakatoa

Keli Mutu

The Great Barrier Reef

Victoria Falls

The Coelacanth

The Okavango Delta

Madagascar

Ayers Rock and Mount Olga

Coober Pedy

The Namib Desert

Precious Minerals

Duck-billed Platypus

Rotorua

Table Mountain

Tasmania

The Glaciers of the Southern Alps

NSET AREA

Island of Ice and Fire

Fair Isle

The Great Fjords

The Giant's Causeway

The Great Glen

The Burren

The Waddenzee

Bialowieza Forest

Hautes Fagnes

The White Cliffs

The Bavarian Forest

Earth Pyramids

Hohe Tauern

The Matterhorn

Verdon Gorge

Cévennes NP

Frasassi Caves

The Danube Delta

Picos de Europa

The Camargue

The Meseta

Mount Vesuvius

The Metéora

Pamukkale

The Dead Sea

The River Nile

THE AURORAE

These eerie bands and curtains of coloured lights dance in the winter skies at high latitudes.

When conditions are right, the *aurora borealis* can occasionally be seen as far south as southern England, but the most spectacular displays appear close to the poles. One of the most accessible spots is northern Scandinavia; a good place to see the lights is from the island of Spitzbergen, off the northern coast of Norway. The *aurora australis* is best seen from the Antarctic continent.

Rainbows

ANOTHER atmospheric wonder of the world is the rainbow. Rainbows are common: it requires only the right combination of sun and rain for one to appear, yet rainbows have a special place in many of the world's cultures.

A rainbow is the refraction of sunlight on raindrops. The larger the raindrops, the more brilliant are the colours in the rainbow. Sometimes, when a rainbow is particularly bright, a paler, secondary bow with the colours reversed, can appear behind it. If someone watching the rainbow moves, the light will be refracted through different raindrops. The sun, always behind the watcher, will light up constantly changing raindrops as the watcher moves forward, until there is no more rain left to refract and the rainbow fades.

Right, a shimmering sheet of light dances in the sky above a fishing village in northern Norway.

Above, a rainbow lies between the clouds and the ocean

IN the silence of the vast tundra of the Arctic, strange lights play in the winter skies. Similar arcs and flares gleam in the far south – especially visible on the Antarctic continent on clear, intensely cold winter nights. These lights can be seen in lower latitudes too. When they appeared in the skies of mediaeval Europe, the chroniclers believed they were caused by giants fighting in the sky, or were flaming lances hurled from heaven. The northern lights are often seen in Scotland, especially in April, and appear about four times a year in northern Florida, but they are most clearly visible from places near the magnetic poles – in northern Canada, for example, and the Ross Dependency of Antarctica.

These northern and southern lights are known to scientists as the *aurora borealis* and the *aurora australis*. They are, strictly speaking, not of the earth at all, but are caused by the sun and occur high above the earth.

Occasionally the sun emits a flare that releases an energy equivalent to an unimaginable number of nuclear bombs, sending solar particles hurtling through space at the speed of light. As the particles are deflected by the earth's magnetic field, they crash into other particles in the atmosphere, leaving these particles charged with electricity. In order to get rid of the charge, the particles "radiate" and it is this process that gives off the light, and presents this spectacle in the night skies. The reason these lights frequent the polar areas is because the magnetic field of the earth deflects particles headed for equatorial regions and points them towards the earth's magnetic poles.

To see the aurorae is a spellbinding experience. Great arches of shimmering light glitter across the skies, ranging from a pure violet-white, through the spectrum to yellow-greens and orange-reds. They span vast sections of the sky – one of the northern lights formed an archway measuring 3,000 miles (4,827 km) long, and 100 miles (161 km) high.

There are many different sorts of aurorae; varying appearances seem to depend upon their height in the atmosphere. The more common arches, or arcs, tend to appear between 40 and 64 miles (65 to 105 km) up, while the displays known as "draperies" appear about 70 miles (113 km) up. The highest displays can be as far away as 620 miles (998 km) from the surface, and there is some suggestion that red-coloured lights are more common higher up in the thinner atmosphere, where there is less chance that the particles will collide with each other. When more particles collide with each other, the light tends to be violet, and at low altitudes the commonest colour is green.

Although the dancing lights of the polar regions have been explained by science, they retain their aura of mystery, and their place as one of the most spectacular natural phenomena.

Norway

GREAT FJORDS
OF THE NORTH

*Cutting great gashes into the Norwegian coastline, the fjords
are places of staggering beauty.*

The coast of Norway is deeply
indented with fjords from
Stavanger in the south to the
border with Russia, but
Bergen, which is easily
accessible by air and ferry,
provides a superb centre from
which to explore the fjords;
Sognafjorden is one of the most
impressive.

*Right, the towering walls of
Geirangerfjord dwarf a ship.*

I N a small boat between the grey and forbidding walls of the great Norwegian fjords, it is easy to see how the legends of Valhalla and the brooding Nordic gods arose. On a dull and misty day, it is also not difficult to imagine the Viking longships in these mysterious waters, oars dipping into the still waters as the Norsemen headed off to explore the coasts of more gentle lands.

Although "fjord" is a Norwegian word meaning simply an arm of the sea, geologists have adopted the word to mean long, narrow indentations in the land that have been flooded by the sea, and the term has been applied to other countries with these

distinctive fingers of sea reaching inland, bounded by steep-sided mountains.

The fjords of Scandinavia were created many thousands of years ago during the ice ages when glaciers ground their way across the land, carving deep U-shaped valleys as they went. Sheer cliffs at the water's edge show tell-tale signs of scratching and scouring by the ice, and the fjords are shallower at the point where they enter the sea — where the glaciers ran out of the power necessary to gouge through the bedrock. However, not all geologists accept that the fjords were formed entirely by the action of glaciers. The bottoms of some of the deepest fjords, such as Sognafjorden in Norway, which is around 4,000 feet (1,212 m) at its deepest point, are considered too far below sea-level to have been wholly carved in this way.

Fjords are to be found on the coast and lead inland to where great icecaps once lay. In Norway little remains of the icecap that ruled supreme until 10,000 years ago; only isolated patches of ice such as the Jostedalsbre, to the north of Sognafjorden. The pressure of these icecaps forced ice to flow towards the sea in individual valley glaciers, and this process can be seen in action in Greenland today at the vast Søndre Strømfjord, on the west coast. A glacier still flows over its head, producing great green-blue icebergs that litter its chilly waters.

In Norway, the fjords make communication by land difficult, for villages that may lie just a few miles apart across the arm of a fjord by boat are sometimes hundreds of miles apart by road. Some settlements, particularly in the past, had no land communications at all because the steep-sided fjords made permanent roads impossible.

Sognafjorden is the largest and most beautiful of the Norwegian fjords.

Sognafjorden, King of Fjords

S OGNAFJORDEN is the biggest fjord in Norway, with sheer walls plunging 4,000 feet (1,212 m) beneath the surface and reaching 2,000 feet (610 m) towards the sky before flattening into a plateau. This finger of the sea is 112 miles (180 km) long, although it is seldom more than 3 miles (5 km) wide. It has several branches, including Naeroyfjord, where the walls crowd so closely together that ships sailing down it seem to disappear into a tunnel. The great fjord carves its way through barren, desolate scenery to the highest mountains in Norway. For most of its way the flanking mountains loom over the water and it always seems to be in twilight.

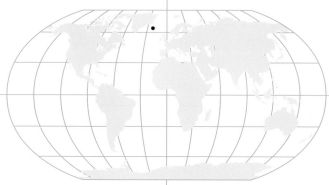

Iceland

ISLAND OF ICE AND FIRE

In Iceland glaciers and volcanoes wage a constant battle for supremacy.

Iceland lies just below the Arctic Circle in the north Atlantic Ocean, between Greenland and Scotland. There are regular flights from America and Denmark and it is also possible to go by sea. The best way to travel within the country is by four-wheel drive vehicle or, more traditionally, by Icelandic pony.

Facts and Figures

THE area of Iceland is 39,690 square miles (102,797 sq km) and about 11.5 per cent of this is icecap and glacier. The population is 262, 202 (1992 census); the interior of the country is almost uninhabited, particularly in winter. The highest point is Hvannadals-hnúkur (6,952 feet, 2,119 m), on Öræfajökull in the south. Hraunhafnartangi, the north-ernmost point of Iceland, just touches the Arctic Circle. The major fissure eruptions of Eldgjá (896) and Laki (1783) both produced major flood basalts, typical of eruptions resulting from the splitting across the mid-Atlantic ridge which separates at about 1 inch (2 cm) per year. Other famous eruptions in recent years have been Surtsey (1963), a new island that formed off the south coast, and Heimaey (1974) in Vestmannaeyjar, which threatened the fishing community on the island.

An eruption of the Strokkur geyser, in the Haukadalur siliceous hot spring area of southern Iceland.

ICELAND is a land like no other. In the capital, Reykjavik, there are almost no brick buildings, the roofs are mainly corrugated iron and you can always see steam somewhere. This is because Iceland is a volcanic island with no natural building materials and the land itself is still being built by nature – constantly pulled into two parts because of its position lying across the mid-Atlantic ridge, and stretched as Greenland and Scotland continue to move farther apart.

The opening of the Atlantic Ocean began some 180 million years ago, and Greenland began to separate from Scotland 60 million years ago, giving rise to the Tertiary volcanic

Typical yellow-brown mud of the hot springs at Namaskard, seen across the lava desert of Hverfjall, northern Iceland.

provinces of northern Ireland, north-west Scotland and south-east Greenland. The oldest rocks in Iceland are less than 60 million years old and the island has continued to grow since that time, piling sheet upon sheet of lava from long fissure eruptions that provided the foundation for the active volcanoes of today. Despite the internal heat of Iceland, the island was covered by a sheet of ice during the last ice age and the remnants of that sheet form the icecaps and glaciers today.

Evidence of volcanism is everywhere, from the major active volcanic cones such as Hekla (major eruption in 1947, recent lesser eruption in 1991), to extinct craters, many with spectacular lakes and extensive hot spring areas. These springs range from sulphurous pools of boiling mud, reminiscent of Dante's inferno, to crystal clear, turquoise-blue siliceous springs and geysers. Stóri Geysir (Great Geyser) at Geysir has given its name to all other spouting springs, and though it spouts less frequently today it still performs spectacularly. Hot water is the geological heritage of Iceland and its value has long been recognised. Today, Reykjavik is centrally heated by the island's subterranean hot water, pumped to all public and domestic buildings. Not far away, at Hveragerði you can buy tomatoes and bananas at the roadside, grown in greenhouses heated by natural hot water.

Only the southern coastal plain supports much vegetation, and most of Iceland's farms are found here. The interior of the country is a barren, lunar-looking landscape coloured in shades of brown and mauve. The only trees are low studs of birch, and the Arctic willow, reaching a height of about 8 inches (20 cm).

Iceland's Icecaps

VATNAJÖKULL is the largest icecap covering many geothermal sources, one of which gives rise to Grimsvötn, a unique lake within the icecap, its surface normally frozen solid. The source of the Jökulsá á Fjöllum River lies beneath the northern part of Vatnajökull, with hot springs under the ice keeping a chimney open to the lake above. In 1983 a canoeing expedition lowered its boats down the chimney and then paddled through the ice tunnel to the open river and down to the North Atlantic Ocean. The smaller icecap of Langjökull is bounded on its southern side by a large lake that often contains icebergs calved from the snout of the glacier.

This remote island can be reached either by a short air flight, or just over 2½ hours' ferry trip, both of which operate from Shetland.

Scotland

FAIR ISLE

The most remote place in the British Isles provides a safe landfall for millions of birds.

FAIR Isle lies almost equidistant from North Ronaldsay in the Orkney Isles and Sumburgh Head, the most southerly point on Shetland. A mere dot on most maps, this is a lofty island with precipitous cliffs of Old Red Sandstone rising up where the Atlantic Ocean and the North Sea meet. The waters around Fair Isle are often rough and troubled due to the contrary currents of these two great water masses, which result in tidal streams running in opposite directions within a few hundred yards of each other. Such areas are known locally as roosts. This is a small island, only 3 miles (4.8 km) long and 1.5 miles (2.4 km) at its widest, with a total area of only just over 3 square miles (8 sq km). The coastline is all steep cliffs with the highest rising to over 500 feet (152 m) on the west side and the highest point on the east side over 400 feet (122 m).

Fair Isle is synonymous with the great bird migrations which follow the East Atlantic Flyway. Many birds use the island as a welcome stopover point on longer journeys while others return there to breed. The numbers of birds using the island are enormous and over 340 different species have been recorded – over half the species ever recorded from the British Isles.

Exotic Visitors

IN addition to the large numbers of regular visitors, Fair Isle is also host to the occasional unusual visitor. Species such as the hoopoe, bluethroat and ortolan bunting may arrive alone or in whole flocks, taking advantage of this tiny haven after being driven off course.

Right, Fair Isle stands mid-way between Shetland and Orkney in one of Britain's roughest stretches of sea.

Facing page, some 20,000 pairs of puffins return here each year to breed.

14

Only 35 species are classed as residents or regular summer visitors, and most notable of these is the endemic Fair Isle wren, *Troglodytes troglodytes fridariensis*.

Fair Isle is used by many birds on both their spring migrations to more northern breeding sites, and their autumn migration south to over-winter in Britain and Europe or further to Africa. Regular visitors come from as far afield as Greenland, Iceland, the Faroes and North America, as well as from Scandinavia, Russia and the Arctic. The journeys which many of these birds undertake are quite remarkable. Birds such as the redstart and willow warbler breed in Scandinavia and then carry on from Fair Isle to winter in Africa.

The spring migration north is an intense affair lasting only a few weeks, with birds dropping down on Fair Isle for a short rest and feeding stop before continuing the journey to the breeding sites. The first are generally those which have wintered in Great Britain or northern Europe – the skylarks, oystercatchers and lapwings. After these come the first of the visiting breeding birds, including puffins, guillemots and lesser black-backed gulls, followed by other Scandinavian breeders such

as redstarts, whinchats and pied flycatchers arriving from Africa.

The island is popular year-round, with the last birds to head north leaving Fair Isle just before the first are found returning. Birds like turnstones and purple sandpipers breed early in the far Arctic where the summer is very short, and rapidly deteriorating weather conditions there can force them south as early as July. The southward migration is a more protracted affair, with the birds lacking the urgency and drive of the breeding season. Paramount now is the need to rest and build up reserves for the winter.

Fair Isle Bird Observatory

FROM the beginning of the 20th century Fair Isle was recognised as the place to study bird migration. William Eagle Clark, curator at the Royal Scottish Museum, pioneered the interest in Fair Isle, and was the inspiration for local man Jerome Wilson to take an active interest in the bird life of the island. He was probably the first professional bird-watcher, engaged by Eagle Clark to record bird numbers. It was George Waterston who purchased the island in 1948 and set up a proper bird observatory. As part of the work of today's observatory there are daily counts of the migrants alighting, and an extensive programme of bird ringing.

Breeding Seabird Colonies

THE towering cliffs of Fair Isle, appearing out of the vast expanse of sea, are a welcome sight not only as a landfall to birds flying on long migrations, but also to large numbers of seabirds which return to breed. Numbers fluctuate, but in summer the cliffs are crowded with upwards of 27,000 pairs of fulmars (5 per cent of the total British breeding population), 1,100 pairs of shags (3 per cent), 105 pairs of Arctic skuas (3 per cent), 19,500 pairs of kittiwakes (4 per cent). In addition there are four species of auk, with 332,300 guillemots (3 per cent), 5,100 razorbills (3.5 per cent) 380 black guillemots (1 per cent) and 20,000 puffins (3 per cent). As if the cliffs and adjacent seas were not crowded enough with all these, there are also significant numbers of gannet, storm petrel, great skua, herring gull, and great black-backed gull together with smaller numbers of common and Arctic tern.

THE GREAT GLEN

*Scotland's natural divide
and man-made waterway.*

The Great Glen stretches from Inverness in the northeast to Fort William in the southwest. Trains serve both towns, but the train to Fort William, though infrequent and slow, does cross some of Scotland's most magnificent scenery along a route that is mostly remote from roads, and is otherwise seen only by the determined walker. Urquhart Castle is a good place to view the Great Glen.

EVEN a cursory glance at a map of Scotland reveals that the country is almost cut in two by a line of lochs extending south-westward from the Moray Firth to the Firth of Lorn. To the south and east lie the Grampian Mountains and all of Scotland's towns and cities, to the north and west lie the remote and sparsely populated north-west highlands. The line of this distinctive feature, called the Great Glen, continues along the north-western coast of the Moray Firth in almost a straight line. This is no

accident or man-made feature but a deep and ancient weakness in the earth's crust – a fault. Most geological faults are near-vertical features, the crust on one side having dropped down relative to the other side. But the Great Glen is a classic example of the less common horizontal tear, or wrench fault. Here the northern side of the fault has moved some 60 miles (97 km) to the south-west relative to the southern side. Evidence of this movement has been revealed by matching the outcrop of the Foyers granite

The Caledonian Canal

VICTORIAN engineers, with an eye for a natural advantage, dug a series of canals linking the lochs of the Great Glen with the Moray Firth, finishing the job begun by nature and cutting Scotland completely in two with the Caledonian Canal. This enabled small ships to sail from the west to the east coast of Scotland without having to make the storm-tossed passage between the Inner and Outer Hebrides around Cape Wrath.

Loch Ness, seen here from the south-western end near Fort Augustus, lies along the floor of the Great Glen.

on the southern side of the fault near Inverness, with the outcrop of the Strontian granite west of Fort William on the northern side.

From the northern slopes of Ben Nevis, the highest mountain in Britain, this great cleft in the mountains recedes into the distance to the north-east. On a fine day the sun shimmers on the surface of the impressive sequence of lochs: Loch Ness, Loch Oich, Loch Lochy and finally, in the south-west the long sea loch of Loch Linnhe.

The fault of the Great Glen is interesting from a scientific viewpoint. Turning back the geological clock some 200 million years one can re-assemble the continents bordering the north Atlantic. North America and Greenland slide back together like the pieces of a colossal jigsaw puzzle until they abut against the western seaboard of northern Europe. Newfoundland now lies to the west of Ireland and a similar linear feature there aligns with a continuation of the Great Glen. The true extent of the fault then becomes apparent, and it is possible to wonder at the enormous forces that must have been needed to achieve this movement. All this took place over a very long

period, similar to the San Andreas Fault in California, moving in a series of fits and starts by a sequence of earthquakes. Happily for the Scots, all major movement has long ceased, although fidgeting along the Great Glen is often recorded by geophysicists with sensitive seismographs, and there were strong earthquakes in the Inverness area in 1816, 1888, 1890 and 1891.

The Great Glen is a natural dividing line separating northern and central Scotland.

The Loch Ness Monster

THE real fame of the Great Glen lies in none of the geological or geographical facts, but in myth, for the Loch Ness monster is known throughout the world. Monster watchers and monster expeditions, including those wrapped in a thinly disguised scientific veil, have spent countless hours looking over and searching through the deep dark waters of the loch for this fabled serpent.

The monster's first appearance was allegedly to a monk in the 8th century, and many hundreds of people have claimed to have seen it since, especially during the last 100 years or so. The most famous photograph was taken near Urquhart Castle; a convincing picture although at long range – but it could be merely a log floating in the water. Some reports tell of the monster crossing the road on the northern shore of the loch. Those people who have "seen" the monster are convinced of its existence.

Scientists have suggested that the various accounts tend to describe an animal like a plesiosaur, an aquatic dinosaur. Some argue that it might be a survivor trapped in the loch when it was last open to the sea, but that was so long ago that at least two must have been trapped for there to be a modern survivor. The loch is very deep, the water very dark with peat and there are deep crevices in its sides; finding the truth is not easy.

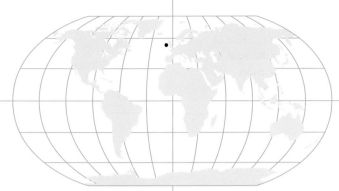

Northern Ireland

THE GIANT'S CAUSEWAY

A natural stairway of gigantic proportions leading into the sea.

Good roads from either Belfast (about 50 miles, 80 km) or Londonderry (about 35 miles, 56 km) lead to the Giant's Causeway in County Antrim. Staffa is difficult to reach, but a boat trip from Oban on the Scottish mainland, about 95 miles (153 km) north of Glasgow, is sometimes possible.

I N the early days of the north Atlantic Ocean, the newly formed seaway between the recently separated continents of North America and Europe was a still-developing feature; the body of the north Atlantic was in place, but its edges were still being formed and re-formed. The western coast of Greenland separated from Canada about 80 million years ago but the south-eastern coast was still firmly attached to the opposing north-western coast of the British

Fingal's Cave

C OLUMNAR basalts are not confined to Northern Ireland; another of the best known examples is in the Inner Hebrides off the west coast of Scotland. Here, on the island of Staffa, the columns are well developed over a large part of the island, and a huge cave where the sea has eroded the columns is known as Fingal's Cave, after another mythical giant. Fingal's Cave has wide renown, and has figured in poems and novels over the centuries, and a visit to the island in 1829 by the composer Felix Mendelssohn inspired his famous orchestral overture, known today as "The Hebrides".

Tightly-packed, hexagonal basalt columns of the Giant's Causeway on the north coast of Antrim.

Isles. Some 20 million years later these coasts were beginning to separate and there were major volcanoes on what are now the islands of Skye, Rhum, Mull and Arran, on the Scottish mainland at Ardnamurchan Point, and also to the south in Ireland at Slieve Gullion, Carlingford and Mourne. These ancient volcanoes must have been splendid sights in their prime, but the greatest record left of this episode lies in the flood, or plateau, basalts. Basalt is a particularly hot, fluid lava which has been recorded flowing downhill at speeds of more than 30 miles (48 km) per hour. Such fluid lavas are able to spread across large areas relatively easily, hence the term "flood basalts", and they constitute the bulk of lava products found in this whole volcanic area. Similar flood basalts are known elsewhere – the Deccan Traps of India produced 171,000 cubic miles (700,000 cu km) of lava between 60 and 40 million years ago.

Any hot liquid contracts as it cools, and molten lava is no exception to this rule. However when lava eventually cools sufficiently to crystallise, it tends to crack in a regular pattern, usually a hexagonal design similar to cracks formed in the muddy bottom of a pond that dries out in a hot summer.

The significant difference with lava is that the cracks extend right down through the flow from top to bottom. The result is a distinctive network of basalt columns, all packed incredibly closely together with just the thinnest of gaps between. Geologists refer to these cracks as "joints" and to the whole as "columnar basalt". The width of the columns is typically about 18 inches (46 cm), but larger and smaller columns are known. The Giant's Causeway is a particularly fine exposure of this unique phenomenon – a grand causeway indeed fit for giants.

Basalt columns like giant organ pipes are capped by massive lavas on Staffa, a tiny island in the Inner Hebrides.

The Myth of the Giant's Causeway

THE origin of the name, Giant's Causeway, is rooted in Irish folklore. The causeway is said to have been built by the Irish giant, Finn Mac Cool, who drove the columns into the sea bed one by one so that he could walk to Scotland to fight his rival Finn Gall. When he finished, Finn Mac Cool decided to take a rest. Meanwhile, Finn Gall walked across to Ireland to size up his opponent, and was amazed and frightened by the size of the sleeping giant, especially after Mac Cool's wife told him that this was, in fact, only the giant's baby. Fearing for his life at the thought of how big the baby's father might be, Finn Gall beat a hasty retreat to Scotland, destroying the causeway behind him. All that remains of the causeway today is on the Antrim coast.

Ireland

THE BURREN

The Burren is accessible by road from Dublin, about 120 miles (193 km) to the east, or from Shannon airport which lies some 30 miles (48 km) to the south.

The Burren Coast

APART from the unique combination of plants for which the Burren is rightly famous, the shores of this part of south-west Ireland have a fascinating diversity and range of species in the many rock pools, carved out of the limestone over the centuries by Atlantic waves. The waters which wash onto this part of the coast are warmed by the remnants of the Gulf Stream, and so are able to support many animal and plant species more commonly found in the Mediterranean. One such species is the rock urchin, with its dark green or brown shell covered in short violet spines, and often camouflaged with bits of dead seaweed. The rock urchin creates depressions in the rock by slowly rotating its shell, leaving a distinctive pitted landscape when it moves on or dies.

Facing page, the Burren is one of the most important areas of Carboniferous limestone in Europe.

Above, the delicate mountain aven (Dryas octopetala) in bloom.

This internationally famous botanical site in south-west Ireland drops from gently rounded hilltops of about 1,000 feet (305 m) down to the sea.

THE name Burren, literally translated from the Irish Gaelic, means "a stony place". Covering an area of around 145 square miles (376 sq km), this is one of the most important and spectacular areas of Carboniferous limestone pavement in western Europe. Fossils of many primitive marine invertebrates, preserved in the limestone before being uplifted some 250 million years ago, betray the origins of the Burren beneath an ancient tropical sea.

On first sight the Burren might appear to be a rather barren area of bare limestone pavement, but closer inspection reveals a luxuriant and diverse plant life in the cracks and crevices (grykes) of the rock. The mild, wet climate – an average of 80 inches (203 cm) of rain annually – is a vital factor in determining the area's unique and spectacular flora.

The assemblage of plants here is quite extraordinary, and unrivalled anywhere else in Europe both for the diversity of plants, with Lusitanean (Mediterranean-type), temperate and Arctic/alpine species mixed together, and more remarkably for the fact that they are all indigenous species, although exactly how such a mix originated is the subject of much

speculation. Some species grow in abundance: the low growing Arctic/alpine mountain avens with its downy evergreen leaves and delicate white flowers, and the bloody cranesbill with its bright reddish-purple flowers, together with more southern species such as the Burren orchid. The juxtaposition of some species is unique, with sea pinks growing next to the mossy saxifrage which is more commonly found on mountain tops. The Burren is also home to many rare plants whose once wide distribution has now diminished because of climate and other changes. Notable rarities include the fen violet with its delicate bluish-white flowers, the shrubby cinquefoil and the parasitic thyme broomrape.

Dotted throughout the eastern part of the Burren are areas of standing water known as marl loughs and turloughs. Turloughs dry out each summer because they are situated on well draining limestone, filling again during the autumn rains and remaining flooded until the following spring. A very specialised flora is found in these areas, with reed sweet-grass dominating large areas and various species of sedges around the margins, with the rocks and boulders exposed by the retreating water covered in a distinctive black moss. The marl loughs are permanent standing waters which occur on less permeable limestone, resulting in such a high calcium carbonate concentration that the carbonate and most of the available phosphate precipitates out as a chalky layer known as marl. These vital nutrients are not available to the microscopic phytoplankton, resulting in very clear water with a distinctive blue tinge, but they are available to rooted plants and extensive growths of stoneworts and other related species which occur here.

Complementing the rich and diverse flora, the Burren is also notable for its animals, and in particular for the large numbers of a wide variety of butterflies. Of the 30 species of butterfly recorded in Ireland 26 occur on the Burren, and it is the only place in Ireland for the pearl-bordered fritillary.

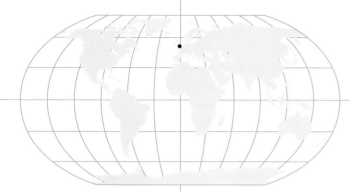

England

THE WHITE CLIFFS OF DOVER

Approaching Dover, known historically as the "Key to England", the chalk cliffs are visible from miles out to sea.

Dover lies about 80 miles (129 km) from the centre of London and is linked to the capital by good roads. The white cliffs are best seen from the sea and there are a number of boat tours available. The chalky downs behind the cliffs offer pleasant walking, with far-reaching views over the sea and the surrounding coastline.

THE cliffs at Dover tower over the sea, and their glittering whiteness has been the first sighting of England for many a mariner. Because of its proximity to France, a mere 21 miles (34 km) away, Dover has historically been of great strategic importance to the defence of Britain's island kingdom. Perched on top of the white cliffs, some 375 feet (114 m) above the sea, is Dover Castle, one of the most impressive fortresses in the world, constructed over a thousand years to repel invaders from Europe.

There are chalk cliffs all around the south coast of England, such as those at Beachy Head in East Sussex where the South Downs meet the sea, but none have inspired so many popular songs, poems, and paintings as have the white cliffs of Dover.

The abundance of chalk-loving flowers on the cliffs was noted back in Elizabethan times when the "father of English botany", William Turner, described them in 1548, and they still thrive here today. One of the best known of these is the sea cabbage, with its bright yellow flowers and large, fleshy green leaves. Samphire and yellow sea-poppy, along with several species of wild orchid that can only be found in chalky soils, are a delight along the many cliff-top footpaths around Dover.

The cliffs themselves, predominantly chalk, were formed during the Late Cretaceous period when the bodies of millions of tiny creatures, with shells rich in calcium carbonate, died and sank to the ocean floor. Layer upon layer of shells accumulated and were gradually compressed in a process known as sedimentation. Once formed, the chalk, a soft form of limestone, was rapidly eroded by the forces of sea and wind.

The geological processes that caused the breaking of the limestone and the formation of the White Cliffs of Dover follows a typical pattern. First, vulnerable points in the cliffs are made weaker when salt water creeps into cracks and crevices, dissolving the softer rocks. This trapped water also expands and contracts with changing temperatures, causing the rocks to crack, and plants and trees can cause even more damage by forcing their roots down into the weakening rock.

The second stage in cliff formation occurs when breaking waves hurl themselves into the foot of the cliffs, forcing the sea water into cracks and openings with such power that the rocks literally explode. The suction of the retreating water also takes its toll, and the waves sometimes carry small pebbles and rocks that grind against the rock, wearing it slowly but inevitably away, and sometimes cutting overhangs and caves into the lower parts of the

cliff face. The overhanging upper layers eventually collapse as the support is worn away from under them, leaving a sheer cliff face. This process is repeated constantly, making the cliffs retreat steadily before the attack of the sea. The erosion also causes the formation of structures such as stacks and needles, which occur when headlands are undercut by the sea.

The geological forces that formed the famous cliffs of Dover occurred simultaneously on the opposite side of the Channel at Étretat, just north of Le Havre in France. Here a fine example of a chalk sea stack, L'Aiguille (The Needle), stands 230 feet (70 m) above the sea.

The wild flowers of the chalky downland attract a wide variety of insects, including many butterflies and moths, and the largest British species of grasshopper, called the wartbiter.

Cliffs

ALL around the world, the erosion of the sea has produced magnificent cliffs. Some of the most spectacular occur in Port Campbell National Park in Victoria, Australia, where limestone cliffs are pounded by waves of immense power. The result is 20 miles (32 km) of coast punctuated with spectacular geological formations including a double-arched structure called London Bridge. The Great Blowhole is a tunnel nearly 325 feet (99 m) long, that ends in a natural well 130 feet (40 m) across. Under certain conditions, waves tear along the tunnel and explode into the well, causing a geyser-like eruption of spray.

Cliffs can also form inland, and the Bandiagara Cliffs in Mali, a few miles from Timbuktu, are a good example. Here the cliffs form the edge of a sandstone plateau that towers over the African plain. Sandstone, deposited in a natural basin about 600 million years ago, was subsequently forced upwards by movements in the earth's crust; the edges of this deposit form the cliffs today. Up to 1,650 feet (503 m) high, the cliffs are the result of undermining by fast flowing rivers and subsequent collapse of the upper layers of rock.

Dover's south-facing cliffs of bright white chalk have been a familiar landmark for ships for hundreds of years.

THE WADDENZEE

The Waddenzee is a complex area of shallow sea and coastal lands stretching along the shores of the North Sea, from Den Helder in the Netherlands to the Skallingen peninsula in Denmark. There are many small ports along the coast and on the offshore islands. Ferries run between various ports on the European mainland and the offshore islands, many of which need to be explored on foot. One of these islands, Texel, can be reached by ferry from Den Helder.

Cockles and Mussels

BIRDS are not the only animals to feed on the bounty of the Waddenzee – shellfish, including mussels, have long been cultured and harvested by humans. Cockles, living just below the surface of the sand, have traditionally been collected by hand rake, a labour-intensive operation which effectively controlled the scale of harvesting. However, modern mechanised harvesting methods have proved so efficient that cockle fishery here is all but exhausted, and the Waddenzee cockle joins the ranks of other species which have been over-exploited by humankind.

Right, a cloud of knot and dunlin at a roost site.

Facing page, the salt marsh is a trap for sediment particles, and important for stabilizing this shallow coastline.

A vital stop-over point on the North Sea for millions of migrating birds.

THE Waddenzee, extending over 310 miles (488 km,) from Den Helder in the Netherlands to the Skallingen peninsula in Denmark, is one of Europe's most important and productive wetland areas. The shallow waters average around 6 to 10 feet (2 to 3 m) deep, and extensive inter-tidal areas of sand and mud flats, shallow sandbanks and salt marsh protected from the North Sea by a string of off-shore islands cover a total area of around 3,900 square miles (10,101 sq km). The international significance of the area as a wetland habitat has been acknowledged with its designation as a Ramsar Site, and the governments of the Netherlands, Germany and Denmark are actively cooperating in the development of an integrated management plan for the area.

The Waddenzee is the focal point for enormous numbers of birds, with over 50 species of waders and waterfowl either over-wintering or resting and refuelling during their migration north or south along the East Atlantic Flyway. Over 10 million birds from as far afield as northeast Canada, Greenland, Iceland and Siberia congregate here to feed on

vast populations of invertebrate worms and molluscs living in the sand and mud. In particular, large numbers of brent, pink-footed and barnacle geese together with mallard, wigeon and pintail frequent the low-lying marsh areas behind the dykes while oyster-catcher, dunlin, knot and eider duck feed on the rich inter-tidal invertebrate fauna. Many birds also breed here during the summer, especially on the many remote offshore islands; among the more unusual are avocet, spoonbill, Kentish plover and Montagu's harrier.

In addition to the large numbers of birds which depend on the area, over 100 species of fish, and both common and grey seals, rely on the shallow waters and sandbanks of the Waddenzee for at least part of the year. Some species of fish which are caught commercially throughout the North Sea spend much of their early life in these productive waters – as much as 80 per cent of plaice and 50 per cent of sole, together with large numbers of herring.

Much of the coastline of the southern North Sea is under considerable developmental pressure and in the past 100 years the construction of port facilities and embankments to protect against sea level rise has resulted in the loss of much of the original salt marsh.

Nonetheless, what remains still represents the most extensive area of salt marsh in Europe.

The major rivers which empty into the Waddenzee, such as the Ems, Weser and Elbe all support considerable industry along their banks, and in the past this has resulted in significant pollution. As part of the agreement between the countries involved in the Joint Declaration on the Protection of the Waddenzee, the levels of many pollutants have been reduced, and efforts to reduce them further are continuing.

Marsh Flora

ALTHOUGH it is the bird life which attracts most of the attention, the coastal salt marsh, lagoons and sand dunes are also of great botanical interest. There is a rich and varied flora, including pioneer species such as glasswort, at the fringes of the salt marsh, while on some of the more established dune and marsh areas there is a variety of orchids, marsh gentians, and the beautiful and delicate grass of Parnassus with its heart-shaped leaves and honey-scented white flowers.

Common Seal

THE population of the common seal in the Waddenzee, as elsewhere in the North Sea has been severely reduced. With a halt to the hunting of seals and a reduction of some pollutants, numbers rose to around 10,000 by the early 1980s, representing about 3 per cent of the world population. However, in 1988 they suffered a significant setback, when large numbers of dead common seals were reported around the North Sea, including around 7,000 in the Waddenzee. The cause was an epidemic of phocine distemper virus, closely related to canine distemper. A link between the severity of the out-break and pollution has been suggested. Man-made compounds such as polychlorinated biphenyls (PCBs) and various pesticides which do not degrade easily accumulate in the tissues of animals like seals, reducing the effectiveness of their immune system and making them more susceptible to infections. Common seal numbers are now recovering slowly, but the incident is a sharp reminder of the vulnerability of wild populations to both natural and man-made events.

HAUTES FAGNES

Hautes Fagnes is in the Ardennes, on the border with Germany, and near the town of Eupen some 30 to 40 miles (48 to 64 km) from Liege.

The remarkable Hautes Fagnes Nature Reserve is set on a high plateau in the Ardennes.

Above, the crowberry is a member of the heath family.

Facing page, characteristic of bogs and wet, acid heathland, the delicate bog asphodel is regarded as poisonous to livestock.

S OME 10,000 years ago, as the massive ice sheets of the last ice age retreated northwards, an extensive area of bog and marshland was left behind to be slowly colonised by forests of oak, alder, lime, hazel and beech. As the first human settlers came into these areas they began to cut these forests, using the timber for fuel and the production of charcoal. In time much of the forest was destroyed, and with its demise the various animals which depended on it also disappeared. Animals once common in the region, including beaver, wolf, moose and brown bear, are no longer to be found. Only the most inhospitable regions remained more or less undisturbed; the Hautes Fagnes in Belgium is one.

This is a relatively small reserve of only 15.1 square miles (39.1 sq km), made up of high peat land surrounded by semi-natural forest of oak and beech and some plantations of spruce. The whole area lies at the relatively high altitude of 1,804 feet (550 m) and receives on average 55 inches (1,397 mm) of rain per year – more than twice the Belgian average. It is also considerably colder than much of the

rest of the country, with heavy snowfalls each winter and severe frosts.

The bogs contain unusually deep reserves of peat, up to 23 feet (7 m) deep in places. Trapped within this peat is an encapsulated history of the plant life of the area since the last ice age, including whole tree trunks and the pollen of the various plants preserved in layers of the bog. The surface vegetation of today is dominated by such familiar species as the common mat grass and purple moor grass, together with bilberry, crowberry, cowberry, bog wartleberry and the cross-leaved heath. Rarer species such as the bog asphodel and white-beaked sedge are also present, along with species more commonly found in northern latitudes, such as marsh gentian and marsh andromeda.

The bog and marshy areas support a rich and diverse insect life, with many species of spiders in particular. In the early morning light there is no more evocative sight than the vegetation laden with dew-covered spiders' webs: intricate and tautly constructed orbs, or the tangles of silk laid by the hammock spider.

The woodlands, although much reduced in extent, still represent one of the last remaining refuges in the low countries for certain large mammals, including both red deer and roe deer, together with wild boar and the increasingly rare European wild cat.

Hautes Fagnes is an important breeding area for a large number of different birds including the black grouse, the great grey shrike, common and short-toed tree creepers and the rare black and middle spotted woodpeckers. It is also an important area for a variety of birds of prey including Tengmalm's owl and long-eared owl, buzzard, hen harrier and goshawk.

Above, a spider's web catches the early morning light.

Building a Spider's Web

THE most elaborate webs are the orb webs, which are precise geometric insect traps made from fine silk-like strands; these intricate constructions are usually rebuilt each day. To start the web the spider releases one end of a thread of silk, which is then carried by the wind until it becomes attached to an adjacent piece of vegetation. Once this first strand is established, the spider reinforces it, passing back and forth across it, laying down further strands. The spider then drops from the centre of this strand to another twig or leaf or to the ground, where it attaches another thread which forms the first spoke in the web. Once all the spokes radiating from the hub have been established, the spider then lays down the spirals of the orb which will ensnare its prey. Throughout the day as the web captures its prey the spider is continually repairing the structure. How the spider avoids becoming ensnared in its own web is still a mystery.

27

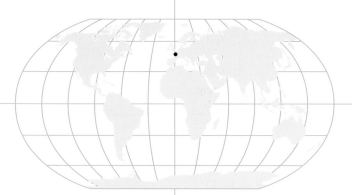

France

CÉVENNES
NATIONAL PARK

Forest-covered granite ridges and gorges interrupted by the flat limestone plateaux of Causses make up this unique wilderness area.

The Cévennes National Park is situated in the southern region of the Massif Central, lying in a triangle formed by Mende, Alès and Millau. It is about two hours' car drive from Montpellier and the Camargue, on the Mediterranean coast.

Order in Apparent Chaos

ANTS, together with some of their close relatives the bees and wasps, form complex social colonies. Individual ant colonies may number hundreds of thousands of individuals, each with an integral part to play. The essential work in the society, nest building, tending the brood and defence of the nest is performed by the female workers. Each nest has a single fertile female or queen whose only function is to lay eggs. The female workers have distinct functions, and subtle differences in their morphology and physiology distinguish between inside workers, outside workers, soldiers and nest builders. The male ants have no role in the day-to-day running of the nest, and they only occur for a limited period each year in order to fertilise the queen. Ants' nests take on very many different forms, from great piles of twigs and leaves to underground chambers, but common to all is the highly ordered nature of the society and the complete interdependence of each individual on the whole.

Right, the vast wilderness of the Cévennes includes high meadows and forest-covered ridges.

AT the high altitudes of the Cévennes winters can be very severe, with heavy snow and low temperatures, and although the area has been used for centuries by shepherds from the valleys as summer grazing for thousands of sheep, there is little permanent habitation. The environment has been influenced by this long history of grazing and forestry, but nonetheless it represents one of the few remaining wilderness areas in France. The highest of the ridges are Mont Lozère (5,576 feet, 1,700 m), Mont Aigoual (5,068 feet, 1,545 m) and Mont Bouges (4,592 feet, 1,400 m); the Causse Mejean lies between 3,280 and 3,936 feet (1,000 and 1,200 m). The Cévennes National Park and Biosphere Reserve covers a total area of 1,260 square miles (3,263 sq km).

The centuries of sheep grazing and the extensive wood cutting for the charcoal industry has reduced the woodland cover to only about 25 per cent of what it once was. Some of the native oak, sweet chestnut and beech forest survives, however, and more recently there has been widespread planting of conifers. This great variety of habitats has resulted in a diverse array of animals and plants.

In the spring many wild plants burst into flower, with colourful carpets of wild daffodils, martagon lilies and arnica. The area is particularly famous for its orchids, with over 40 species including the rare lady's slipper orchid, with its strikingly beautiful maroon and yellow flower. The Causses also support a magnificent show of spring flowers with dwarf daffodils, wild tulips and pasque flowers among many others.

As with all complex ecosystems there are many intricate and often subtle interactions between animals and plants; the forest floor with its covering of dead leaves and rotting wood provides rich pickings for a wide variety of invertebrates, recycling much of the material to make it available once again to the plants. These animals in turn are food for predators higher up the food chain. The woods with their secluded clearings support populations of larger herbivores such as wild boar and deer.

The large variety of birds in particular reflects the diversity of habitats and prey. They include a number of species of woodpecker and their close relative the wryneck, little bustards, choughs, rock thrushes, capercaillies and black grouse, with many different birds of prey – most notably peregrine falcon, hen harrier and Montagu's harrier, golden eagle and the eagle owl. The griffon vulture, once common in the area, has been reintroduced to the wild in recent years. The European beaver, which has seen its number and range severely reduced in recent years, is another species which has been successfully reintroduced.

Despite successes, some species are in decline, including the wryneck and the green woodpecker. This is largely because the main prey of these birds – ants – are also disappearing, for the use of fertilisers and sewage to enrich the land produces lusher growth which is less suitable for the ants. The decline is not limited to fewer ants and woodpeckers however, because the reduction in woodpeckers in turn means there are fewer nest holes available in the woodland for tits, nuthatches and small mammals. With a reduction in some of these species there is less prey for other birds, and so the effects are compounded.

Above, more than 40 species of orchid flourish in this remarkable landscape.

Orchids

THERE are around 30,000 species of orchids in the world, the vast majority found in the warm, damp tropics. The structure of the flower of many orchids is very elaborate and often beautifully coloured and patterned, and many have evolved a specialised relationship with a single pollinating insect or bird. Orchids produce tiny seeds which by themselves are unable to germinate successfully, and they depend on a fungus in the soil which penetrates the seed and provides essential nutrients to help the seedling develop. This association imposes limits on the distribution of orchids to areas where the fungus is present.

France

THE CAMARGUE

A famous area of wetland on the Mediterranean coast.

The Camargue lies at the mouth of the River Rhône, on the Mediterranean coast of France, in the Golfe des Saintes-Maries. The nearest international airport is at Marseilles on the eastern edge of the Camargue. There is an extensive network of roads, railways and canals linking Marseilles with the other main towns of Arles, Avignon and Montpellier in the west.

Brine Shrimp

VERY few animals can adapt to highly saline waters. Those that have done so usually occur in very large numbers and the brine shrimp, *Artemia salina,* is no exception. This shrimp, which is no more than ⅗ inch (15 mm) long, can live in conditions in which salt levels range from less than a third of that of sea water, to over six times as much. This enables it to survive periods of inundation by fresh water as well as times of extreme drought. It achieves this feat by having a skin which is impermeable to both salt and water, and transfer of both is restricted to very confined, strictly controlled areas.

Right, this wetland wilderness, vital as a feeding and nesting site for many species of bird, supports other creatures too, including the semi-wild white horses.

THE Camargue is an enormous coastal wetland area of some 566 square miles (1,466 sq km) and is one of the most important areas of its type in Europe. Historically, at the time when the Roman and Greek empires were at the height of their powers, the Mediterranean coast supported a rich mosaic of wetlands, which remained largely intact until the 19th century. Large areas were then drained to create agricultural land, and also to eradicate malaria by destroying the breeding grounds of the mosquito; as a result very little remains. The Camargue, however, is one area which has survived more or less intact, although human intervention such as the development of the salt pans has changed the landscape from that enjoyed by our ancestors. It was designated a Ramsar Site in 1970 and subsequently a Biosphere Reserve in 1977.

The Camargue is an intricate mix of beaches, sand dunes, reed beds, brackish lakes, riverine forest and pasture lands, together with the extensive salt pans. This array of habitats, combined with the strategic geographic location of the Camargue, makes it a very important staging post in the migration routes of many species of bird – over 300 species of migrant birds have been recorded. Millions of ducks, geese and waders visit the area each year from as far afield as Siberia and northern Europe. Some are merely transient visitors on longer journeys, while others come to nest and breed. Notable among the latter are the Kentish plover, slender-billed gulls, red-crested pochards, black-winged stilts, stone curlew and the avocet, together with the collared pratincole which breeds nowhere else in France. The freshwater reed beds which have survived provide ideal nesting sites for the bittern, little bittern, purple heron, squacco heron, little egret, cattle egret, various warblers, and the majestic marsh harrier which can be seen gliding just above the reeds.

It is the combination of suitable roost sites and adjacent feeding areas which make the Camargue so attractive to so many birds. The ducks spend a large part of the day in the

relative safety on the many brackish ponds. In the early morning and late evening they can fly to the nearby marshes to feed. Many of these marshes are privately managed and wild fowling is permitted, and as a result the numbers of birds over-wintering on the Camargue have dropped by 50 per cent over the last ten years.

The unusual conditions of very high salinity created by the salt pans make the area especially

Salt is extracted on an industrial scale at Salin de Giraud.

Salt Pans

ONE of the easiest ways of obtaining salt, historically an important trading commodity, is by allowing the sun to evaporate sea water, which leaves a residue of salt and other trace elements. In the salt pans of the Camargue, sea water is moved by pumps through a series of shallow ponds or pans, becoming more and more salty at each stage, until it reaches the final pan, where the last of the water evaporates to leave the crystalline salt. This artificial system's great advantage for birds is its predictability, thus guaranteeing suitable conditions for roosting, feeding and breeding. It is this man-made system which has given the Camargue its importance today as a major site for the greater flamingo and other avian visitors.

suitable for the brine shrimps, an important prey for some species of bird, particularly the pink or greater flamingo. These strikingly beautiful birds are a symbol of the success of the management of the Camargue. Since 1944 the number of breeding pairs of greater flamingos has risen steadily, and at the same time the area has increased in importance as an over-wintering area for them – over 24,000 birds were recorded in 1991. Central to the success of these birds in the Camargue is the presence of secure nest sites in the salt pans and the proximity of rich feeding areas.

Apart from the vast numbers of birds for which the Camargue is rightly famous, it is also noted for its local breed of black cattle and, more particularly, the herds of semi-wild white horses thought to be direct descendants of primitive horses. These pale creatures are indeed a dramatic and evocative sight galloping through the shallow lagoons.

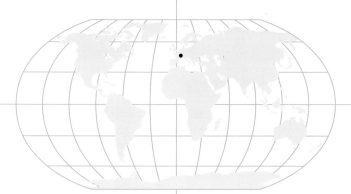

France
THE VERDON GORGE

A extraordinary chasm cut by the Verdon River.

The Cañon du Verdon lies in the upper reaches of the River Verdon in the Alpes-de-Haute-Provence in south-eastern France. The Verdon eventually flows into the River Durance, which joins the River Rhône near Avignon. The gorge can be reached by road from Marseilles, about 80 miles (129 km) away, or Toulon, about 60 miles (97 km).

Right, looking down the Verdon Gorge, with the Lac de St Croix on the far left – note the road which clings to the wall of the canyon.

A T the south-western end of the Alps in the
mountains of Provence, the River
Verdon rises, fed by the melting snows of the
surrounding hills. It flows south towards the
coast for some 30 miles (48 km) before
swinging west for a further 30 miles (48 km) to
join the River Durance that flows into the
Rhône at Avignon. As the river turns to the
west it enters the Verdon Gorge and then
quickly gathers speed to race through the
bottom of the canyon. The sides of the gorge
soon become steeper, and in many places the
walls are vertical. Some of the larger and higher
cliffs have become popular with rock climbers.

The gorge itself is only 12 miles (19 km) long
but in that short distance it reaches a maximum
depth of 2,300 feet (701 m) from the rim to the
river, making it both the longest and the
deepest gorge in France. In some parts it is also
very narrow and the opposing canyon walls are
a mere 650 feet (198 m) apart. Despite the
precipitous sides of the gorge it is possible for
the more intrepid explorers to follow a track
leading deep into the canyon. For many, this
provides the best views of the gorge and, with
the sheer walls towering above and the raging
rapids of the river below, it is a reminder of the
powerful forces in nature. The less adventurous
can still find spectacular views of the gorge
from the highway, known as the Corniche
Sublime, that follows close to the edge; a road
on the opposite side clings to the very rim of
the chasm. The best spots for panoramic views
are marked along both routes and frequently
show the contrast between the rugged pale-
coloured limestone cliffs and the verdant green
of the gentler wooded slopes.

The gorge has been cut into a sequence of
thick limestone strata and there are many caves
in the surrounding limestone countryside. It is
sometimes difficult to appreciate that limestone
was deposited under the sea and frequently
contains the remains of countless billions of
invertebrate animals whose calcite shells form
the bulk of the rock. This is all part of the story
of the gorge, however, because as the limestone
was gradually uplifted (in the same geological
uplift that raised the Alps), the river was able to
continue eroding its bed to form the gorge.
The many caves in the area suggest that the
process was assisted by chemical erosion of the
limestone, but to date there is no evidence to
suggest that the gorge was originally an
underground cave system whose roof collapsed.

*Tourist boats show the scale of the
towering limestone cliffs in a narrow
section of the gorge.*

Formation of a Gorge

A RIVER gorge may be
formed in a number of
ways, but there are certain
differences between the
formation of gorges and the
formation of more common
river valleys. The first point is
that the river must continue to
deepen its channel through the
rocks faster than the sides are
eroded away, and it must also
have sufficient energy to erode
its bed so that it does not
deposit its sediment load. Thus
the river must have a steep
gradient relative to its flow.
The sides of the valley will also
erode if there are tributary
streams, and a normal valley
will result.

In desert regions the water
supply is often dependent on
occasional thunderstorms that
produce enormous quantities of
water for a short time – ideal
conditions for the river to carve
a gorge. The river has a very
powerful, high-energy flow;
but once the storm is over the
water quickly subsides and
there is no erosion on the sides
of the valley, so they remain
very steep.

Many of the world's great
gorges have been formed in
areas where the land has been
steadily rising at a rate equal to
the rate at which the river can
continue to cut a channel. The
Grand Canyon is a classic
example of this. In limestone
country, gorge formation may
be assisted when the roof of an
underground river collapses.

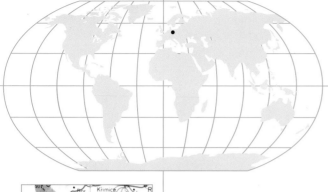

THE BAVARIAN FOREST

*The Bayerischer-Wald, a great and ancient forest straddles the
border between Germany and the Czech Republic.*

The city of Grafenau lies some
31 miles (50 km) to the south
of the National Park. Access is
unrestricted and the area is
criss-crossed by a series of
footpaths and minor roads.

Carnivorous Plants

THE sundews are a group of
plants which thrive on the
surface of raised bogs despite
very poor nutrient conditions.
These low growing, insectivorous plants have a rosette of
leaves, tipped with sticky,
reddish, translucent hairs. Once
an unsuspecting insect is
captured by these sticky hairs,
the edges of the leaves curl
over to encase the prey,
allowing enzymes secreted by
the leaf to digest the insect and
absorb its nutrients into the
plant.

*Above, an adult Tengmalm's owl
observes from its nest hole in a
dead tree.*

*Facing page, spruce trees in a corner
of the Sumava Forest National
Park, in the mist of early morning.*

THE centre of Europe was once a wilderness
covered by vast tracts of mixed broad-
leaved and coniferous forest, broken only by
rivers and lakes and interspersed with areas of
blanket bog. In the high mountain regions the
forest was dominated by spruce because of its
ability to survive the cold frosts and heavy
snows of winter. The Bavarian Forest, the
largest remaining remnant of what was once a
much larger forest, straddles the German-
Czech border, covering a total area of some
780 square miles (2,020 sq km).

Although there has been some exploitation
over the last 150 years some areas of original
forest still remain intact, principally because of
their remoteness, and more recently because of
the protection they have been afforded – the
Bavarian Forest National Park was established
in 1969. It is remarkable in that over 98 per
cent of the total area of 51 square miles
(132 sq km) is forested. Together with the
Sumava Forest National Park on the Czech
side of the border, covering 645 square miles
(1,683 sq km), a large proportion of the total
area of the Bavarian forest is secure. With the
protection afforded to the forest the effects of
human interference are disappearing, tree
felling has ceased and the drainage channels
which were cut are becoming blocked
and the areas of raised bog are beginning to
be revived.

The Bavarian Forest National Park lies
mainly on granite and gneiss, overlaid with
acidic soils which are able to support the pre-
dominantly coniferous woodland. On the
upper reaches of the highest mountains, which
reach beyond 4,600 feet (1,402 m), the forest is
of spruce with a limited understorey of bilberry,
mountain tassel flower and chickweed winter-
green. On the lower slopes, the forest is of
maple, elm, ash, alder, beech and lime, together
with spruce, silver fir and the occasional
ancient yew tree. In this mixed forest there is a
much wider variety of understorey plants,
including ferns such as thorny fern and lady's
fern, as well as various flowering plants such as
woodruff, Turks-cap lilies, herb Paris (a good
indicator of ancient woodland) and the
extremely rare Hungarian gentian.

The forest is criss-crossed by a myriad of
small streams which cascade down the
mountain slopes to feed the raised bogs on the
valley floor. Along the sides of these streams
the lush vegetation includes the striking alpine
sow thistle with its blue-violet flowers, yellow
Austrian leopard's-bane and the mountain
buttercup. In the damp valley bottoms spruce
and bog birch dominate, along with other
moisture-loving plants such as horse-tails and
common twayblade. Areas of raised bog formed
by deep cushions of sphagnum moss also
support mountain pine, crowberry, bilberry
and the insectivorous sundews.

The forest and open bog areas are a treasury
of animal and bird life. Herds of red deer
wander through the forest, while other animals
are more rare, including the lynx, the fish otter
and pine marten. A huge number of bird
species inhabit the forest, including capercaillie,
hazel grouse, red-breasted flycatcher, and four
species of woodpecker – great-spotted, white
back, three-toed and black. There are also
many birds of prey, most notably honey
buzzards and goshawks, and Tengmalm's and
pygmy owls. Other species including the eagle
owl, the Ural owl and the raven are slowly
being reintroduced to these ancient woodlands.

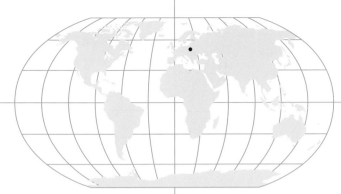

Poland

BIALOWIEZA FOREST

In the north-east of Poland this ancient forest has stood largely undisturbed for over 500 years.

Bialowieza Forest lies some 140 miles (225 km) east of Warsaw (Warszawa) and is accessible by both road and rail. Much of the forest, however, is totally inaccessible due to its remoteness from roads, the density of the trees and ruggedness of the terrain.

Beech Woods of Central Europe

BEECH is the climax forest tree over much of Europe (although not in Bialowieza), particularly on relatively rich soils with average moisture content. Much of these woodlands have been cleared, and most of what remains has been affected by the selective felling of beech, a valuable timber used for a variety of purposes. Beech forms a closed canopy over the forest floor, letting as little as 2 per cent of the light to penetrate, and profoundly affecting what can grow. The thick layer of dead beech leaves on the forest floor decomposes only very slowly, resulting in limited understorey flora.

Right, the open canopy of the deciduous forest allows light to penetrate to the forest floor, where ferns and other plants thrive.

GREAT forests once covered much of both lowland and mountainous regions of eastern Europe. Over the centuries human encroachment has resulted in the drastic reduction of these once-vast areas, with forests cleared for agricultural land, the building of settlements and a variety of industrial activities.

Bialowieza Forest, covering 470 square miles (1,217 sq km), is a mere fragment of the original forest which once covered these lands. At the centre of this remaining forest lies the 20.5 square miles (53.1 sq km) of Bialowieza National Park. This whole area has only survived intact because for many years it was under the patronage of kings and the tsars of Russia as a hunting ground. Its importance as both a national and an international asset is now recognised through the protection afforded it by the Polish government, and by its designation as a Biosphere Reserve and a World Heritage Site.

These ancient forests have a diverse flora including at least 26 species of tree, with pine, spruce, ash, hornbeam, alder, oak, birch, lime and aspen the most common; curiously beech and yew, common elsewhere in Europe, are absent. Species characteristic of all four corners of Europe thrive within the forest: the northern Lapland willow and the southern silver fir are mixed with durmast oak, a western European species, and dwarf birch from the east. In total there are over 700 species of flowering plants and countless species of moss, liverworts, ferns and lichens.

brown bears, wolves, lynx, moose and wild boar together with otters and beavers. The European bison and the tarpan (the wild horse) are also to be found in the forest. Most of these animals depend on the protected habitat of the forest for their survival.

The forest is also an important area for a large number of different birds, with over 160 breeding species recorded, from woodpeckers, flycatchers and nutcrackers to snipe and various aquatic warblers which frequent the bogs and marshes. There are also many birds of prey, including a number of species of eagle, Montagu's harrier and nine species of owl.

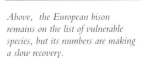

Above, the European bison remains on the list of vulnerable species, but its numbers are making a slow recovery.

The forest is at least 5,000 years old, and some parts have never been subjected to any sort of felling or management. Within the forest are natural clearings where there are peat bogs, marshes and meadows. This variety of habitat contributes to the overall diversity of species of both animal and plant in the Bialowieza forest.

This is one of the last refuges in Europe for a number of large mammals which includes

The international importance of this virgin, primeval forest is undoubted, and further steps are being taken to ensure that it and the diversity of life it supports are protected. A further area covering 335 square miles (870 sq km) across the border in Belorussia has been brought into a protection scheme, to preserve for the future what little remains of Europe's original native flora and fauna.

The European Bison

LIKE many of the large herding herbivores, the European bison once occurred in large numbers throughout much of Europe. Relentless erosion of their habitat reduced their numbers dramatically, and by the 17th century and they were in real danger of extinction. Two strongholds remained for the bison: Bialowieza Forest and the Russian Caucasus (Bol 'soi Karkaz). In 1914 there were still around 700 bison in Bialowieza, but by 1918 all those in the wild were dead. Some Bialowieza stock remained in captivity, and a slow but dedicated captive breeding programme increased numbers, so that in 1939 some animals could be released back into the wild. Today there is a herd of around 260 in Bialowieza which, together with the 200 or so remaining in the Caucasus, represent the total wild stock. Although still vulnerable and threatened, numbers are increasing each year, and with their habitat now protected their future is more secure.

THE DANUBE DELTA

*The largest and most natural wetland area
remaining in Europe.*

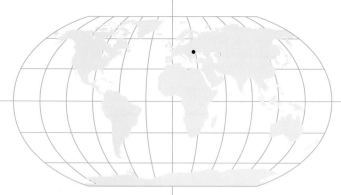

The main town and capital of
the district is Tulcea, which lies
some 220 miles (354 km) north
east of the capital Bucharest
(Buchuresti). Boat trips on the
Danube are available as either
day trips or longer cruises.

The Reed Beds – Biological Filters

IN recent times large areas of
the delta have been dredged
to make the upper reaches of
the river more accessible to
shipping, and drained to acquire
the rich alluvial lands for
cultivation. These operations
have gone on unchecked
regardless of possible wider
effects on the delta as a whole,
and therefore large areas of the
extensive reed beds have been
lost. These are important not
only as habitat for birds and as a
source of raw material for
thatching and paper-making,
but also as a natural filtration
plant. The reeds grow in areas
which are either permanently
water-logged or intermittently
flooded, re-growing each year
from a dense mat of rootstock
(rhizomes) below the surface.
When they die back, much of
the mineral goodness is
returned to the rootstock to
fuel the next year's growth.
The decomposing plant
material, together with the mat
of rootstock, act as an effective
natural filter, removing many
pollutants from the waters of
the Danube before they empty
into the Black Sea.

THE Danube is the second longest river in Europe after the Volga, and flows for some 1,716 miles (2,761 km) from its source in the Black Forest (Schwarzwald) in Germany through Austria, Slovakia, Hungary, former Yugoslavia and Bulgaria before entering Romania. The Danube drainage basin is 310,927 square miles (805,300 sq km), and the delta where the waters eventually enter the Black Sea covers an area of some 2,317 square miles (6,000 sq km) – a mosaic of lakes, reed swamps, meadows and primary oak forest.

This vast area of wetland straddles the border between Romania and Ukraine. A measure of its importance is demonstrated by the number

of global designations it has acquired in recent years, most notably its recognition as a World Heritage Site.

Above all else the Danube Delta is famous for its bird life, with over 280 species recorded. An estimated 180 species breed in the area, and the remainder – from as far apart as the Arctic, China, Siberia and the Mediterranean – use the delta as an over-wintering area or a stopover on longer migrations. A number of these bird species are endangered world wide, and the delta takes on an additional importance as a safe haven. Large proportions of the remaining world populations of four species in particular depend on the delta: the pygmy cormorant, of which there is a colony estimated at 12,000 pairs; the red-breasted goose, of which the entire world population can sometimes be found wintering in the area; 150 pairs (10 per cent of the total population) of the very rare Dalmatian pelican; and also a substantial number of white pelicans.

For centuries the Danube has been a vital trade route, and for much of this time man and nature have survived in relative harmony. However, in more recent years, the Danube Delta has suffered from the commercial forces and pollution of modern civilisation. The waters of the delta and the adjacent coastal seas support a large number of fish species, many of which have been exploited. Over half the fresh-water fish harvest of Romania is taken from the Danube Delta, including carp and caviar-yielding sturgeon. Increased drainage of the area for agricultural land – which in turn has meant increased pollution from that source – has resulted in the decline of many indigenous species. The political revolution of 1989 resulted in a more environmentally sympathetic government, and steps are now being taken to reverse some of the damage and protect what is still a vital ecological unit in Europe.

Above, white pelicans in flight.

Left, the harvesting of reeds is essential to the local economy and to the successful management of the wetland.

Pelicans

PELICANS are among the largest bird species, uniquely adapted to an aquatic way of life. Their most characteristic feature is the large, pointed beak with its distensible pouch adapted for engulfing fish. Pelicans live in colonies and make efficient fish-catchers, sweeping an area of shallows in line. The reed beds of the Danube Delta provide essential safe nesting for the two species of pelican found there. The Dalmatian pelican, a beautiful, silvery-white bird, is now on the list of globally endangered species, a victim of its own success as a superb fisherman. Whole colonies have been destroyed by local commercial fishermen, particularly in the Middle East, where the birds are perceived as direct competitors.

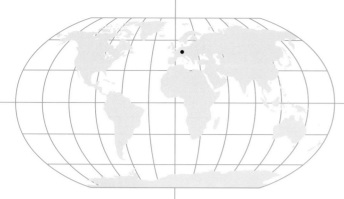

Austria
THE HOHE TAUERN

*The spectacular mountainous backbone
of western Austria.*

The Hohe Tauern crosses the provinces of Tirol, Salzburg and Kärnten. The nearest cities are Innsbruck to the west and Salzburg to the north, both served by international flights.

Hohe Tauern National Park

IN 1971, the heads of government of the three provinces of Tirol, Salzburg and Kärnten agreed to establish the Hohe Tauern National Park. By 1984, some 475 square miles (1,230 sq km) of the region, including the principal peaks in each group, had been declared a national park. There are plans to extend this by the addition of some 270 square miles (700 sq km) of the Tirol, but there is opposition from other interest groups. The park area has been zoned, and includes specially protected areas to safeguard the fauna, flora and geological formations.

Right, the cold beauty of the snowfield below the Grossglockner is a magnet for alpine climbers.

Far right, the Pasterze Glacier flows through an ice-scoured valley below the Grossglockner.

THE eastern Alps cover about 65 per cent of Austria, greatly limiting the area in the rest of the country which is available for agriculture and other human needs. Hohe Tauern is the name given to the highest parts of the Austrian Alps along the southern side of the Pinzgau valley. The region is normally divided into three mountain groups; from west to east they are the Venediger, Granatespitze and Glockner. The Venediger and Glockner are areas of high mountains and extensive glaciers, connected in the middle by the slightly lower Granatespitze, a little-glaciated rock ridge. Only the Ötztaler Alps to the west have a greater area of snow and ice in Austria.

The highest peak in the Venediger group is the Grossvenediger at 12,054 feet (3,674 m) – a magnificent pyramidal peak covered with ice and surrounded by snow. The first ascent was made in 1841 by Ignaz von Kürsinger with a party of 40, an exceptionally large group by today's standards for a first ascent. However it is an easy climb, presenting no difficulty to anyone experienced in walking on glaciers.

The Granatespitze group is perhaps the least spectacular of the range, its highest peak, the Grosser Muntanitz, a mere 10,604 feet (3,232 m) high, and with correspondingly less snow and ice. While it does offer some fine climbing and excellent views of the surrounding countryside, it is overshadowed by the greater grandeur of the adjacent Venediger and Glockner groups.

The Glockner group forms the jewel in the crown of the Austrian Alps. The area of the group is much smaller than the Venediger, but there is so much variety and it is so visually spectacular that the first impression is one of overwhelming splendour. The Grossglockner at 12,458 feet (3,797 m) appears to tower above its neighbours, narrow rock ridges plunge downward from the summit and the mountain is flanked by precipitous ice slopes, scarred by crevasses and tumbling ice-falls like cataracts carved in marble. Around the lower slopes the Pasterze Glacier curves like a frozen moat, more than 6 miles (10 km) long , and the largest glacier in the eastern Alps. Count von Salm, the Prince-Bishop of Gurk, was the first to climb the mountain in 1800, and it still provides a good challenge for mountaineers.

There is no doubt that the best way to see the mountains is to walk and climb among them, but in the Hohe Tauern there are excellent roads that provide panoramic views for the less energetic. From Lienz, on the south side of the range, the road to Mittersill affords good views of the Grossvenediger just before entering the Felbertauern tunnel. At Mittersill you can follow the Pinzgau valley east to Bruck and then take the Grossglockner road, which passes close to the mountain and crosses the ridge at Hochtor before descending back to Lienz – a round trip of about 113 miles (182 km). Some minor tracks lead off the main roads to give closer access to the mountains, and the road off the Grossglockner highway just north of Heiligenblut leads to Franz-Josefs-Höhe, at the side of the Pasterze Glacier, arguably the most beautiful place in the entire region.

THE MATTERHORN

This jagged four-sided pyramid pierces the sky from the midst of the Alps.

Situated on the Italian-Swiss border, the Matterhorn is easily reached by road from either country. On the Swiss side, a main road runs alongside the River Rhône as it flows towards Lake Geneva (Lac Léman), while on the Italian side the mountain is easily accessible from Turin and Aosta. Once at the mountain, a number of lifts and tramways offer access to the slopes.

Known in Italy as Monte Cervino and in France as Mont Cervin, the Matterhorn is instantly recognizable among alpine peaks.

THE Matterhorn (known in France as Mont Cervin) is not the highest mountain in the Alps, but it is surely the most dramatic.

Consisting of some 14,690 feet (4,480 m) of hard crystalline rock, the Matterhorn is a classic pyramidal peak formed by glacial activity in the ice ages over the last 2 million years. Four tapering faces of rock converge at its peak, faces that were so difficult to climb that an ascent was not completed until 1865; the south face remained unconquered until 1931. Its distinctive shape is the result of cirques, ground out by glaciers, converging on an ever-narrower point, until all that remains is the

sharp tip of the mountain, known as a pyramidal peak – Mount Everest, in the Himalayas, was formed in a similar way.

The Alps themselves were formed when the tectonic plate of Africa was forced northwards to collide with southern Europe. The process began about 180 million years ago, and reached a climax about 40 million years ago when the earth's crust buckled and rose to form the great spine of mountains that are the Alps. The mountains' core contain hard rocks such as granite, mica schist, and gneiss, with softer rocks such as sandstones and shales at the edges. The mountain range is 750 miles (1,207 km) long and runs through Germany, France, Switzerland, Italy, former Yugoslavia, Albania, and Italy. Europe's great rivers – the Rhine, the Rhône and the Danube – originate in these mountains, while famous lakes such as Maggiore and Lucerne lie in the hollows gouged by the glaciers of the last ice age.

On 14 July 1865, the first successful team of climbers, led by the Englishman Edward Whymper, reached the top of the Matterhorn by traversing a ridge on the Swiss side. Three days later, an Italian team under the leadership of Giovanni Carrel arrived at the summit via a ridge on the Italian side. The Italians later claimed that Whymper's team had thrown rocks at them, an allegation the Englishman vigorously denied. Today, cables and artificial footholds help amateurs to the top of the peak that was once the domain of the dedicated and hardy few.

Another climber closely associated with the Matterhorn was Hermann Perren, a Zermatt guide and hotel owner, whose ambition was to climb the Matterhorn, not just once, but 150 times. Unfortunately he fell to his death at the age of 68, fewer than ten climbs short of his goal.

The Alps are the most important mountain range in Europe, and the source of some of its greatest rivers.

Alpine Peaks

THERE are many famous mountains in the Alps, of which the Matterhorn is one of the best known. The highest is Mont Blanc in France, which is 13,100 feet (3,993 m), while the Jungfrau is generally considered one of the most beautiful of the snow-capped mountains. The Eiger has achieved a particular place of importance because of the difficulty of its climbs; its almost sheer north face, one mile (1.6 km) high, defied all attempts to master it until 1935. In Austria, the towering Zugspitze is the tallest of the Bavarian Alps and is famous for skiing and climbing. In the valley below, Garmisch-Partenkirchen was the site of the 1936 Winter Olympics, with tramways to the crest of the mountain.

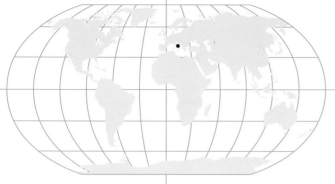

Italy

MOUNT VESUVIUS

This active volcano on the busy Bay of Naples seethes wisps of steam and smoke from its summit.

Vesuvius lies about 10 miles (16 km) outside Naples (Napoli), and roads to Pompei and Herculaneum (Ercolano) from the city are excellent.

Digging Out the Past

ARCHAEOLOGICAL remains at Pompei were discovered as early as the 1600s, and since then excavations have continued. The discovery of many skeletons provides clues not only to events of the fateful eruption, but also to the way of life some 2,000 years ago. Pregnant mothers, babies, old men and children have all been identified, their bodies frozen in time by the hot lava.

Scientists examining the bones have been able to distinguish between people who lived a comfortable life with plenty of food, and those who were probably slaves. The skeletons of the slaves show signs that they were poorly nourished, and wear and tear patterns on their arms and spines indicate they performed hard physical labour.

Fascinating trappings of everyday life have also been uncovered, including brightly painted buttons, a crib, a fine wooden cabinet, a bed, a cloth press, a marble bathtub, a large bronze bath and even a boat.

Right, the cone of Vesuvius rests in the collapsed outer rim, or caldera, of an older volcano.

About one o'clock on the afternoon of 24 August in A.D. 79, the residents of the small Roman towns around the base of Mount Vesuvius (Vesuvio), the great sleeping volcano to the east of Naples in Southern Italy, heard a tremendous roar. Accounts written at the time suggest that people were frightened, but thought they would be safe within their houses. The explosion which followed turned molten stone into pumice and ash that rained down onto the townships of this busy coastline.

Towards midnight the volcanic activity increased, and families from the town of Herculaneum, a few miles west along the coast,

At 4,190 feet (1,277 m), Vesuvius is less than half the height of Etna, but its viscous lava makes it far more explosive. Sulphurous fumes constantly rise from the huge main crater, and there are places near the summit where the rocks are hot enough to cook eggs.

The first (and most notorious) recorded eruption of Vesuvius, in A.D.79, caused the collapse of an older crater. A new, basin-shaped crater called a caldera was formed, and inside this a new, smaller cone arose. The last major eruption was in 1944, and a stroll or cable car ride to the rim may suggest that the volcano has been tamed – but the whisps of smoke and signs of subsidence in the towns below are reminders that it could erupt again at any time.

began to flee their homes, heading for the only possible escape route – the sea. Suddenly, a great surge of ash exploded from the volcano and raced towards the town, followed by a fiery tongue of molten rock. Perfectly preserved skeletons uncovered in the houses near the harbour suggest that people had very little time to understand what was happening – some died in each other's arms, while others died as they ran away. A lamp was found with one group of skeletons, suggesting that the people had taken it with them to light their way as they fled the terrifying eruption. Successive surges buried the town under great layers of ash and rock, and so it remained until the excavations that are still going on in Herculaneum today.

The residents of the nearby town of Pompei were spared until the following day when Vesuvius erupted again, exploding in clouds of deadly ash and gas. An estimated 2,000 people perished in Pompei that day – but the number is constantly revised as archaeologists uncover more and more human remains in the vast excavations.

Mount Etna

By contrast, Mount Etna in Sicily (Sicilia) is benign. Although it destroyed the town of Catania in A.D.122 and erupted ferociously in 1979, it has never caused the loss of life and devastation of Vesuvius. The two volcanoes are very different: the magma under Etna is very fluid, so gases can escape easily. The thick, sticky lava under Vesuvius traps these gases, and it was this that caused the devastation of A.D.79.

Etna, 600,000 years old and the largest volcano in Europe, emerges from the sea bed to tower to 10,900 feet (3,322 m) above the eastern coast of Sicily. A series of eruptions have left it a complicated structure with scores of secondary cones, vents and craters within craters.

Mount Etna, in Sicily, is Europe's largest active volcano, and remains covered in snow for some nine months of the year.

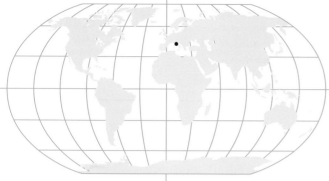

Italy

FRASASSI CAVES

These beautiful caves in the limestone hills of central Italy have some of the most impressive stalactite and stalagmite formations in the world.

The Frasassi Caves are located in central Italy near the River Esino, a few miles inland from the Adriatic coast. The caves are south-west of Ancona, the nearest major city. Florence (Firenze) is about 90 miles (145 km) to the west, and road connections are excellent.

IN 1971 a startling discovery was made by a team of speleologists from Ancona, caving in the limestone hills of the Apennines. The vast cave system in the Frasassi Gorge (Gola di Frasassi) was always a favourite among cavers and tourists, but this lucky group stumbled upon the most splendid of all the Frasassi Caves: the Great Cave of the Wind, in Italy called La Grotta Grande del Vento. The cave is not just one cavern, but is linked to around eight miles (nearly 13 km) of tunnels and passageways. It has several enormous caverns, each large enough to house a cathedral, as well as many smaller caves, and each with its own special beauty. Among the most impressive caverns is the Room of the Candles, or Sala

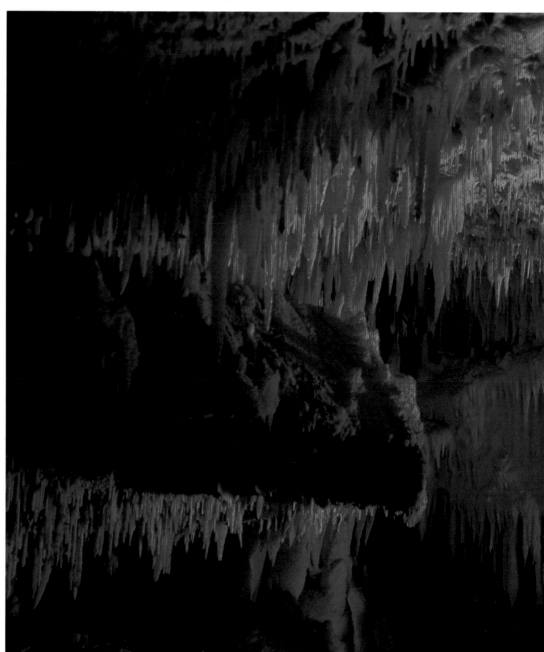

Right, an extraordinary collection of natural stalactites and stalagmites in one of the Frasassi caves.

delle Candeline, the roof of which is hung with thousands of creamy alabaster-white stalactites. Another highlight is the Room of the Infinite, or Sala dell' Infinito, where the stalactites and stalagmites have been growing for so long that many of them have met to form majestic columns. The intricate formations of the columns are reminiscent of elegantly carved structures in Gothic architecture, and the overwhelming feel of this cave is that these columns are supporting the roof.

Beauty abounds in the Frasassi Cave system; wandering from cavern to cavern, an incredible array of geological formations are revealed, ranging from fragile curtains of mineral deposits so thin that light can shine through them, to great thick pinnacles that look like the teeth of an enormous dragon. In many caves, dripping water with minerals other than calcium carbonate has given some of the structures a dazzling display of colour, from soft blue-greens to delicate pale pinks.

Another particularly spectacular feature here is the Grotta delle Nottole, or the Cave of the Bats, where thousands of these tiny nocturnal mammals cling upside-down to the roof of the cavern or flit silently back and forth. At dusk, the entrances to the cave become a frenzy of activity as the thousands of bats leave their daytime resting place to hunt moths and other insects in the dark of night. Bats have poorly developed sight and hunt their prey by locating them with a complex sonar system, still not fully understood by scientists.

The Frasassi Caves are in prime karst country, where large deposits of limestone have been eroded by the River Esino and its tributary the Sentito, to form canyons deep in the foothills of the Apennines. The water from the two rivers has eroded some of the caves in the Frasassi system, over many thousands of years, steadily carving and dissolving tunnels and caverns in places where the rock was weakest.

As stalactites drip from the ceiling, so the minerals collect and build up beneath them.

Stalactites and Stalagmites

THE columns of rock that hang from the roofs of caves like icicles are called "stalactites"; those that stand pillar-like on the floor are "stalagmites". Both formations, known as dripstone, are a common feature of karst landscapes, which occur when limestone is dissolved along weak points by slightly acidic water. Dripstone begins to form when this water, saturated with the dissolved minerals from the rock, drips through the limestone ceiling of a cave forming calcite crystals on the ceiling. At first the crystals form a tube, and the water drips down the middle and runs down the side. As more water runs down the tube more calcite crystals are deposited, and eventually a stalactite develops as the tube increases in length. As the water drips from the stalactite, a mound of calcite crystals begins to collect on the floor of the cave, eventually growing upwards to form a stalagmite. In time the stalactites and the stalagmites can fuse together to form columns, and such formations take thousands, even millions, of years to develop.

Italy

EARTH PYRAMIDS
OF RENON

*Fragile remnants of
the last ice age*

Bolzano lies about 75 miles
(121 km) north of Verona along
the autostrada via Trento, and
the journey may also be done
by train. Slightly longer routes
by other roads may be more
scenic, such as a diversion to the
west along the shore of Lake
Garda (Lago di Garda).

Trentino-Alto
Adige

THE earth pillars are only one
attraction of this beautiful
mountain region. The area of
the Trentino-Alto Adige is 44
per cent woodland, the second
most heavily wooded region in
Italy. At lower altitudes, oak
and chestnut dominate, but
these give way to beech and
conifers higher up the valleys
which in turn are replaced by a
bush-forest of alder and dwarf
pine extending to the tree-line.
Wild flowers are common, and
the native fauna includes
chamois, roe deer, red deer
and ibex.

*Right, the strange earth pyramids
at Renon, remnants of a galcial
moraine, appear to echo the shapes
of the surrounding trees.*

For most people, mention of the Alps conjures vistas of soaring, snow-capped peaks towering over ice fields and glaciers, but in northern Italy the Alps have a rather different character. Here are the pinnacles of the Dolomites (Dolomiti), where amazingly steep and often overhanging cliffs punctuate the skyline like rows of giant teeth. They offer some of the finest rock-climbing in the Alps: not too high and facing the sun for most of the day, with no glaciers to negotiate. Bolzano lies to the west of the Marmolada at 10,500 feet (3,200 m), a ridge forming some of the finest peaks in the area, and to the north-east is an extensive, hilly plateau called the Renon or

Perpendicular cliffs of dolomitic limestone, in the Italian Dolomites.

Ritten. It is formed of hard, crystalline rock, with large individual crystals that contrast totally with the sedimentary magnesium and calcium carbonate (dolomite) of the Dolomites proper. The summit of the plateau is the Rittnerhorn at 7,418 feet (2,261 m), which provides splendid views of the Dolomites and as far east as Grossglockner in Austria.

The truly extraordinary feature of this landscape is to be found, however, at a much lower level. Close to the picturesque village of Lengmoos, in the Finsterbach Valley, partly hidden among the trees on the wooded slopes, are the famed earth pyramids or pillars of Renon.

The pillars themselves are clusters of earth pinnacles that look like tall, slender cloaked figures processing through the trees, and many are neatly capped with a small boulder. The explanation for the formation of this strange geomorphological phenomenon lies with the last ice age, when the region was heavily glaciated.

The retreating glaciers left behind moraines – fragments of rock engulfed and carried by the ice, and dumped as the ice melted – and deposits of boulder clay. Boulder clay also contains boulders, as the name implies, but is mainly composed of a fine clay. When boulder clay is exposed to the weather the clay tends to wash away in the rain, except where a boulder or large stone protects the clay beneath it. The clay is washes away from around and below the level of the boulder leaving the boulder perched on top of a pinnacle. Eventually the supporting pillar of clay becomes too narrow to support the boulder and it topples. As rain begins once again more to erode the top of the pinnacle, another boulder may be exposed and a new pinnacle will develop.

Earth Pillars and Badlands

The badlands landscape, such as may be familiar from Western film images of North America, is created by the erosive power of rainwater in an otherwise relatively dry region. Harder layers in a sedimentary sequence of pre-dominantly softer rocks form a cover which protects the underlying layers from erosion. On a large scale, a table-topped hill or mesa results, but where the harder layer has itself been gradually eroded, the result is a collection of towers or pillars, such as Bryce Canyon in Utah.

The earth pillar is the ultimate development of this erosion, although the protecting harder rock is usually a boulder, rather than the remnant of a layer. An example similar to that at Renon occurs in Val d'Herens in France, on a tributary of the Upper Rhône. Here the pillars are joined together in lines, giving the appearance of a buttress or a long curtain. Another example is in Turkey in the Göreme valley, about 150 miles (241 km) south-east of Ankara, where the rock is a volcanic tuff (volcanic ashes) from Mount Argaeus, and the cap rocks are fragments of a lava flow. The tuff is very soft, and hundreds of churches have been carved out of the pinnacles and elaborately decorated by the Cappadocian monks.

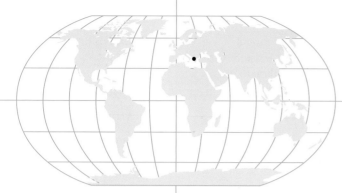

THE METÉORA

*Huge pinnacles of rock
with settlements perched on top.*

The Metéora lies on the north side of the small town of Kalabáka, in a valley on the eastern side of the Píndhos Óros mountains in Thessaly (Thessalía). The town is about 170 miles (274 km) north-west of Athens, or about 100 miles (161 km) south-west of Thessaloníki, beside the main road.

THE town of Kalabáka lies at the foot of the Píndhos Óros mountains on the edge of the broad valley of the Peneus River; the surrounding hills dominate the scenery. The slopes – some tree-clad, some bare rock – rise gently at first, then become steeper and blur into the distant heat haze. But to the north, the strange pinnacles of the Metéora draw the eye.

Climbing to the Top

STIFF climbs to the top of many of the towers offer views over the Peneus River valley that are quite breath-taking. Some of the lower slopes are wooded and provide welcome shade, but the rocks themselves are exposed to the searing Greek sun. It is more comfortable to make the ascent during the cool of the early morning, and there are clearer views before the heat haze of midday casts a veil over the distant hills.

The inselbergs of the Metéora stand watch over the valley like petrified giant sentinels.

The tops of the rocks are about 1,000 feet (305 m) above the valley floor, and the tallest reach as high as 1,800 feet (549 m). The sides of the pinnacles vary from steep to vertical, smooth to craggy, but any aspect would challenge a rock climber. Narrow, rounded ledges and vertical grooves and cracks provide some clues to the origin of these strange and dramatic outcrops.

The rocks are sandstones and conglomerates that were deposited in horizontal layers and originally covered a wide area. The various layers have reacted in different ways to weathering and erosion, thus forming the ledges and crevices. Following compaction and diagenesis (the change from a soft sediment into a sedimentary rock by increased pressure and temperature as the sediments are buried under succeeding layers of sediment), the resulting vertical joints provided lines of natural weakness. During diagenesis it is common for water, saturated with lime or silica, to permeate through the rocks and deposit some of its minerals. This acts as a cement to the grains of sand or pebbles in the conglomerate so that the rock becomes quite hard. It might be expected that a particular rock would have the same properties throughout the area where it occurs, but in nature this is rare – a fact which may be frustrating to the geologist, but it results in an endlessly fascinating landscape.

In some areas the jointing in the rocks was extensive and provided easy paths for erosion, while in other areas it appears the rock was better cemented and better able to resist erosion. Over the millennia, it is these resistant areas which became the towers of the Metéora that we see today.

Monasteries of the Metéora

VISITORS to the Metéora can marvel at the beauty of nature and the endless ways in which the forces of nature can affect the landscape. But there is another source of wonder here – the precarious monasteries that perch atop these pinnacles. At first sight it appears virtually impossible to reach the top of a pinnacle without resorting to serious rock-climbing, but the intrepid monks of the 14th and 15th centuries managed to do so, and then to build their homes and churches on the summit. It must have been amazing to watch while the building materials were hauled up to the building site and then to see the structures gradually take shape. Once installed on the tops of their pinnacles, the monks would pull up the ladders behind them and rest safe in the knowledge that their lofty positions were virtually impregnable.

The monasteries began to fall into disuse during the 19th century, and today the monks are vastly outnumbered by tourists. The ascent is less precarious than in the past; staircases and ramps have been built to replace the old system of ladders.

Below, the monastery of Aghios Trias, perched high on its rocky pinnacle.

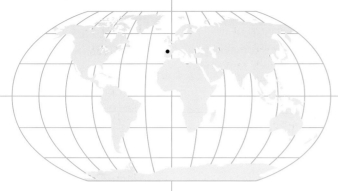

PICOS DE EUROPA

The Cordillera Cantabrica mountain range spans the northern coast of Spain from the Pyrenees to Portugal, crowned in the middle by the Picos de Europa.

Lying in a triangle between the port of Santander, Oviedo and León, the mountains can be reached by taking any of a number of picturesque roads which lead to small sleepy villages.

THE national park of Picos de Europa covers 29.8 square miles (77.2 sq km) of rugged mountains, with alpine meadows which have been claimed from native forest. The mountains are precipitous pinnacles of limestone, with the highest peaks of Naronso de Bulnes at 8,252 feet (2,515 m) and Torre Cerreda at 8,685 feet (2,647 m). From December to May each year, and often for longer, this area lies under a thick covering of snow, but with the thaw in late spring the area

erupts into life with a carnival of colour and fragrance from the many hay meadow flowers.

The area has been managed in essentially the same way for at least the last 5,000 years, and has escaped modern fertilisers and pesticides. The hay meadows of the lower regions of the Picos de Europa were cultivated from the natural vegetation of mixed oak and beech forest. The remaining areas of woodland, together with those in the adjacent Covadonga National Park to the west and Saja National Reserve to the east, are the last remaining stronghold in Europe for a number of animal species that were once widespread across the continent. Most notable are the endangered Iberian wolf and brown bear, together with wild cat, genet, otter, pine marten and wild boar. On the barren scree slopes in the rugged regions, thousands of nimble footed chamois thrive.

Butterflies and the Picos

IN areas where modern agricultural practices have resulted in the decline in hay meadows there has been a parallel decline in butterfly species. The Picos de Europa is a haven for over 130 species of butterfly – many very beautiful, some extremely rare and others found nowhere else in the world. The Gavarnie blue has evolved a race endemic to these mountain meadows, as is the chalk hill blue. Clouds of small butterflies such as purple-shot coppers and various species of hairstreak create a haze of moving pastel shades above the meadow flowers, and there is no more eye-catching sight than the large and exotic swallowtails.

Above, the striking markings of the male Apollo butterfly have unfortunately made it a popular target for collectors.

Right, autumn colour in the Picos de Europa

The bird life of the Picos is exceptional, with a particularly wide range of birds of prey, including Egyptian and griffin vultures, short-toed, golden and booted eagles, buzzards, Montagu's harriers, hen harriers and kites. Other bird species of note include Bonelli's warbler, black redstart, the black woodpecker and both the common and alpine chough.

The floral diversity of the hay meadows is unrivalled in northern Europe. Partly because of the lack of any dominant species, more than 550 flowering species congregate in this small area – a number equal to about one third of the total British flora. This richness and diversity is due a combination of the antiquity and unchanging quality of the management of the area, with the variations in underlying geology and the range of altitudes of the hay meadows. The list of flowers includes greater yellow rattle, pink-purple kidney vetch, white asphodel, bloody cranesbill, gentian and narcissus, all in profusion together with such rarities as rock cinquefoil and martagon lily. Many species of orchid also feature in the Picos, including both early and late spider orchid, man orchid, fragrant orchid, black vanilla orchid and fly orchid.

Natural Remedies

NATURE has a remedy for most human afflictions, and this is demonstrated in the traditional cures found in many of the traditional meadow plants. Thus the roots of bistort are used to cure intestinal disorders, while the leaves of cowslip are rich in vitamin C. An infusion of mallow flowers will help alleviate various respiratory problems, and kidney vetch flowers help close wounds quickly thus reducing scarring.

THE MESETA

The Meseta covers most of central Spain, making the capital city of Madrid an excellent focal point. Roads radiate from here like the spokes of a wheel.

*An ancient tableland
that forms the core of the country.*

THE land to the south of the Pyrenees is the Iberian Peninsula, comprising Spain, Portugal, and Gibraltar in the far south facing north Africa. Most of this great peninsula is an ancient tableland that formed a stable block of land, resisting the forces of the African continent slowly colliding with southern Europe. On the northern side of the block the pressure of the continental shift was absorbed

by crumpling and folding the rocks into a range of mountains – the Pyrenees. On the southern side, the Rock of Gibraltar is a slice of the earth's crust thrust northward onto the southern part of Spain.

The Meseta is not simply a flat plateau, for rivers have cut deep valleys over millions of years, and there are some high mountain ranges within its area, including Spain's highest

Right, weathered limestone at El Torcal de Antequera stand like the tower blocks of a petrified city.

mountain, Mulhacén (11,425 feet, 3,482 m), in the Sierra Nevada. The average height of the Meseta is about 3,000 to 4,000 feet (914 to 1,219 m), but the highest points in the centre are Pico de Almanzor (8,504 feet, 2,592 m) in the Sierra de Gredos, and Pico Peñalara (8,097 feet, 2,468 m) in the Sierra de Guadarrama, that lie on the northern side of the River Tagus (Tejo), west and north of Madrid. The principal rivers of the region are the Ebro in the north, which flows east into the Mediterranean at Tortosa, and the Tagus and Guadalquivir that flow west into the Atlantic at Lisbon, in Portugal, and through Seville in the south-west to the Atlantic.

Much of the Meseta is composed of the hard and ancient crystalline rocks of the metamorphic basement, but there are areas of limestone and two of these are notable. About 100 miles (161 km) east of Madrid an area of limestone outcrop is known as the "Ciutad Encantada", the Enchanted City. This feature lies on the plateau and covers an area of about 500 acres (201 hectares). From a distance there

is the unmistakable sight of a city skyline with buildings standing above the horizon, but closer inspection reveals that this is not a man-made city at all, but a bizarre work of nature. Slightly acid rainwater attacks limestone everywhere, but this limestone is a mixture of pure limestone (calcium carbonate) and dolomite (magnesium-calcium carbonate). The erosive power of the rain acts faster on the limestone than on the dolomite, resulting in these strange shapes that look like ancient buildings left to decay. It is little wonder that this natural city is regarded as enchanted.

Torcal de Antequera in the Sierra Nevada, about 20 miles (32 km) north of Malaga, is a limestone plateau that is also eroded into strange shapes. Here rainwater has exploited natural cracks and joints in the rock, and has eroded a shallow cave system just below the surface. Many of the cave roofs have collapsed, leaving trenches between upstanding blocks. This too has the appearance of a ruined city, with the trenches looking like ancient streets between lines of weathered buildings.

Typical limestone scenery at Serrania de Ronda, near the eastern edge of the Meseta.

Exploiting the Land

SOME parts of the Meseta are relatively flat, and the region around Valladolid, in the north-west, is an agricultural centre. Fields of grain cover this basin during summer, together with fruit trees and vines. Elsewhere on the Meseta shepherds tend flocks of long-haired goats and Merino sheep, renowned for the quality of their fine wool. Cattle are also an important part of the rural economy. These gentle pastoral activities contrast strongly with mining on the northern and southern margins of the Meseta – the Canadian Shield east of the Rocky Mountains is another famous example of crystalline crust with a wealth of minerals. Iron ore is mined in the Cantabrian Mountains, much of it for export, but some is also smelted in the port of Gijon where locally mined coal from Oviedo is used to fire the furnaces. Iron ore is also mined in the Sierra Nevada, and at other places along the southern margin are the copper mines of Rio Tinto, the lead and silver mines of Linares and the mercury (quicksilver) mines at Almaden. Although lead is still a valuable commodity it is often being replaced by other materials today, so that many lead mines depend on the silver frequently associated with lead minerals to provide a financial bonus that keeps the mines open.

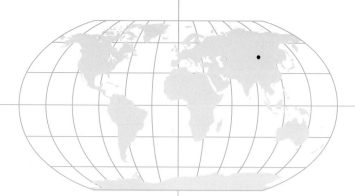

LAKE BAJKAL

This remarkable lake is situated in southern Siberia (Sibir) near to the Russian border with Mongolia.

The city of Irkutsk lies at the southern end of the lake. The famous Trans-Siberian railway passes the southern shore of the lake, while the more recent Bajkal-Amur Mainline takes a route around the northern shore.

Bajkal and Pollution

DESPITE its remoteness, Lake Bajkal and its unique flora and fauna is threatened by pollution. In recent years the area has become more accessible, and with the people have come their litter and rubbish, and increased erosion of fragile habitats.

Many pollutants are carried into the lake by the waters of the hundreds of rivers which feed into it. Major industries including a paper and pulp mill, thermal power plants, chemical and petrochemical installations, pumping lead, zinc and mercury among other materials, have all contributed to the destruction of vast areas of the bed of the lake. The local fish catch has also been seriously affected.

The problem has now been recognised and, importantly, it has been acknowledged that something needs to be done. Steps are underway to repair the damage and prevent any further destruction but as is always the case it takes much longer to repair the damage than it took to cause it.

Right, looking along the wooded shoreline, the vastness of Lake Bajkal stretches over the horizon.

IN trying to describe Lake Bajkal, superlatives become commonplace. It is some 25 million years old, by far the oldest lake in the world (the next oldest is Lake Tanganyika at a mere 2 million years). It is the deepest freshwater lake at 5,315 feet (1,620m), over 1,300 feet (396 m) deeper than the second deepest lake, Lake Tanganyika at 4,013 feet (1,223 m). It is 395 miles (636 km) in length, equivalent to the distance between Aberdeen and London; at its widest it is 49 miles (79 km) and 15 miles (25 km) at its narrowest point with a total coastline of 1,240 miles (1,995 km).

With a surface area at 12,159 square miles (31,492 sq km) it is equivalent to the combined land area of Belgium and the Netherlands and has a catchment area of 210,600 sq miles (545,452 sq km). Despite its relatively lowly seventh position in the league table of surface areas, Lake Bajkal contains 5,515 cubic miles (23,000 cu km) of water (which is almost as much as the five Great Lakes of Canada combined), and equivalent to about 20 per cent of all the surface fresh water in the world.

The lake is fed by over 300 rivers but is drained by only one, the Angara River, which eventually joins the Jenisej River which flows out into the Karskoje Sea high above the Arctic Circle.

Lake Bajkal provides not only breathtaking scenery but also supports a dazzling array of species of animal and plant, with over 2,600 species having been recorded of which an amazing 960 species of animal and 400 species of plant are endemic to Lake Bajkal. Despite its great depth, the water is very well mixed, partly as a result of the action of the hot water springs which rise at a depth of 1,350 feet (411 m).

The lake contains over 50 types of fish, including familiar species such as pike and perch, but nearly half are endemic species of bullheads and others. Two species belong to the genus Comephorus are completely transparent, and live at a depth of around

1,650 feet (503 m) in total darkness. The majority of the fish are found in the shallow margins of the lake, and despite the great expanse of the deep waters, only five

species have successfully colonised this area: the omul (a relative of the salmon), yellow-wing and long-wing bullheads and the two species of Comephorus. These five species represent over 75 per cent of the total fish in the lake.

There are many different species of invertebrates, including large numbers of gammarids, shrimp-like animals which have colonised the lake at all depths, some living in the lake's water, while others burrow in the bottom sediments. These form the main food supply for many of the fish.

The most famous and enigmatic species to be found in Lake Bajkal is undoubtedly the Bajkal seal. This is another of the endemic species which thrives in the lake, with over 70,000 individuals feeding off the plentiful fish resources in the lake.

Above, the Bajkal seal is found nowhere else in the world.

The Bajkal Seal

LAKE Bajkal is the only place in the world where this small species of freshwater seal is found. Growing to a length of only 4 feet (122 cm) and a maximum weight of 160 pounds (73 kg.), it has a uniform dark grey coat and the pups, which are born in solitary snow lairs, are pure white. The parent seals maintain the air holes into the lairs during the winter by gnawing at the ice from below. The population of 70,000 represents a considerable success, and numbers are recovering from a low in the 1930s which was due to human exploitation.

The question of how the ancestors of this species got to Lake Bajkal is intriguing. There is no evidence of the sea ever having occupied the Bajkal region of Siberia, although a vast inland sea known as the Paratethys stretched across the area now containing the Caspian, Black and Aral Seas. It is thought that the ancestors of the Bajkal seal and the closely related Caspian seal originated here, and when the Paratethys contracted, some remained in the Caspian Sea while others escaped to the Arctic Ocean. It is supposed that some of these seals reached Lake Bajkal by migrating from the Arctic Ocean during the last glacial period, when the Yenisey-Angara River systems connected Lake Bajkal to the Arctic Ocean.

LENA DELTA

The nearest major airport to this vast geographical area is at Jakutsk, the capital city of the newly formed Sakha Republic. Tiksi, which is closed off for the winter months by sea ice, is the nearest port and stands at the mouth of one of the Lena's channels.

Set in a frozen wilderness, this huge river system rises near Lake Bajkal and divides into more than 150 separate channels in the Russian tundra.

THE Lena is one of the great north-flowing rivers of central Siberia, along with the Ob'-Irtysh and the Jenise. Rising in the mountains just north of Lake Bajkal, it flows 2,730 miles (4,393 km) to the Laptevych Sea and the Arctic Ocean. The Lena serves as a boundary between two distinct areas. To the west is the central Siberian plateau, an area of dense and continuous taiga – a wilderness of spruce, pine, and, most of all, larch. To the east are the majestic Verchojansk, Suntar-Khayat, and Cherskiy mountains, which host impenetrable forests of cedars and pines in what in winter is the coldest region of the earth outside of the Antarctic.

A two-hour journey by hydroplane downstream from the headwaters of the Lena will reach the 50-mile-long (80 km) area known as the Lena Pillars or Columns. These are vertical limestone cliffs that interrupt the otherwise continuous expanse of forest. They are some 600 feet (183 m) high and have been eroded into fantastic shapes resembling the towers of a medieval church. Further downstream is the Lower Lena hydroelectric power station, which is driven by the enormous force of the river.

The geographical area covered by the Lena Delta is immense, second in size only to the Mississippi Delta in the United States. It covers 14,700 square miles (38,073 sq km), and the enormous river breaks down into more than 150 separate channels. Although it is the largest delta system of permanently frozen sub-soil (permafrost), vast quantities of clay and silt are regularly washed downstream and deposited in the delta area, which means that it is constantly changing. This far north, the Lena River is frozen for six to eight months of the year, so it cannot be not used extensively for trading or transport. Each May and June, however, the river becomes swollen from the melting ice further upstream, causing what the Russians call *rasputitsa* – literally, the season of bad roads, a term that refers to the total inability to travel.

Right, a miriad of waterways in the delta stretch as far as the eye can see.

Facing page, the sable is one of 29 species of mammal protected in the Lena Delta region.

In 1985 a huge section of the Lena Delta was designated as the Ust-Lenskiy Nature Reserve. This area of 5,530 square miles (14,323 sq km) was set aside by the Soviet government to protect 29 species of mammal, 95 species of bird, and 723 species of plant. Included in this sizeable list are bears, wolves, reindeer, sables and Siberian polecats, as well as breeding places for birds such as Bewick's swans and Ross gulls.

The intense winter cold of the taiga surrounding the Lena means that the mammals and birds that live here all year round need special adaptations to cope with the sub-zero temperatures. Some birds, like the Arctic redpoll and the Siberian tit, have a very dense plumage: when it becomes very cold, they sit hunched into fluffy balls to conserve their energy. Mammals like red foxes, grey wolves, weasels, martens, minks and sables have developed especially soft, thick fur. The fur of the sable is particularly fine, and the animals have been hunted mercilessly for their pelts. Other animals, such as voles and shrews, have learned to live in the warmer air trapped in spaces underneath the snow, and can continue to feed throughout the winter on the small plants and insects that thrive there during the winter months.

Frozen Siberia

THE Lena is one of several rivers that cross Siberia, the largest of the former Soviet regions. Siberia is 4 million square miles (10.4 million sq km) of coniferous forest, towering mountains, vast rolling plains and empty plateaux. The temperatures are extreme – the coldest temperature ever recorded in the northern hemisphere (-90.4 degrees Fahrenheit, -68 degrees C.) was measured here – while during the summer the temperature often rises above 86 degrees Fahrenheit (30 degrees C.). The Russian writer Maxim Gorky called Siberia "the land of death and chains" because of the many labour camps.

The *Jeannette* Expedition

IN 1879, under the command of George Washington De Long, the expedition ship *Jeannette* left San Francisco to sail to the North Pole via the Bering Strait, on a trip sponsored by James Gordon Bennett of *The New York Herald* (the same man who sent Stanley to find Livingstone). *Jeannette* was caught in the ice and drifted north of Siberia for almost two years before she was crushed and sank. The crew made for the Lena Delta in three small boats, one of which was never seen again. The second boat reached the delta, but could not find its way out of the maze of river branches and islets. All but two of the members of this boat, including De Long, died of starvation, exposure, and exhaustion before they could be rescued. The crew of the third boat reached the delta and managed to make their way upriver to Jakutsk. The commander of that boat, George Melville, then launched a number of searches for the members of the other two boats, ultimately finding and burying De Long and his colleagues.

PAMUKKALE

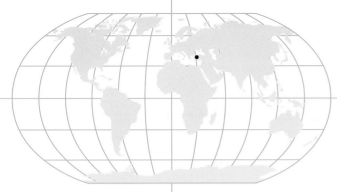

*A cascade of snow-white rock pools
on a Turkish hillside.*

Pamukkale lies in the Büyuk
Menderes valley at the edge of
the mountains of the Phrygia
region of western Turkey. It
can be reached by a road or rail
journey of about 140 miles
(225 km) from the airport at
Izmir, on the coast of the
Aegean Sea.

Mineral Waters

WATER is an essential
ingredient of life in any
form, but some waters with
particular mineral contents are
considered to be positively
beneficial to health – whether
for imbibing or bathing in.
Pamukkale has been a popular
health spa for some 2,000 years,
since the Romans first came to
bathe in the hot springs and
drink the supposedly curative
waters. Eventually driven away
by earthquakes during the 14th
century, tourists eager for
alternative therapies have
returned in the 20th.

*Right, looking across the shallow
pools of mineral water, gently
overflowing the terraces at
Pamukkale.*

*Facing page, the dazzling white
travertine terraces of the hot springs.*

THOSE coming to marvel at the beauty of the
springs at Pamukkale, in a remote region of
western Turkey, on a bright sunny day will
find the sight quite dazzling – rather like
looking at an ice fall on a glacier. The area has
been popular for many centuries, but the
springs and the tufa must have been here for
very much longer. The medicinal and
therapeutic properties of some mineral waters
have been recognised since ancient times, and
the Romans built the thermal resort of
Hierapolis around the springs here. The
Roman resort has not survived the ravages
of time as successfully as the tufa, although
the ruins can still be seen, but there is now
a modern tourist spa resort built on the
same site.

The waters of a geothermal area are
invariably rich in dissolved mineral salts, but
the composition of the salts varies from place to
place depending on the composition of the
underlying rocks through which the waters
flow. Hot water is able to dissolve any number
of different mineral salts, although some are
more soluble than others. The water is usually
saturated with salts by the time it reaches the
surface and, once in the open air it starts to
evaporate naturally. As the solution dries out,
the salts crystallise, forming deposits on the
ground. The colour of these deposits will
depend on the composition of the salts, and
although many salts are white, impurities can
cause a range of colours.

At Pamukkale the hot springs bubble out of
the ground near the top of the hillside. These
waters, rich in calcium bicarbonate, emerge
at a temperature of about 109 degrees
Fahrenheit (43 degrees C.) and have evaporated
in their path down the hillside, leaving a
spectacular veneer of snowy white salts of
travertine (a calcium carbonate rock) encrusting
the ground.

Over the millenia these salts have
accumulated until now the deposits are quite
thick. Such deposits, known as tufa, are not
uncommon, but what makes those at

Pamukkale so special is the unusual formation
that has resulted, and the scale of the site.
Tier upon tier of gleaming pools adorn the
surface of the hill for a height of around 300
feet (91 m), looking for all the world like a
builder's yard where scores of shallow
white porcelain basins have been stacked
together.

It is not clear why the deposits have formed
in these neat terraces; no other hot spring
areas around the world exhibit quite the
same shapes, which have been likened to a
frozen waterfall, or the walls and turrets of a
fantastic castle.

Jordan, Israel

THE DEAD SEA

*The salty waters of the lowest lake in the world shimmer
constantly in the intense heat.*

The Dead Sea forms part of the
border between Jordan and
Israel. Jerusalem and at Amman,
12 miles (19 km) and 30 miles
(48 km) away, are the major
cities. The road on the western
side of the sea is part of the
main highway to Eilat, and is
excellent.

The Dead Sea Scrolls

THE first scrolls at Qumran
were discovered in 1947 by
a Bedouin boy who was
looking for a lost goat. Eleven
caves yielded hundreds of
manuscripts, all carefully stored
in earthenware jars, and
preserved by the arid
atmosphere which prevails
around the Dead Sea. The find
was one of the most exciting
archaeological discoveries of
this century, and contained
Biblical and other manuscripts
that are almost 2,000 years old.

*Curious clusters of mineral salts
have formed in the shallows – the
salts include potash and
magnesium, as well as the familiar
sodium chloride.*

ALTHOUGH the River Jordan and several other small streams can discharge up to 7 million tons of water into the Dead Sea each day, the intense heat of the Jordan Valley rapidly evaporates the water, and none of it ever flows out. However, minerals and salts that are washed into the sea remain, making it one of the saltiest lakes in the world. Its mineral content is around 30 per cent, compared to the 3.5 per cent of most of the world's oceans. The Hebrew name "Yam HaMelah" means "Sea of Salt".

The Dead Sea often appears a deep metallic blue colour, with the salts making the water dense and giving it an oily appearance, unruffled by any breeze. While the high salinity ensures that buoancy is no problem, actually swimming in the Dead Sea is tricky; it is simpler just to sit comfortably in the water, like in a bean bag. The taste of salt is so strong that it stings the tongue, and even the tiniest of cuts on the skin hurts when the salt water touches it.

At the southern part of the lake there are hot springs and pools of rich black mud which have long been held to have healing powers – Herod the Great was known to bathe in these waters for medicinal purposes. The development of tourism has resulted in strings of hotels, built especially so guests can enjoy their mud-baths in the comfort of an air-conditioned bathroom rather than face the searing heat of the Dead Sea's shimmering shores.

The Dead Sea is 1,300 feet (396 m) below sea level and is part of the Great Rift Valley. In fact this is really not a sea at all, but a lake made up of two basins that together are around 45 miles (72 km) long and 9 miles (14 km) wide. No fish can survive the extreme saltiness, but scientists have discovered that the Dead Sea is not dead at all, and supports a number of salt-loving bacteria.

The shores of the Dead Sea are as remarkable as the lake itself. In places the water has evaporated leaving great pancakes of salt-encrusted, cracked earth, and behind it, dry brown hills rise in jagged, dusty peaks. Further north the dry mountains are redder, sometimes turning vivid shades of scarlet in the afternoon sun, while pillars of salt stand at the southern extremes of the lake.

One of these salt pillars is embedded in legend: the story in the Bible recalls the cities of Sodom and Gomorrah, which were rife with sin. Lot, a righteous man, was warned that the cities would be destroyed as a punishment, and that he should flee with his family. On no account, Lot and his relations were warned, should anyone look back. Unfortunately Lot's wife could not resist the urge to have one last look, and tradition has it that she was turned into the large salt pillar near the modern town of Sedom.

The Dead Sea is a strange and atmospheric place; it is also a silent place with little or no bird song, and the constant evaporation usually envelopes the lake in a mysterious haze. The concentrated minerals and the rate of water evaporation often makes the Dead Sea smell strongly of sulphur, and with the temperature usually rising above 104 degrees Fahrenheit (40 degrees C.), it is not a comfortable place to stop and reflect for long.

The Dead Sea marks the lowest point on the earth's land surface.

Mezada and the Romans

ON a great plinth of rock overlooking the Dead Sea, Herod the Great built the virtually impregnable fortress of Mezada, surrounded on all sides by steep cliffs. The biggest enemy of the fortress would have been lack of water, but deep wells were sunk into the rock to ensure that it would always have its own supply. The ruins of houses, halls, and a formidable array of defensive walls have been excavated, along with Herod's "pleasure palace", a spacious hall with large baths.

After Herod, Mezada was occupied by a community of Jews. When the Romans destroyed the Second Temple in Jerusalem in A.D. 72, they turned their attention to imposing their own law and order. The group of 960 people living in Mezada refused to surrender to the Romans, and so the Romans spent a year building a ramp from which to attack. Rather than give themselves up, every person in Mezada died in what must remain the largest mass suicide in history.

China
FORESTS OF SICHUAN

The mountainous Sichuan province in central China is the last refuge of the giant panda.

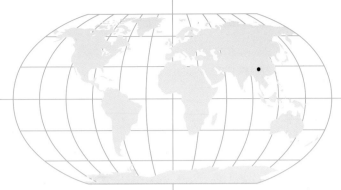

As with so much of this vast country, Sichuan is only now becoming more readily accessible to travellers. The airport at Chengdu provides the nearest most direct access to the various reserves which have been established to protect the habitat of the pandas.

The Sichuan Golden Snub-Nosed Monkey

THIS shy creature lives in the forests between 5,000 and 11,000 feet (1,524 and 3,353 m) in the rhododendron thickets, only very rarely venturing onto the ground to drink at a pool or stream. For half the year its habitat is under snow, but except in the most severe winters it does not leave its mountain retreat.

Numbering less than 15,000, this monkey is rare and endangered. Like the giant panda it has suffered from the destruction of its habitat, but it is also a prized quarry for hunters. Its pelt was reputed to have the power of preventing rheumatism, and the mighty lords under the Manchu emperors wore whole cloaks made from its fur.

Right, the subtropical forests of Sichuan are the last stronghold of the giant panda.

64

THE Daxiangling, Xiaoxiongling, Qionglai Shan and Min mountains in Sichuan province form part of a corridor which stretches from the eastern edge of the plateau of Tibet to the Qin Ling mountains in Shaanxi province. This narrow band of land is the last remaining area where bamboo forest, the preferred habitat of the giant panda, is found. Even in this area large sections of the forest have been destroyed, lost to agriculture, settlements or used for firewood. The rate of loss was particularly fast during the Cultural Revolution of the late 1960s and early 1970s, and the once-continuous expanses of bamboo forest are now reduced to isolated pockets.

The forests on the slopes of these mountain ranges are extremely rich, mainly because of the climatic variations, with some parts permanently covered by glaciers such as those on Mount Siguniang at 28,000 feet (8,534 m), contrasting with the subtropical evergreen forest at 3,650 feet (1,113 m). Within this wide variation there are 4,000 species of plant, many with medicinal properties, and others familiar to gardeners around the world such as the colourful rhododendrons, magnolias, buddleia, cotoneasters and roses.

The forest was once widespread, and the distribution of its most famous inhabitant, the giant panda, was equally extensive. With the loss of forest the giant panda has retreated to what are now its last strongholds in the mountain forests of Sichuan province. Even here its foothold is rather tenuous because of the fragmentation of the forest, and the peculiar life cycle of the bamboo which is the staple diet of the giant panda. Indeed, the dependence of the panda exclusively on the bamboo has been the reason for the creature's demise – it has been unable to adapt its diet to anything else.

Bamboo undergoes periodic mass flowering and subsequent die-off on a 40 to 60 year cycle. Whole areas of forest can flower at once and then die. The bamboo seeds germinate well but they grow only slowly, so that an area where die-off has taken place is unable to support giant pandas for at least ten years. A mass bamboo die-off event occurred in the mid 1970s in a number of the remaining pockets of forest, with the result that large numbers of panda starved to death when their food source disappeared and they had no-where to go. Tragic though this incident was, it did receive considerable attention and, more importantly, provided the motivation for a massive conservation programme to try to rescue the giant panda and its habitat from the brink of extinction.

Two reserves which already existed for other reasons were declared giant panda reserves and these were closely followed by nine others,

including Wolong, a substantial area covering 2,000 square miles (5,180 sq km). More importantly, these new areas link up existing reserves, providing a vital corridor along which the giant panda can travel to find new stands of bamboo when one area flowers and dies. It also has the advantage of encouraging the interbreeding between animals from different areas, thus improving the genetic stock.

The soulful-looking giant panda has captured the imagination of the world, and as a result there are important moves underway to halt and then reverse their decline. At present the best estimates are that only around 750 animals are left in the wild, and it is officially classified as endangered. However, it is not only the giant panda which is threatened by the loss of the bamboo forests; other endangered species such as the takin, the tufted deer and the Sichuan golden snub-nosed monkey (which is endemic to the region) are also benefiting from the conservation efforts in this unique area.

Above, the delicate natural balance which has been maintained between the giant panda and its staple food, bamboo, has been upset by human activity.

Birds of the Forest Floor

PHEASANTS are particularly well represented in Sichuan, living secure lives in the dense undergrowth of the mountain forests. The variety and grandeur of their plumage is remarkable: the Impeyan pheasants have plumage like burnished copper, and the cock satyr targopan has an air sac under its bill that inflates into a beautifully patterned bandana. The red jungle fowl, from which the domestic fowl is descended, still frequents these mountain forests in great numbers, although other once-plentiful species such as the western targopan are now much less common.

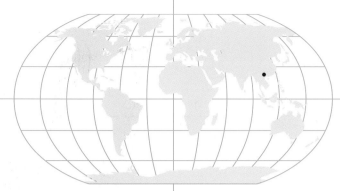

China
THE GUILIN HILLS

*Pillars of limestone rise abruptly from the valley floor
to form one of China's most beautiful natural wonders.*

Guilin (formerly spelled
"Kueilin" or "Kweilin") has a
major airport and is about 1,050
miles (1,689 km) from Beijing
and 800 miles (1,289 km) from
Shanghai. It is in the Guangxi
province in southern China,
and is connected to other major
cities by road.

I N Chinese "Guilin" means "forest of cassia
trees", but "forest of hills" might be a more
apt name for these pinnacles of rock that cluster
together on the shores of the River Li. The
thick layers of limestone that form the hills were
laid down under an ancient sea. Millions of years
later the land was uplifted and acidic rain began
to dissolve those rocks, which were already
weakened by cracks and fractures. When the land
was uplifted a second time some weakened rocks
collapsed, leaving free-standing conical towers
made of a limestone more resistant to erosion –
a prime example of what is known as tower
karst scenery. The limestone region of which
the Guilin Hills are a part stretches right across
south-central China to northern Vietnam.

*Right, fish farms and rice fields
occupy the flat land at the base of
the hills of Guilin.*

The steep-sided hills average about 325 feet (99 m) in height, rising abruptly from bright green valley floors and disappearing into the distance as row upon row of jagged summits and peaks. Many are draped with vines and small trees that maintain a tenuous hold on their rocky sides; others explode with colour when orchids come into bloom. Sometimes shrouded in a soft mist and reflected in the sluggish waters of the River Li, these hills emanate a mystical quality which has been an inspiration for artists and poets for centuries.

The hills are riddled with caves and passageways created by the erosive rain, and during World War II many people hid here to escape Japanese bombing. It was also the site of fierce fighting in the late 1960s, when clashing Red Army factions turned the region into a battlefield. The people of Guilin once again fled to the caves in the hills to hide from the fighting. One well known cave is the Reed Flute Cave, part of a series of caverns and channels strewn with delicate stalactites and stalagmites. It is indeed aptly named: hundreds of tiny stalactites hang from the ceiling, many the size of the small flutes that produce the haunting melodies evocative of China.

This ageless landscape has until recently been closed to Western visitors. The Ming court which retreated to Guilin when the Manchus took over Beijing in 1664 included some Jesuit priests, who were attempting to convert the royal household to Christianity. Apart from a small group of imprisoned Portuguese seamen in 1550, these Jesuits were the first Westerners to see the Guilin Hills. When Communist forces took over Guilin in 1949, they closed the city to most foreigners. It was only reopened in 1973 and has quickly become one of China's most visited beauty spots.

The Guilin region contains rich agricultural land, and the underground water is often pumped to the surface for irrigation. Some of the underground rivers that flow through the tropical karst are used as sources of hydro-electric power.

The spectacular formations of the Reed Flute Cave.

Karst Landscape

NAMED after a region in former Yugoslavia, a karst landscape is one that is formed of limestone. Characteristically, the surface of karst scenery is dry and arid because it is drained by underground channels and streams.

Limestone consists almost entirely of calcium carbonate. Groundwater and rain can both contain carbon dioxide, forming a mild acid which is capable of dissolving limestone, especially where the rock is already weakened by cracks and crevices. Thus water which moves across the surface of harder rocks may suddenly disappear underground when it reaches the softer limestone, often into geological formations known as "sinkholes", and sometimes reappearing elsewhere as springs. As the water flows underground, caves and caverns are eroded, and the dissolved minerals are deposited on the walls of caves or drip from the ceiling to form stalactites and stalagmites.

Some of the best caves formed in this way include the Frasassi Caves in Italy, and Réseau Jean-Bernard in the foothills of the French Alps. These caves are a complicated labyrinth of passages, tunnels, and chambers, some of them with underground rivers winding through the darkness. Réseau Jean-Bernard falls to 5,256 feet (1,602 m) underground – the deepest known cave in the world.

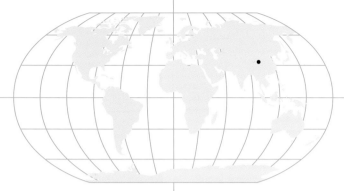

China
YELLOW RIVER, HUANG HE

One of the two great rivers of China, the Yellow River brings prosperity and disaster to the people along its banks.

The delta of the Yellow River is about 200 miles (322 km) south of Beijing. The river can be followed for much of its length by road and rail but some sections, particularly the upper reaches, are very remote and require an expedition rather than an organised tour. A good place to observe the river is at Lanzhou, as it descends from the mountains onto the Loess Plain.

T HE Yellow River rises at the eastern edge of the Tibetan plateau, about 100 miles (161 km) west of the lake of Gyaring Hu, and begins

Yellow River's tributaries, lie barely 30 miles (48 km) north of the source of a tributary of the Yangtze Kiang, Asia's longest river.

Right, the Yellow River shows many moods in its long journey – here, on its upper reaches near Xining, it is broad.

Facing page, craggy hills of loess near Lanzhou.

its journey of 3,395 miles (5,463 km) to the Yellow Sea. It is the fourth longest river in Asia, although its drainage basin of 378,000 square miles (979,016 sq km) ranks only sixth (or seventh if the Ganges-Brahmaputra basin in India and Tibet is included). The Bayan Har Shan mountains, the source of one of the

The Yellow River earns its name in English for the colour of the water, so heavily laden with silt washed from the loess soil of the land over which it flows. The Chinese name, Huang He, means "the Sorrow of the Sons of Han", referring to the tendency of the river to flood and bring disaster to the people along its

course. In fact the river is known to have burst its banks and its enclosing dykes more than 1,000 times and undergone at least 20 major changes to its course during the past 2,000 years. But, as with many of the world's major rivers, the flooding also provides new life to the fields when the waters subside, re-depositing much of the loess soil that it has gathered higher in its course.

The upper part of the river, for the first 730 miles (1,175 km), lies in remote, sparsely populated country. It descends more than 8,000 feet (2,438 m) over rapids and through deep gorges to emerge from the Tibetan highlands onto the desert plains of Inner Mongolia. Then it crosses the Loess Plateau, cutting deep gorges into the soil, until its fall and flow reduce dramatically as it crosses the

above the level of the surrounding plain. This is the area that is most susceptible to the major flooding which occurs from time to time.

The Yellow River is one of the world's muddiest rivers, carrying about 57 pounds (26 kg.) of silt per cubic yard of water, compared with 2 pounds (0.9 kg.) for the Nile and 17 pounds (7.7 kg.) for the Colorado River. Floodwaters may carry as much as 1,200 pounds (544 kg.) of silt per cubic yard of water – 70 per cent by volume. These figures mean that the river carries about 1,520 million tons (1,492 tonnes) of silt to the sea every year. Part of the reason for this enormous load is the relatively high speed of the river, which remains fairly constant even through the extensive irrigation system on the plain.

The river has never been navigable, except

Loess

DESERT dust storms are a vivid example of the power of the wind as an agent of erosion, but where does all the dust go? As the wind speed drops, so do the heavier sand grains, but the light, dusty clay particles can be carried over enormous distances. Where this windblown clay accumulates it is called loess. Much of northern China is covered by loess, blown from the desert regions to the west. Once grasses have become established on the dust their root systems hold the soil together; as more dust accumulates the deeper roots die and become calcified, further helping to bind the soil. Most modern loess soils began to develop as the ice sheets of the last ice age retreated to reveal vast areas of fine-grained glacial deposits, which were then exposed to weathering.

Loess soil is very fertile, and in many parts of China it has been extensively cultivated for growing rice in terraced paddy fields. Loess is very soft and friable but relatively stable if left undisturbed, and dwellings have frequently been carved in its cliffs. On the other hand, earthquakes in loess areas cause untold damage as whole hillsides slip, destroying cave dwellings and damming rivers that then flood to cause further damage and further landslips. In Kansu province in China, 300,000 people were killed during two separate earthquakes in the 1920s, most as an indirect result of the havoc wrought on the loess soils. However the immediate benefits of the fertility of the loess is more important to people than the longer-term possibility of natural catastrophe.

alluvial plains of the Ordos desert. As it flows south it gathers pace again and enters narrow gorges, eventually turning east once more and continuing through the eastern peaks of the Tsinling Shan. Once on the North China Plain, it slows again and widens its course, in some places flowing as much at 10 feet (3 m)

for about 100 miles (161 km) on its lower reaches, but the construction of a dam, creating a reservoir 130 miles (210 km) long, and a 1-million kilowatt power station at San-men-hsia, together with other planned dams, should increase the navigable stretches of the river and some of its tributaries.

India, Bangladesh

SUNDARBANS

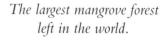

*The largest mangrove forest
left in the world.*

The delta complex of the rivers
Ganges, Brahmaputra and
Meghna straddles the
India/Bangladesh border on the
Bay of Bengal. The great Indian
city of Calcutta lies to the
north-west of the delta area,
but the best starting point is
probably Dhaka in Bangladesh.
However, much of the area
remains inaccessible to all but
the most adventurous.

THE Sundarbans, which literally means
"beautiful forests", covers an area of 3,965
square miles (10,269 sq km) – the largest delta
complex in the world. As with many other wetland
areas in the world it has suffered from over-
exploitation and the continuing encroachment of
human development, resulting in the destruction
of important natural habitats. However, the delta
has recently received its due recognition, with
India declaring all its lands in the Sundarbans a
tiger reserve and closing an area of 500 square
miles (1,295 sq km) to all exploitation, while
Bangladesh has made the whole of its area a
forest reserve, including three wildlife sanctuaries
covering 125 square miles (324 sq km).

The delta is fringed by a massive mangrove
forest covering some 2,300 square miles
(5,957 sq km), the largest remaining continuous
mangrove swamp in the world and the only one
inhabited by tigers. Over 334 plant species
which thrive in the warm and humid climate
have been recorded, including 27 types of
mangrove and the strikingly elegant sundari tree,
which gives the region its name. The humid,
tropical maritime climate has resulted in a unique
mix of plants, with species from south-east Asia,
Polynesia, Ethiopia and the New World co-
existing as they do nowhere else.

The mangrove forest is under constant threat
from exploitation of its natural resources by the

local population. Forestry is a major industry: trees are harvested for timber, pulp and fuel. Fishing is also extremely important, with the sheltered and protected waters of the delta yielding over 147,060 tons (149,000 tonnes) of fish each year. These are not only rich feeding grounds for the many different species of fish, but also prime nursery areas for shrimp. The forest also provides the local people with a substantial harvest of honey and beeswax.

Despite this considerable exploitation, the Sundarbans still supports a rich and diverse fauna with at least 35 species of reptile, over 40 species of mammal and more than 270 species of bird. Impressive as these figures are, they conceal some notable failures, with the local extinction of species such as the Javan rhinoceros, the swamp deer, the Asiatic water buffalo. The great Indian rhinoceros is now on the endangered list, and the 1,700 remaining animals have retreated to the flood plains of the Brahmaputra River in northeast India, and to the marshlands of central Nepal.

The Sundarbans is still the last remaining stronghold of the Bengal tiger, with over 700 animals, and despite the fact that some of its traditional prey are greatly reduced in numbers, more than sufficient remains for the tigers. The reputation of the tigers as man-eaters is difficult to shake off, however, and they are still under constant threat of persecution.

The sheltered coastal waters off the mangrove swamps and the intricate maze of estuarine water channels are home to a wide range of reptiles and aquatic mammals including three species of crocodile, the Indian smooth-coated otter, the Ganges River dolphin, the Irrawaddy dolphin, the Indo-Pacific humpbacked dolphin and the finless porpoise.

The Sundarbans is also a very important staging post and wintering area for many shorebirds, gulls and terns. It supports a remarkable array of over 30 species of birds of prey, including the white-bellied sea eagle, the crested serpent eagle and Pallas's fish eagle.

The majestic, yet delicately balanced mangrove ecosystem is under constant threat from over-exploitation and pollution, and from the risk of reduced freshwater in-flow which results in increased salinity and consequently mangrove die-back. It is to be hoped that the positive steps taken by the Indians and Bangladeshis will help to preserve this unique area.

Above, despite its protection here, the Bengal tiger is still persecuted.

Facing page, the dense mangrove provides habitats for many creatures.

Mangroves

MANGROVES are evergreen trees of the muddy inter-tidal zone and play an important role in stabilising these coastal lands. They show some remarkable adaptations which enable them to survive in what is essentially a very inhospitable environment. Their aerial roots are able to absorb oxygen from the air, which is not available to the roots in the waterlogged mud. And as the mud builds up and these aerial roots are buried they are able to produce new rootlets, ensuring that they remain above the mud level and the plants can continue to breathe. The seeds of the mangroves are pointed, so that when they fall from the branches they drop straight down to become embedded in the mud. This ensures that they are not washed away, and also that when they germinate the seedlings grow up through the mass of roots, thus receiving maximum protection.

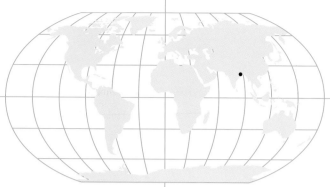

Bangladesh
THE BAY
OF BENGAL

Three great rivers – the Ganges, the Brahmaputra-Jamuna, and the Meghna – merge in Bangladesh and flow into the Bay of Bengal.

Virtually surrounded by India, the capital of Bangladesh is Dhaka. It is a densely populated country and major roads link the capital with the delta area, although communications are often disrupted by the monsoon.

Right, some of the damage caused by the 1991 cyclone in the Chittagong district.

Facing page, a low-lying settlement in danger of flooding at Demra Bustee, Bangladesh.

BANGLADESH sits on top of one of the world's biggest flood plains, where three vast rivers break into thousands of channels as they wind their way to the sea. Even Dhaka, the capital city that is home to 6 million people, is only 25 feet (8 m) above sea level, and waist-high floods are common in the monsoon. Bangladesh is startlingly green, but the water that makes the country so fertile is also responsible for the great devastation that regularly afflicts the land.

To the north of the country lie the Himalayas, and it is from these great snow-capped mountains that the powerful rivers originate. The Brahmaputra-Jamuna rises in Tibet, traveling more than 1,800 miles

(2,896 km) and dropping some 16,000 feet (4,877 m) before emptying into the Bay of Bengal. The Ganges meanders across India before breaking into a myriad of constantly changing channels into the part of the bay known as the Mouths of the Ganges. The Meghna is the smallest of the three rivers, but can still cause immense devastation when it is in flood. In 1991, in one small area alone, the Meghna eroded 200 feet (61 m) of land in ten days, sweeping away homes, crops, and animals.

Although Bangladesh has around 2,500 miles (4,023 km) of embankments, most attempts to control these wilful rivers are futile. Melted snow from the Himalayas and rain from the monsoons swell the rivers, flooding one fifth of the country every year and sweeping away vast chunks of land. But the water that destroys land also creates it. Combined, the rivers deposit 2 billion tons of silt a year, and when the small silt islands ("chars") are washed away, others form. The floods also replenish the fish stocks and leave algae to nourish the crops.

Plans are afoot to try to control the rivers in a similar way to the Mississippi River in the United States, but the flooding of the Mississippi in July 1993, despite controls, has brought these plans into question. When in flood the Brahmaputra-Jamuna in particular becomes a vast, unpredictable multi-channelled torrent of muddy brown water that many believe is untameable. Bangladesh is a poor country, and some question the wisdom of using the country's resources to construct dams and levies that may not only be worthless when the rivers are in full spate, but which might cause even more damage by changing the rivers' natural courses. The Meghna-Dhonagoda Irrigation Project cost $50 million, and aimed to control flooding and erosion over 80 square miles (207 sq km) of rich crop land. Despite the high embankments the rivers still have the upper hand, and one section of land alone has been eroded by more than a mile (1.6 km) since 1979. The problem lies partly in the strength of the water as it races towards the sea, and partly in the speed at which the rivers can become flooded.

Great tropical atmospheric depressions occur in the steamy Bay of Bengal, giving rise to some of the fiercest cyclones in the world. In the past 30 years, 16 cyclones with winds stronger than 75 miles (121 km) per hour have battered Bangladesh. Great storm surges force their way inland, driven by the winds, leaving swathes of death and destruction in their wake. Although some areas now have concrete cyclone shelters, the storm of April 1991 shows the vulnerability of the people and their land to the forces of nature.

The 1991 Cyclone

ON 29 April 1991, a satellite image revealed that Bangladesh was about to face one of the strongest storms the area had experienced this century. Although warnings were broadcast on the radio, there was little time to organise evacuation, and in any case many people had nowhere to flee. When the storm hit the densely populated region between Cox's Bazar and Chittagong, the winds were estimated at 145 miles (233 km) per hour. The wind whipped up a 20-foot (6-m) storm surge that submerged much of the low-lying land. An estimated 139,000 people and nearly half a million animals died in the devastation of the cyclone and its aftermath; 10 million people lost their homes.

Controlling the Floods

IN 1993 the United States government came under fierce attack because, despite an investment of billions of dollars on flood control, the Mississippi River burst its banks and caused extensive flood damage. On 18 July the river reached 49.6 feet (15.1 m) at St Louis – 3.5 feet (1.1 m) higher than its previous record. There was enormous damage to crops and property, and 30 people died. All the bridges on a 275-mile (442-km) stretch of the river were closed because of the flood.

The first attempts to control "Old Muddy" began about 60 years ago when engineers developed a complex system of dams and levies to try to prevent the river's annual flooding. In places there were "short cuts" to stop the river from meandering, and huge areas of wetlands were drained so that they could be used for crops. The disaster of July 1993 has forced the government to rethink its policy on flood control.

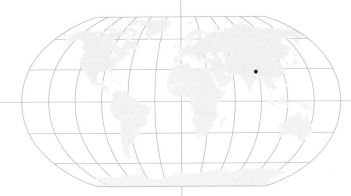

THE HIMALAYAS

Most travellers to the Himalayas will fly to India or Pakistan and then head north towards the mountains by train, road and, finally, on foot. Access from the north, through Tibet, is more difficult.

*The world's highest mountains
separate the Indian sub-continent from Asia.*

THE Himalayas are the greatest mountain range on earth, containing 96 of the 109 peaks in the world over 24,000 feet (7,315 m) high. The Andes in South America form a longer chain, approximately 4,700 miles (7,562 km) long, but are not as high. Facts and figures are one thing, but the awesome sight of the Himalayas is quite another. Although the highest mountain in the world is known worldwide as Mount Everest, perhaps the Nepalese name for the mountain conveys an image that might be applied to the whole range: Chomolungma, Goddess Mother of the Snows.

The Himalayan mountain range, including the Karakoram mountains, stretches for more than 1,500 miles (2,414 km) across the northern edge of the Indian sub-continent, separating it from Asia to the north. From the north-west, in northernmost Pakistan, the Karakoram mountains extend to the south-east through Kashmir in northern India. The

Himalayas sweep round to the east, taking in the mountain kingdoms of Nepal, Sikkim and Bhutan, and continuing into the Arunachal Pradesh province of north-eastern Assam. The northern boundaries of these countries lie along the watershed of the mountains; to the north lie the Chinese regions of Tibet and Chinese Turkestan. To the west of the Karakoram the mountains divide into the Pamirs and the Hindu Kush; to the east there is a sharp swing to the south into the lesser mountains of northern Burma.

The native peoples of the Himalayas never felt the urge to explore their mountains beyond their own immediate needs, and this was left largely to the more restless Europeans. In the 19th century, while pioneering mountaineers were conquering peaks in the Alps, the Department of Survey of the Government of India had triangulated the position of a peak that seemed higher than the others. In 1856, the final calculations of the theodolite surveys of 1849 and 1850 showed that the height of Peak XV on the Tibet-Nepal border was 29,002 feet (8,840 m), the highest in the world. It was named after Colonel Sir

George Everest (pronounced Eve-rest), the former Surveyor-General of India. Now there was a new target for the mountaineers. Between the wars, the major effort focused on an approach from Tibet because Nepal was closed to expeditions. After World War II Nepal opened its borders to Everest expeditions and exploration from the south side began but it was not until 29 May 1953 that the summit was finally conquered by the New Zealander Edmund Hillary and the Nepalese Sherpa Tenzing Norgay.

The greatest mountain range, as might be expected, also has other world firsts among its natural features. The longest glacier outside of the polar regions is Siachen, measuring 47 miles (76 km) in length, while the sheerest mountain wall is on Mount Rakaposhi (25,550 feet, 7,788 m), both in the Karakoram. The mountain wall rises 3.72 vertical miles (5.99 km) from the Hunza Valley in 6.2 horizontal miles (10 km) at an overall gradient of 31 degrees. The highest wall climb is on the south face of Annapurna I (26,545 feet, 8,091 m) in the Himalayas, and the longest wall climb is on the Rupal-Flank of Nanga Parbat in the Karakoram, a vertical ascent of 14,704 feet (4,482 m). Other major peaks in the range include K2, in the Karakorums, at 28,251 feet (8,611 m), and Kanchenjunga, at 28,169 feet (8,586 m).

Above, sunset over Mount Everest (left) and Nuptse (right), seen from Kumbu, Nepal.

Left, an endless vista of Himalayan snowfields, glaciers and mountain peaks, northern India.

Geological Evolution

More than 200 million years ago the former single continental mass of Pangaea broke into two super-continents, Laurasia and Gondwana. Laurasia was made up of the present continents of North America, Greenland, Europe and Asia; Gondwana comprised South America, Africa, India and Australia grouped around Antarctica. When Gondwana began to fragment, South America and Australia moved toward the ocean to their present positions, but Africa and India continued their northward drift until they collided with Eurasia. Over a period of millions of years, and still continuing today, these collisions buckled the rocks of southern Eurasia and produced the mountains we know as the Alps and the Himalayas.

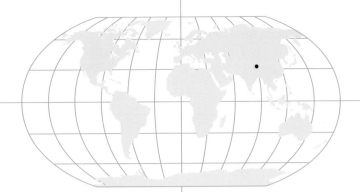

Tibet
THE TIBETAN PLATEAU

*The highest upland region
in the world.*

Tibet, the autonomous region
of Xizang Zizhiqu, lies in
western China on the northern
side of the Himalayas. It can be
reached overland from the
south through Kashmir, Nepal
or Bhutan, and from Chengdu
or Lanzhou in China to the
east. Any of these routes is a
major undertaking.

The Serengeti of Asia

THE Argin Shan Reserve is
China's largest nature
reserve, covering some 17,375
square miles (45,000 sq km),
and is one of the remotest
places left on earth. Bordered
by the 92,400 square miles
(240,000 sq km) of Tibet's
Chang tang Reserve, this
remarkable expanse of
wilderness has been dubbed
the 'Serengeti of Asia', because
of the vast herds of hoofed
animals which range across it.
The upland plains are inhabited
by large herds of chiru
(Tibetan antelope) and kiang
(wild ass), and many other
species including Tibetan
gazelle, wild yak, ibex and wild
sheep graze the high mountain
meadows. Predators attracted
to the area include the now
endangered snow leopard.

*Above, nomadic yak herders in a
broad green valley near Lake
Namtso, on the Tibetan plateau.*

*Facing page, snow-covered Kula
Kangri lies near the eastern margin
of the plateau.*

THE Tibetan Plateau covers an area of 77,000
square miles (199,429 sq km) in southern
Asia on the northern side of the Himalayas.
The average altitude of the plateau is 16,000
feet (4,877 m) but it is not a flat plain, and
includes mountains within the overall area of
the plateau. It is bordered in the north by the
Kunlun Shan mountains, beyond which are
the steppes of central Asia.

Six of the mightiest rivers of southeast Asia
and the Indian sub-continent rise within its
borders. The Indus rises on the northern side
of the Himalayas, and flows northwestward
until it can cut between the Karakoram
mountains and the western Himalayas to flow
south into the Arabian Sea. A short distance
east of the source of the Indus is the source of
the Brahmaputra River. It flows east until it
can pass through the eastern end of the
Himalayas, turning south and west to join the
Ganges on its way to the Bay of Bengal. On
the eastern side of the plateau four rivers rise in
roughly parallel valleys; the Salween and the
Mekong flow south through Burma and
Thailand, respectively, while the Yangtze

(Chang) Kiang and the Yellow River (Huang
He) flow generally eastwards through China to
the East China Sea and the Yellow Sea. In
their upper reaches all these rivers are fierce
torrents, especially in spring when they are fed
by melting snow from the mountains. On the
broad plains of Tibet they wind across wide
valleys, but are still powerful rivers and create
major obstacles to communications.

The plateau is a barren country but the
scenery is awesome and magnificent; it is not
just the altitude that leaves the traveller
breathless. Snow-capped mountains fringe the
huge plains of the valleys and in the clear, crisp
air there is no haze or pollution to hamper the
view. In winter the whole region turns white
except for the dark lines of the rivers, which
are flowing too swiftly to freeze, and the
mountainsides, which are too steep to hold
snow. The brief spring and summer are marked
by a sudden surge of greenery spotted with
colour by the blooms of flowers, all taking
advantage of the brief period of sun and
warmth to reproduce before the onset of
winter. The people of Tibet must also use this
time well, for little can be done during winter.
Goats, yaks and other livestock must be put to
pasture to fatten and raise their young, and
essential journeys to markets must be made
before snow again blocks the mountain passes.
Many Tibetans are still nomads who live in
skin tents and move across the country during
the summer with their entire families.

Religion is a major part of life in Tibet and
the religious leader, the Dalai Lama, is also the
king and political leader. One of the greatest
honours for a Tibetan boy is to become a
Buddhist monk, in the characteristic saffron-
coloured robes. Priests and monks are a
common sight in the towns and countryside,
frequently whirling prayer wheels in their
hands. The simple rural life of Tibet makes a
pleasant contrast for most visitors from
Western countries, but few would be willing
to stay and endure the rigours of the harsh
climate and environment.

76

Japan

MOUNT FUJI

A classical strato-volcano — built up in layers
— of near-perfect symmetry.

Mount Fuji lies about 60 miles (97 km) to the south-west of Tokyo, on the main island of Honshu, and is easily reached by road and rail. There are several nearby resorts from where the mountain may be climbed.

The volcanic cone of Mount Fuji towers magestically over a frosted forest in winter sunshine.

A<small>LL</small> along the Pacific margin of Japan is evidence of the country's dramatic volcanic history, from long-dead lava fields, through hot spring areas, to volcanoes of which some 60 to 65 are classified as active. Not all volcanoes exhibit the classic cone-shape but many in Japan do, and the most famous of these is Mount Fuji.

Fuji-san (the Japanese name may be translated as Fuji-mountain, or as a respectful name) lies on the main Japanese island of Honshu, about 60 miles (97 km) south-west of the capital, Tokyo. It is the highest mountain in Japan, rising to 12,460 feet (3,798 m), and forms an important focus in Japanese culture. Seen from the south, the mountain stands majestic and isolated, its symmetrical sides leading steeply to the truncated summit, which hides the central crater. On the southeastern flank is the explosion crater of Hoei-zan that was formed during the volcano's last eruption in 1707. The oldest lavas on Mount Fuji have been dated as 8,000 years old, making it a very young volcano. However, careful geological survey and the examination of drill cores from the mountain have shown that Mount Fuji is based on two much older volcanoes. The older Kofuji volcano was active from about 50,000 to 9,000 years ago and is now completely hidden beneath the lavas and ashes of Fuji. Part of the younger volcano is exposed in the northern side of Mount Fuji.

The beauty of Mount Fuji lies in its near-perfect shape, the top of the cone permanently covered in snow. On a fine day it is a magnificent sight, dominating the surrounding landscape. At dawn and by sunset the mountain assumes an ethereal quality, suffused with a rose-pink light. Icon of peace and serenity, Fuji-san is regarded as the home of the gods. Followers of the Shinto religion worship the beauty of nature so that, for many Japanese people, the sight of Mount Fuji in spring, forming a backdrop to the cherry trees flowering below, is a very moving experience.

The popular image of Japan as a volcanic island chain is only partly true. Ancient Precambrian rocks and the overlying sedimentary rocks have been folded in several mountain-building events that gave rise to Alpine-style ranges of mountains. Volcanic activity has been predominant only during the last 60 million years, and is known to geologists as "island-arc type" volcanism.

As the crust of the Pacific Ocean floor expands in one area so it must be consumed elsewhere if its area is not to increase. This happens around the margins of the ocean, where the oceanic crust slides beneath the adjacent continental crust. As the oceanic crust descends into the earth's mantle it is heated by friction against the overlying rocks, causing melting and expansion. The resulting increase in pressure is reduced by volcanic activity, with the accompanying tension in the rocks relieved by earthquakes. As a result, the younger rocks of Japan are largely volcanic in origin and earthquakes are common. Japan is not unique in this respect, for all the lands and islands surrounding the Pacific Ocean experience island-arc type volcanism to some extent, giving rise to the description of the Pacific rim widely used by geologists – "The Ring of Fire".

Fuji-san at cherry blossom time is a sight of exceptional beauty, and important to the Japanese cultural heritage

Fault Lines

M<small>OST</small> of the volcanoes making up the Pacific "Ring of Fire" have formed as the result of subduction of the ocean crust beneath the adjacent continent. A deep oceanic trench backed by a volcanic arc is the typical association. In some cases, however, major trans-current faults are connected with the consumption of the oceanic crust, and the San Andreas Fault in California is the most famous example of this. The fault crosses from the ocean to the land at an oblique angle through San Francisco, and the land on the south-western side of the fault is moving slowly past the land on the north-eastern side. The stresses that drive the movement of such faults are relatively constant, but the strength of the earth's crust can resist only to a certain point, then it breaks and the strain is released. When it breaks there is an earthquake and the degree of accumulated strain will dictate the power of the earthquake.

GEOTHERMALS OF BEPPU

Spouting geysers, simmering mud pools, hissing fumaroles, and boiling waters abound in Japan's active volcanic regions.

The Beppu thermal area is on the north-east coast of the Japanese island of Kyushu. The nearest airport is at Fukuoka, a short drive from Beppu on good roads.

Hammam-Meskoutine

THE hot springs of Hammam-Meskoutine in north-eastern Algeria have created some extraordinary rock formations. The mineral-saturated water has given rise to deposits of carbonate that look like a frozen waterfall cascading over a precipice, in a wealth of colours from bright white to dull ochre. Legend has it that a wedding procession was once turned into stone by the gods, and indeed, the rocks have the appearance of a crowd of people sporting veils and billowing robes.

Above, foliage offsets the brilliant orange colour of a geothermal pool.

Right, a troop of macaques making the most of a thermal spring.

IN the bitter cold of winter in southern Japan is a curious sight. As the snow falls, small monkeys head for the warmth of volcanically heated waters, occasionally sitting up to their necks in warm water while the snow settles on their heads. However, once the monkeys leave the hot water, they cool rapidly in the freezing air, and end up being colder with wet fur than they would have been had they resisted the temptation of a hot bath. But monkeys are ingenious creatures, and there is evidence that they have developed a rota system, sending one or two delegates to fetch food while the others wait in the warm.

Japan has been described as sitting on "mother Earth's cradle", and with more than 500 volcanoes on the main islands, the description is apt. Many volcanoes are extinct, but some remain active, including Fuji, Asama, Aso, and Bantai. As well as volcanoes,

there are hundreds of areas of thermal activity, the best known of which are Beppu, Kusatsu, and Noboribetsu.

The city of Beppu is located at the bottom of a slope of volcanic debris hurled from one of the several nearby volcanoes in the recent

past. It is estimated that its hot springs and geysers emit more than 2 million cubic feet (56,600 cu m) of water each day, and it has become a major tourist attraction, where visitors immerse themselves in hot sand baths or the healing, mineral-laden waters. There is also a zoo at Beppu; it houses, among other creatures, hippopotamuses and pelicans, which can splash and relax in the warm spring waters.

There are about 3,500 fumeroles (vents which allow gases to escape), hot springs, and geysers in the Beppu area, making it one of the largest thermal regions in the world. Boiling ponds, called "jigokus", occur in a fantastic range of sizes and colours. Chinoike Jigoku is bright red because the water has oxidised some of the underlying rocks, whereas the large Umi Jigoku is deep blue reflecting the colour of the sky. The geyser at Tatsu-maki Jigoku erupts regularly every 20

minutes or so, and a great spray plume of steam is forced high into the air with an ear-splitting hiss.

Another geothermal area occurs in the southern part the island of Hokkaido, Japan's most northerly large island, at Noboribetsu Spa. Here, in a volcanic crater that is 1¼ mile (2 km) across, are the Jigokudani Hot Springs. Like Beppu, there are geysers, boiling springs and bubbling pools of blistering hot mud. There are also "solfataras", which are vents that give off steam and sulphurous gases. These have painted the inside of the crater an array of colours from bright, gaudy yellows to deep reds, and have fed a lake of sulphur-laden water that sits in a hollow in the crater floor. The Noboribetsu region is alive with sounds and smells. Constant hisses and rumbles accompany the all-pervading stink of the sulphurous emissions, giving the Jigokudani its well deserved name – "valley of hell".

Above, grooming time for Japanese macaques at a hot spring in the Shiga highlands.

Other Thermal Springs

L IKE Beppu and Noboribetsu, Yellowstone National Park in the United States is an area with an enormous number of hot springs and geysers. The first pioneer to discover Yellowstone was John Colter in 1807, who was looking for good beaver-hunting country. He returned to tell disbelieving people of boiling cauldrons of mud and hissing geysers, and it was not until the 1870s that the region was surveyed and its natural wonders documented. Yellowstone has about 300 geysers, the best known of which is Old Faithful, named because it erupts regularly every 70 minutes or so.

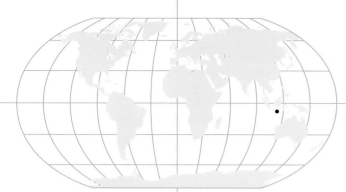

Indonesia

KELI MUTU

Three coloured lakes lie in the craters of a volcano on one of Indonesia's islands.

The crater lakes are on the eastern part of the elongated island of Flores, which is the second largest island of the Indonesian Lesser Sunda Islands. The nearest airport is at Ende, around 20 miles (32 km) from the lakes. The nearest international airport is at Jakarta.

Crater Lakes

THERE are many other lakes around the world that have filled craters or calderas. Crater Lake, in Oregon in the United States, is one of the best known. The crater was formed around 7,000 years ago in the Cascade Mountains by the violent volcanic activity of Mount Mazama, which collapsed into itself after a series of eruptions, to form an enormous caldera 6 miles (10 km) across and 4,000 feet (1,219 m) deep. The depression quickly filled with rainwater and melted snow, and today is the deepest lake in the United States. In the middle of the caldera are three volcanoes, although only one – Wizard Island – now pierces the surface of the lake.

New Zealand also has green and blue crater lakes, Tikitapu and Rotokakahi, which lie side by side, separated by a narrow isthmus. It is possible to stand on the isthmus and compare the colours of the two lakes, which are near Rotorua, in an area of seething geysers, boiling mud pools, and fumaroles.

THREE silent lakes lie within a few feet of each other in the craters of a great "shield volcano" on the island of Flores, in Indonesia. Two are contrasting shades of green and one is red-black, colours which have been caused by different minerals in the rock in which the lakes lie. The shield volcano was formed when very fluid lava poured out of a central vent to spread over a large area. (Such volcanoes can cover vast areas of land – Mauna Loa in Hawaii is about 120 miles (193 km) across at its base.) Calderas – indentations in the rock – were formed where parts of the central volcano collapsed, and water collecting in such calderas has formed the lakes at Keli Mutu.

The three lakes have romantic names. Tiwoe Ata Polo means "Lake of the Bewitched People" and is a very dark red, now almost black. Next to it is Tiwoe Noea Moeri Kooh Fai, which translates as "Lake of the Young Men and Virgins", and is an opaque emerald green. The third, Tiwoe Ata Mboepoe is a limpid sparkling green, its waters transparent and clear.

So why do the three lakes at Keli Mutu, all so close to each other, look so different?

Tiwoe Noea Moeri Kooh Fai has a small "solfatara" or vent that smokes, as if to caution onlookers that the volcano is still active. The main gases given off by any volcano are hydrogen sulphide and hydrochloric acid vapour, and these are constantly being emitted from the solfatara by the lakeside. When the hydrogen sulphide is released into the air it reacts with the oxygen in the atmosphere and turns into sulphuric acid. Tiwoe Noea Moeri Kooh Fai and Tiwoe Ata Mboepoe have high levels of free sulphuric and hydrochloric acid in their waters, and it is these acids which have caused the lakes to turn bright green.

Tiwoe Ata Polo was a rich glowing red, but has steadily been turning darker and darker; its unusual colour comes from the iron in the rocks. Molten rock – magma – contains many silicates, some of which are high in iron. When the iron reacts with oxygen in the air it forms bright red oxides of iron, turning the water red.

82

Green pools formed from volcanic activity are found in other parts of the world, but nowhere else are red and green pools found together. The answer to this conundrum probably lies in the rock that forms the bottom of Tiwoe Ata Polo. Magma from the same volcano often varies in its chemical content. It is likely that the rocks under Tiwoe Ata Polo contain more iron than that below the other lakes, and it is also possible that the acidic content is higher in the red lake than in the green ones. The iron-bearing rocks in the red lake are dissolved by the strong sulphuric and hydrochloric acids there, to give it a different colour.

Keli Mutu volcano forms part of the "Ring of Fire" which encircles the Pacific Ocean. Indonesia has many burning mountains, and geologists believe that at least 132 volcanoes have been active here in the last 10,000 years.

Below and left, it is difficult to believe that the extraordinarily vivid colours of these lakes were created entirely naturally.

Indonesia

KRAKATOA

In 1883, Krakatoa exploded with a blast heard for thousands of miles – one of the most ferocious volcanic eruptions in history.

The remote island of Krakatoa, or Krakatau as it is called locally, lies in the Sunda Strait between Sumatra and Java. The nearest international airport is at Jakarta, the capital of Indonesia, and the volcano can be seen from the air or by boat.

Right, a cloud of ash is blown high into the air above Anak Krakatoa.

'F_OR day by day, thro' many a blood-red eve. . .
The wrathful sunset glared"_ wrote the poet
Tennyson after the massive eruption of
Krakatoa. An estimated 5 cubic miles (20.5 cu
km) of rock and dust were hurled so high into
the atmosphere that a volcanic halo surrounded
the earth, and its effects could be seen in
sunsets all over the world, turning them to the
bright glowing reds that Tennyson beheld. The
1883 eruption of Krakatoa is thought to have
been at least twice as powerful as the largest
nuclear explosion, and the sound of the blast
was heard 3,000 miles (4,827 km) away.

For Java (Jawa) and Sumatra (Sumatera) the
eruption itself, spewing great vivid streams of
molten rock into the sea, was not the biggest
problem – rather it was the tsunamis, immense
waves thrown up as a result of the movement
of the earth's surface. On 27 August 1883, a
tsunami towering 130 feet (40 m) raced
towards the densely populated islands, killing
36,000 people, strewing bodies of the victims
to within view of ships more than 140 miles
(225 km) away from the site. The wave was so
powerful that it carried a steamship 2 miles
(3.2 km) inland before hurling it down on dry
land. For almost a year, a thick rain of pumice
and ash fell on the islands.

Krakatoa stands on the place where two
plates of the earth's crust meet; the plate
forming the floor of the Indian Ocean is
forcing its way underneath the plate that is
Asia. There are volcanoes all along the 2,000-
mile (3218-km) line where the two plates
meet, of which Krakatoa is the most famous.
This volcano is known to have erupted back in
A.D. 416 causing the death of local inhabitants.
Over the centuries, Krakatoa continued to
rumble, and by 1680 the main cone was joined
by two more cones on Rakata island, which
was about 17 square miles (44 sq km). Early in
August 1883, these two smaller cones began to
vent, hurling ash and pumice into the air;
finally Krakatoa had its turn with the last
devastating explosion. When the activity had
died down, less than a third of Rakata island
remained. The two small cones had disappeared
completely and much of the main cone was
also gone. In 1927, a cinder cone called Anak
Krakatau, or Child of Krakatoa, began to
emerge from the ocean. Today it is about 700
feet (213 m) high and very active.

In the face of the disaster of 1883 there was
one positive outcome: when those living on
the islands and the UjungKulon peninsula near
the volcano were killed or lost their homes,
these areas were abandoned. Gradually Java's
wildlife began to recover, unimpeded by
human development. This area is now the
Ujung Kulon National Park, and is patrolled by
rangers ever alert to the poachers that threaten
the endangered Javan rhino.

The national park contains many exotic
animals and birds. Leopards live here, although
they are shy and seldom seen, and at least eight
species of brightly coloured kingfisher have
made the park their home. The swampy areas
are the ideal habitat for mudskippers, bird
spiders, and fiddler crabs, along with
venomous golden-banded mangrove snakes.
Finally, huge butterflies and moths flit across
the park, some as large as 8 inches (20 cm)
across, painted in a dazzling array of oranges,
reds and yellows.

*The Javan rhino, Rhinoceros
sondaicus, was given a second
chance for survival after the
eruption.*

How Volcanoes Are Formed

V_OLCANOES_ are an indication
that the earth is still
changing, and that underneath
its crust the rock is still molten.
The earth's crust is formed of
rigid "tectonic plates" that
move around. When two plates
collide, the resulting pressure
causes mountains to be formed;
when two plates move apart,
molten rock, called magma,
rises to fill the gap. Volcanoes
are fissures or vents in the
earth's surface, and are
frequently found where one
tectonic plate meets another,
whether on land or under the
sea. They are usually classified
as active, dormant or extinct.

Between the earth's crust and
its core is the mantle, which
contains magma. This magma is
forced near the earth's surface as
a result of tectonic plate
movement into what is called a
magma chamber. Increased
pressure causes the magma to
be forced out.

There are several types of
volcano, but the one that is
most familiar is the cone
volcano. Here, magma flows
out of a vent and solidifies into
rock, leaving a cone shape with
a crater on the top. When the
volcano erupts again, a second
layer of ash and lava is
deposited on top of the first
layer, and so the volcano grows.
Secondary vents often occur on
the cone, caused by an increase
of pressure in the magma
chamber.

Egypt

THE RIVER NILE

The longest river in the world, the Nile travels more than 4,000 miles (6,436 km) from its sources deep in the heart of Africa to its mouth at the Mediterranean.

Many cities along the Nile are easy to reach. Major airlines fly to Cairo and Khartoum, as well as to Addis Abeba, Alexandria (Al-Iskandariyah), and Kampala, which are close to different parts of the river. While it is relatively easy to sail along the Nile north of Khartoum, especially between the Aswan Dam and Cairo, continuing unrest in the southern Sudan has made travel to those parts inadvisable.

THE world's longest river originates in the great lakes of Africa and winds its way for thousands of miles through deserts and swamps, sometimes meandering gently and sometimes plunging down cataracts and rapids. South and east of Khartoum the Nile is two rivers: the Blue Nile to the east, and the White Nile to the south.

The Blue Nile rises in Lake Tana in the Ethiopian highlands, approximately 5,950 feet (1,814 m) above sea level. From here the river flows south-east over the magnificent Tisisat Falls, and then more than 400 miles (644 km) in a grand arc cutting through the Ethiopian plateau before pouring down into the hot plains of the southern Sudan, some 4,500 feet (1,372 m) lower than where it began. On its

way the river slashes a huge gorge through the centre of the plateau, reaching a mile deep and 15 miles (24 km) wide in some places. Although the difficulty of crossing the desert south-east of Khartoum and following the river through the untamed gorge prevented an exact mapping of the Blue Nile until Colonel R.E. Cheesman's efforts in the 1920s and 30s, Europeans had reached its sources hundreds of years before. The first to make the discovery was Pedro Paez, a Portuguese priest who travelled to Tisisat Falls in 1618, but the best known was a Scotsman, James "Abyssinian" Bruce, who reached the falls in 1770.

In contrast to the fast-paced Blue Nile, between Juba, in the southern Sudan, and Khartoum the White Nile is slow and sluggish,

mainly because in 1,000 miles (1,609 km), it only falls about 240 feet (73 m). In the Sudd, a region of seasonal swamp, the river degenerates into a series of constantly shifting channels choked with underwater weeds and roots. From the time of Nero, who sent an expedition down the Nile, until 1899, when a permanent channel was finally carved out of it, the Sudd halted almost all boats trying to sail up river.

By the middle of the 19th century, the discovery of the sources of the White Nile had become renowned as the greatest geographical problem in the world. In 1858 John Hanning Speke, on a side journey from an expedition led by Richard Francis Burton, was the first European to reach Lake Victoria, which he immediately proclaimed as the source of the Nile. There then followed a great debate over whether Speke or Burton, who insisted that Lake Tanganyika was the ultimate source, was correct. A number of explorers, including the famed Scottish medical missionary David Livingstone, attempted to resolve the question. Final proof was not achieved until Henry Morton Stanley's magnificent crossing of Africa (1874–7), during which he circumnavigated Lake Victoria, proving that it did not have a major river running into it that could be the Nile's source, and that it had only one major outlet: Ripon Falls, where the Nile actually starts. He also proved that the river at the northern extreme of Lake Tanganyika flowed

into the lake rather than out of it. Speke, who had actually been guessing in the dark, had been vindicated.

At the north end of the river, the Nile Delta is one of the most fertile places on earth, and still as vital to Egypt's economy as it has been for thousands of years. The building of the Aswan High Dam, 600 miles (965 km) from Cairo (Al-Qahirah), has threatened the delta area, preventing the deposit of valuable silt from upstream. The water control, however, has meant that year-round irrigation can be achieved and as many as three crops a year can be harvested in some areas.

Above, the enigmatic Nile crocodile is now increasingly rare in Africa.

The Nile Crocodile

THE ancient Egyptians revered the Nile crocodile. The god Sebek had a crocodile's head, crocodiles were kept in temples and given gold bracelets to wear, and even a city – Crocodilopolis – was named after it. Archaeologists have discovered thousands of crocodile graves near by, buried with great care and sometimes with expensive jewellery. The Nile crocodile no longer abounds on the shores of the Egyptian Nile, and except where small populations are being monitored and protected such as in Lake Turkana in northern Kenya, this magnificent animal is rare in Africa today.

Left, the area around the city of Aswan on the Nile has been changed by human hands, with extensive quarrying and the famous dam across the river.

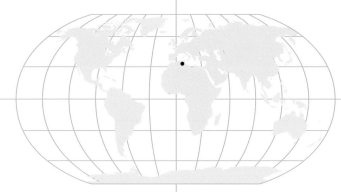

THE GREAT SAHARA

The Sahara is the biggest desert in the world — more than 3.5 million square miles (9 million sq km) of barren rock and sand.

The Sahara is so huge that it covers most of the northern part of Africa. It is possible to reach the Sahara by travelling south from any of the cities on the north coast of Africa, especially Algiers (El Dhazaï), Tunis, and Oran.

Right, a rolling golden sea of sand dunes in the northern Sahara.

Facing page, seeds germinating on sun-baked ground after a desert shower.

THE Sahara Desert sprawls over the northern part of Africa, stretching 3,200 miles (5,149 km) from Egypt and the Sudan to the west coasts of Mauritania and Spanish Sahara. The largest desert in the world, it covers an area of 3,579,000 square miles (9,269,594 sq km).

The name Sahara invokes images of great baking yellow sand dunes, interrupted all too infrequently by jewel-like oases of green. But the immense area of the Sahara contains just about every kind of desert terrain; there are also barren rocky plateaux littered with broken rocks and strange geological formations, and parched scrub land.

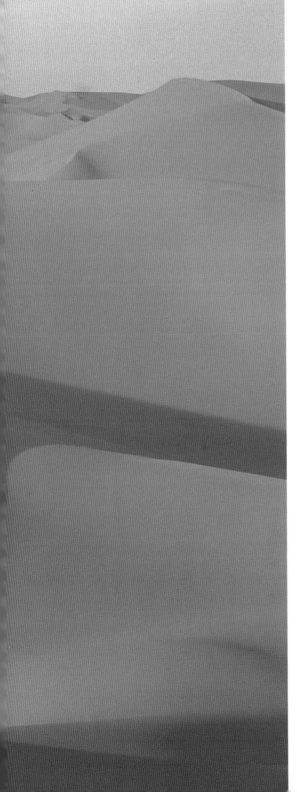

The Sahara is arid, with less than 10 inches (25 cm) of rainfall each year in many parts. The bulk of the desert is far inland, and the prevailing winds dry any moisture before it can reach the interior. Mountain ranges between the desert and the sea also cause clouds to drop their rain before they reach the interior.

With few clouds in the sky, days in the desert are ferociously hot. Cloudless skies also allow the heat to escape easily into the atmosphere once the sun has gone down, and temperatures at night can drop below freezing. One of the hottest places in the desert is Kebili, where high temperatures reaching 131 degrees Fahrenheit (55 degrees C.) are not only due to the burning hot sun, but because it lies in the path of the Sirocco – the wind that originates in the scorching interior of the desert, blowing hot air northwards like a blast from a furnace.

The best known areas of the Sahara are the sand dunes associated with the battles in North Africa during the World War II. These huge tracts of rolling waves of sand cover areas as large as 39,000 square miles (101,010 sq km), known as "ergs". In places, these great dunes are highly mobile, and roll forward at a rate of 36 feet (11 m) per year, driven by the wind. The oasis of Faja is under constant threat from this ever-advancing tide of smothering sand. However in other areas the dunes appear not to have moved for thousands of years, and the trenches between them have become permanent paths for caravans.

Because the Sahara is arid it has not been cultivated, and nomadic tribes still wander with their small herds of animals. There is mixed farming around a few oases, but most of the desert is unproductive in economic terms. Concern has been growing recently about a process known as "desertification" around the edges of the Sahara. This occurs when inappropriate agricultural methods are used, and in combination with natural factors such as drought and wind storms, the desert begins to advance across arable land. Removal of native plants loosens fertile soil which is then baked by drought; winds blow it away like dust, and desert occurs where there were once crops.

Oases: Green Eyes in the Sand

OASES are areas in deserts that are fertile because of the presence of water. Sometimes it is just a few trees around a small spring, but it can also be a far larger area watered by a river, such as the Abiod River that flows through Algeria towards the Sahara. In places the river is a ribbon of dark green palms snaking through the barren desert with groves of date palms, apricots, pomegranates and figs, and a bright array of flowers.

A different kind of oasis is found at Nefta in Tunisia. This has been an important watering station for caravans crossing the northern fringes of the Sahara, and was known and used in Roman times. Each year the water table under the Nefta area rises, saturating the porous rocks, and forming artesian wells underground. Water is forced out of the wells as springs, nourishing huge numbers of citrus fruit trees and date palms.

Discovery of Lake Chad

BEFORE the 19th century Europeans had very little knowledge of the interior of the Sahara. Their first accurate information came from attempts to solve the mysteries surrounding the sources of the River Niger. The first significant exploration was by an expedition involving three British explorers – Dixon Denham, Hugh Clapperton, and Walter Oudney. The small party left Tripoli (Tarabulus) in 1822, spent 68 days going through the uncharted desert, and on 4 February 1823, became the first Europeans to see Lake Chad. Denham went on to explore the area to the south, while Clapperton and Oudney turned west toward the Niger. Oudney soon died, but Clapperton reached the great walled town of Kano, and then Sokoto, the capital of the Fulani empire.

East Africa

THE EAST AFRICAN RIFT VALLEY

A split in the earth's crust of continental proportions.

The East African Rift Valley crosses nine African countries: Mozambique, Malawi, Tanzania, Zaire, Burundi, Rwanda, Uganda, Kenya, and Ethiopia. The capitals of most of these countries are readily accessible by air and there are organised safaris to see the wildlife and the Rift Valley.

THE East African Rift Valley is one of the great geological features of the planet. The view from the top of the fault scarp on one side is of a sweeping panorama across a deep, flat-bottomed valley, in places too wide to see the

far side. The western arm of the rift extends for about 1,900 miles (3,057 km) from Lake Malawi (Nyasa) in the south close to the Mozambique coast, northward along the line of the great African lakes to the west of Lake Victoria. The

Right, looking out over the Rift Valley from the top of the escarpment near Losiolo, Kenya.

Facing page, Ol Doinyo Lengai is the only active carbonatite volcano in the world.

eastern arm starts to the east of Lake Victoria and continues northward for about 1,600 miles (2,574 km) from Tanzania through Kenya and into Ethiopia and the complex area known as the Afar Triangle, an area of volcanic rocks and frequent earthquakes. Here the rift divides, one part continuing north towards the Red Sea, the other striking eastward into the Gulf of Aden.

The German meteorologist Alfred Wegener, who developed the theory of continental drift at the turn of the century, noticed that the opposing shores of the Red Sea formed a perfect match, and that the sea could be closed by sliding Africa against Arabia, except that the Yemen would overlap the Afar Triangle. Geologists now recognise that the volcanic rocks in both these areas are younger than the Red Sea, and so could not have existed before the Red Sea opened; thus the match would have been perfect.

Active rifts are characterised by earthquakes and volcanic activity, and in the African rift, the Afar Triangle is currently the most active part. Earthquakes are frequent here, but the shape of the rift is less spectacular because volcanic activity, with huge outpourings of lava over the millenia, has tended to fill the valley. Volcanism currently occurs around Lake Victoria – in the Virunga Mountains of south-western Uganda to the west, and in northern Tanzania to the east. Here in Tanzania is Lengai, the only active carbonatite volcano, where the lava is like a volcanic limestone that turns to the colour of dirty snow within 24 hours of erupting.

The other main feature of the African rift, particularly in the western arm, is the intermittent line of lakes along the valley floor. Lake Tanganyika is the second deepest lake in the world and has 16,500 feet (5,029 m) of sediment beneath it, indicating a long or very fast history of rifting. The sheer scale of the rift is difficult to grasp, and most visitors turn their attention to the abundant wildlife that typifies Africa. The crater of Ngorongoro, a caldera 12.5 miles (20 km) across that formed in a titanic explosion about 3 million years ago, is Africa's finest game reserve where elephants, Cape buffalo, lions and hyenas are among the wildlife. North of Lengai is Lake Natron, a very shallow lake partly fed by soda-rich hot springs that support a rich growth of algae, and provide ideal breeding grounds for thousands of pink flamingos. Between Lengai and Ngorongoro is Olduvai Gorge, famous for hominid fossils, and regarded by some as the birthplace of the human race.

Formation of a Rift Valley

A RIFT valley is formed by tension in the earth's crust where the opposite sides of the valley are slowly moving apart. As the valley widens, the floor of the valley drops between two roughly parallel escarpments. The fault systems along the valley margins are complex, but generally result in wedge-shaped slices of crust that slip downward to jam in the widening gap. In this way, over millions of years, the valley gradually widens and deepens, but continued erosion tends to blur the sharp lines of the escarpments and sediments accumulate on the valley floor, masking the effects of the vast forces of nature at work.

As the widening continues, the crust of the valley begins to thin from a normal continental thickness of perhaps 25 miles (40 km), to approach the thickness of oceanic crust, typically about 3.8 miles (6 km). When this happens the faulting can no longer accommodate the thinning crust, and a new crust is formed by volcanic magma erupting from the underlying mantle. This is how the Atlantic Ocean was formed and continues to spread. Today, Europe and the Americas continue to move farther apart by about 4 inches (10 cm) per year, and new crust is formed in the central rift of the Mid-Atlantic Ridge.

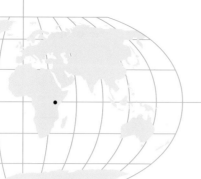

Kenya

LAKE NAKURU

An extraordinary, spectacular lake supporting a million flamingos.

Lake Nakuru is one of a string of lakes that lie along the Rift Valley of Africa. The nearest airport is at Nairobi, the capital of Kenya, which lies around 120 miles (193 km) south-east of Lake Nakuru. It can be reached by road, with the main highway between Nairobi and Kampala in Uganda passing through the national park.

Lake of Many Birds

As well as the lesser flamingos there are also extensive numbers of the larger greater flamingo, which feed on the midge larvae and the copepod. Over 100 other bird species are represented at Nakuru, including the fish-eating cormorants, anhingas, several species of heron, great white pelicans, yellow-billed storks, spoonbills and African fish eagles. Most of these birds only use the lake for feeding on the way to their nest sites, although the cormorants nest in the trees around the mouth of the Njoro River. The great white pelicans have a relatively short journey to their nest site on nearby Lake Elementeita, only 6 miles (10 km) away. In contrast the lesser flamingos breed on Lake Natron, to the south across the border in Tanzania, involving marathon overnight flights of 120 miles (193 km) or more between their feeding and nesting sites.

Above, a vivid flock of flamingos.

Facing page, thousands of flamingos form a continuous pink ribbon around the margins of the lake.

LAKE Nakuru is the centrepiece of the national park which bears its name, and is truly one of the great wildlife spectacles of the world. It is, however, only one of a series of important bodies of water that lie in a string down the east side of Africa in the Rift Valley from Lebanon to Mozambique. These lakes are found at different altitudes, and vary in saltiness from freshwater through those of moderate salinity to others which are hypersaline or soda lakes.

Nakuru, lying just south of the equator at an altitude of 5,770 feet (1,759 m), is one of the highest lakes, with a catchment area of some 695 square miles (1,800 sq km), and receives most of its water from two main rivers, the Njoro and Nderit. There is no major outflow from the lake; its surface area varies with the level of inflow (which is in turn dependent on rainfall), the amount of water taken for human use, the input from other intermittent springs and the rate of loss by evaporation. On average it covers an area of 15.4 square miles (40 sq km) and has a maximum depth of around 9 feet (2.7 m).

Lake Nakuru is hypersaline, the result of very high levels of carbonates and bicarbonates – not chlorides as is the case with sea water. Such an alkaline environment is very harsh. Living things require a very high level of specialisation to be able to survive such conditions, and so the diversity of aquatic species is very low. The waters do not support any large plants, but six species of phytoplankton have been recorded. By far the most numerous of these is the tiny blue-green alga *Spirulina platensis*, which occurs in such vast numbers as to turn the water dark green with a thick, slimy consistency. This tiny species forms the basis of the entire food web in

Filtering Machines

THE favourite food of the lesser flamingo is the protein-rich, blue-green alga *Spirulina platensis*. On the most productive lakes which support a million or more birds they may consume in excess of 59 tons (60 tonnes) of alga per day. The lesser flamingo has a floating bill to help it to concentrate its feeding effort in the surface waters, unlike its close relative the greater flamingo with its heavier bill, which sinks and enables it to feed on the copepods and midge larvae in the lake sediments. Lesser flamingos feed with their head inverted, filtering food from the water with their tongue which acts as a piston, pumping the water through fine filters in the bill and trapping most of the *Spirulina*. The greater flamingo has a coarser filter allowing most of the *Spirulina* to pass through.

The Soda Lake Fish

THE soda lake fish *Oreochromis alsalicus grahami* lives in some of the most extreme conditions in which fish have ever been found. It can survive temperatures up to 104 degrees Fahrenheit (40 degrees C.) and the very wide fluctuations in salinity that occur when the lake is flooded by rainwater and then subsequently drained through evaporation. The soda lake fish was originally introduced to Lake Nakuru in an attempt to control the mosquitoes which were breeding in the less saline areas of the lake. They are now well established as an integral part of the food web, and are the main reason for the great increase in diversity of birds using the lake.

the lake. It is unusually high in protein and contains large amounts of beta-carotene. It is the main prey of the five species of zooplankton, four species of water boatmen, two midge larvae and a calanoid copepod, which together make up the entire natural aquatic invertebrate fauna. There is also one fish species which was introduced to the lake in 1953 and again in 1962, after the lake had entirely dried up and then reflooded. It is the combination of these different species that make Lake Nakuru such a wildlife spectacular.

They provide a vast food resource for countless numbers of birds, many of which are fish-eating and have only appeared on the lake since the fish were introduced.

Most notable among the birds are the lesser flamingos which come to the lake to feed. They can occur in numbers up to 1.5 million, forming an almost endless brilliant pink carpet around the margins of the lake. They depend entirely on the Spirulina for their food; it is the beta-carotenes in these that give the birds their brilliant pink colour.

The Ruwenzori range lies 200 miles (322 km) to the west of Kampala, and is accessible by both road and rail.

Uganda
RUWENZORI
MOUNTAINS

Dramatically called the "Mountains of the Moon", these are one of the three great massifs straddling the equator, flanked by the Great Rift Valley.

Above, the strange vegetation of the Mountains of the Moon.

Facing page, the Mountain gorilla is a shy creature, its habitat now restricted to just a few small areas of central Africa.

THE Ruwenzori mountain range is one of the few places on the African continent to have a permanent cap of ice and snow. The climate varies according to the altitude and the aspect; the southern slopes are wetter, with the region around 8,200 feet (2,499 m) receiving the greatest rainfall. Temperatures can fluctuate markedly each day by as much as 59 to 70 degrees Fahrenheit (15 to 21 degrees C.), equivalent to going from deep winter to high summer in a 24-hour period. The summits of the mountains are often shrouded in mist, which can persist for weeks on end.

The highest point on the range is Mount Ngaliema at 16,794 feet (5,119 m). There is a varied range of habitats moving up the mountain, and the foothills are covered in lush grassland which extends to a height of around 4,000 to 5,000 feet (1,219 to 1,524 m), where it gives way to high forest. Here the dominant tree species are cedar, camphor, and podocarps which grow to a height of 160 feet (49 m). This rainforest dominates up to an altitude of around 8,000 feet (2,438 m) where it merges into mountain bamboo forest, which grows in such dense stands that it is impenetrable to both beasts and light. The bamboo grows 40 to 50 feet (12 to 15 m) high. Above 10,000 feet (3,048 m) sub-alpine moorland takes over, dominated by sedges and coarse tussock grass with open forest of juniper and podocarps. The branches of the gnarled and twisted trees are festooned in mosses, liverworts, ferns and long trailing ribbons of *Usnea* lichens, which all thrive in the permanently moist atmosphere. The effect is

branch is a rosette of large fleshy leaves covered in a fine dusting of silvery hairs. The rosette surrounds the sensitive growing point, and at night when temperatures plummet they envelop it to protect it from the cold.

It is not only the flora which is special; the mountain slopes support a large and varied fauna, the Ruwenzori range has no less than 37 endemic bird species and 14 butterflies. The birds include the spectacular red-headed parrot and Hartlaub's turaco, which is most often seen as a fleeting flash of colour in the forest. Birds of prey abound, such as Verreaux's eagle, and the hawk eagle which preys on the monkeys of the forest.

The Mountain Gorilla

THERE are now fewer than 400 mountain gorillas left in the wild and none in captivity. This magnificent and enigmatic creature is both rare and highly endangered. It has suffered both from direct persecution and from the loss of its habitat. A peaceable animal, it eats nothing but the tender shoots and pith of plants, and unlike its close relative the chimpanzee, it does not supplement its diet with meat in any form. Gorillas live in bands of around 10 individuals, with a dominant male or silverback, and a number of females and juveniles. When feeding the gorillas appear to be very destructive, and once they have finished in an area it appears to have been stripped almost bare. However, after it has been left for a few months there is a vigorous flush of new growth, the preferred food of the gorilla.

dramatic and somewhat unreal, earning it the name of Mountains of the Moon. Even higher, above 14,000 feet (4,267 m), is the alpine zone of lake, tarns, frozen waterfalls, and the most peculiar flora. Plants that are normally low-growing herbs take on gigantic proportions here, and common species such as groundsel, lobelia and St Johns wort grow to 30 feet (9 m) in height, with thick cork-like bark, covered in a thick layer of dead leaves. At the end of each

The high forest is also home to a wide variety of mammals, including elephant, black rhino, forest duiker and bongoe, the black and white colobus monkey and the bushbaby. The elusive okapi (a relative of the giraffe), forest pigs and buffalo feed in the more open forest glades which are carpeted with grass and moss. The most famous inhabitant of the mountain forests, however, is the mountain gorilla which is endemic to this habitat.

Declining Forests

FOREST clearance in Uganda and neighbouring countries has been going on for centuries, although since the 13th century when the Tutsi tribe invaded, pastoralism has been the dominant form of agriculture. Recent forest clearances have been for fuel and cash crops such as quinine, coffee, tea and pyrethrum, but this practice is now in decline. In Uganda the innovative mountain gorilla project is making money from organised trips to view the gorillas while ensuring their long term protection.

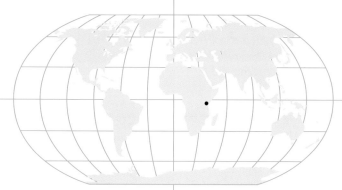

Tanzania

MOUNT KILIMANJARO

This majestic blue-grey mountain with its snowy summit looms over the semi-desert of northern Tanzania.

There is a small airport at Moshi, about 10 miles (16 km) from the base of the mountain. The capital of Tanzania, Dar es Salaam, is about 350 miles (563 km) by road, while Nairobi in neighbouring Kenya is about 180 miles (290 km) by road. Tours to the mountain can be arranged from either country.

Ol Doinyo Lengai Volcano

IN 1955 Ol Doinyo Lengai erupted, spewing ash and sodium carbonate dust into the air. The volcano is unusual because its contents are rich in sodium but low in silica. From a distance, Lengai appears snow-capped, like Mount Kenya and Kilimanjaro, but a closer inspection reveals that the whitish substance is not snow at all, but the alkaline sodium carbonates from its recent eruptions. The volcano lies in a region of the Great Rift Valley in Tanzania called Sykes Grid, where the earth's crust is thought to be very thin.

Right, the snowy summit of Kilimanjaro looms above the plain.

96

I N Swahili, Kilimanjaro means "the mountain that glitters", an apropriate name for this towering volcano with its spectacular snow-covered cap. At 19,350 feet (5,899 m), it is the tallest mountain in Africa, and it can be seen for many miles across the savannahs of Tanzania and Kenya. Its profile is very distinctive: gently rising slopes lead to an elongated, flattened summit that is really a great caldera – the basin-shaped summit of a volcano.

On very hot days and from great distances, the blue mountain base is sometimes indistinguishable from the savannah itself, and the snowy summit seems to hover in the air. The wispy clouds that often stretch below the snow line add to this illusion.

Kilimanjaro covers an area 60 miles (97 km) long and 40 miles (64 km) wide, and is so large that it can influence its own weather. (This is also true of many other large mountains, such as Mount McKinley in Alaska and Mount Everest in the Himalayas.) As moisture-laden winds blow in from the Indian Ocean they are forced upwards when they meet Kilimanjaro, and drop their water as rain or snow. The increased rainfall means that very different vegetation grows on Kilimanjaro from the semi-desert scrub that surrounds it. The lower parts of the slopes of the mountain are cultivated for crops such as coffee and maize, while there is tropical rainforest up to about 9,800 feet (2,987 m). Above this, grasslands are replaced by high-altitude lichens and mosses at about 14,500 feet (4,420 m).

At the very peak of the mountain are Kilimanjaro's permanent glaciers – unusual since the mountain lies only three degrees south of the equator – but recent evidence suggests that these glaciers are retreating. The rainfall on top of the mountain is only 8 inches (20 cm) a year, and this is insufficient to keep pace with the amount of water lost through melting.

Some scientists believe that the volcano is warming up again, which is speeding up the melting process, while others believe that global warming is responsible. Whatever the cause, there is no dispute that Kilimanjaro's glaciers are smaller now than they were in the last century, and it is predicted that if the situation remains constant, Kilimanjaro's icy cap will be gone by the year 2200.

Kilimanjaro is really three volcanoes linked together by a complex history of eruptions. The oldest volcano, Shira, lies to the west of the main mountain. It was once much taller, and is thought to have collapsed following a violent eruption, which left only a plateau of 12,500 feet (3,810 m). The second oldest volcano is Mawenzi, which is a distinct peak attached to the east side of the largest mountain. Even though it appears insignificant next to Kilimanjaro's summit, it rises to a height of 17,500 feet (5,334 m).

The youngest and largest of the three volcanoes, Kibo, was formed during a series of eruptions, and is topped by a caldera that is about 1¼ miles (2 km) across. A second volcanic cone with a crater developed inside the caldera during a subsequent eruption, and later still, a cinder cone formed inside the crater during a third eruption. The great caldera of Kibo forms the flattened summit that is characteristic of this beautiful African mountain.

Above, glaciers remain in the sheltered corries on Mount Kenya.

Mount Kenya: Africa's Second Mountain

A NOTHER equally famous African mountain is Mount Kenya (Kirinyaga). Lying north of Nairobi, and part of the Great Rift Valley, it is second in Africa only to Kilimanjaro, rising 17,000 feet (5,182 m) above the rolling African plains. Like Kilimanjaro, Mount Kenya's origins are also volcanic, and it is estimated to be between 2.5 and 3 million years old. While Kilimanjaro appears as a smooth snow-capped dome, Mount Kenya's peak is a craggy splinter of rock clawing into the sky. The peak is actually a "volcanic plug", a core of very hard rock that formed in the vent of the volcano. When softer rocks surrounding the plug eroded, the core was left standing proud like a broken tooth atop the mountain.

Also like Kilimanjaro, Mount Kenya has glaciers at its summit, and scientific evidence suggests that they too are melting. Some unusual plants live in the glacial climate of Mount Kenya's upper reaches, such as giant groundsels and giant lobelias. Further down the slopes are rainforests and bamboo thickets.

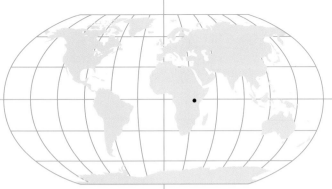

Tanzania

NGORONGORO CRATER

Spectacular and varied scenery ranges from the precipitous slopes on the Ngorongoro crater wall to the sweeping plains of grassland and acacia scrub.

Ngorongoro is situated in the north of Tanzania, lying at the western edge of the great Rift Valley on the border with Kenya. It is possible to fly by small plane to the airstrip on the crater rim. Alternatively it is a road trip of 292 miles (470 km) from Nairobi.

T HE Ngorongoro Conservation Area is vast, covering some 2,500 square miles (6,475 sq km); its importance has been reinforced by its status as a World Heritage Site and a Biosphere Reserve. Formerly this whole area was part of what is now the Serengeti National Park, but as a conservation area it has the dual aims of conserving the natural resources of the area while safeguarding the interests and traditional ways of life of the indigenous Maasai tribe who still tend their herds of cattle, sheep and goats here.

The centrepiece of the conservation area is Ngorongoro crater or caldera, the remains of just one of a number of extinct volcanoes in the area. Ngorongoro caldera is not only one of the most spectacular big game haunts in Africa, but it is also one of the largest calderas in the world, measuring 9 miles (14.5 km) across and ranging from 2,000 to 2,500 feet (610 to 762 m) deep, covering a total area of 102 square miles (264 sq km).

It is the diversity of habitats within the

Birds of the Crater

N GORONGORO is not only a haven for big game but also a very important area for large numbers of birds which either live and breed in the area, or over-winter, or use it as a stopover point on a longer migration. Year-round residents include ostrich, bustard, Augur buzzard, Verreau's eagle and Egyptian vulture. During the wet season many European migrants, such as white storks, yellow wagtails and swallows, escape the cold of a northern winter here. Less regular visitors include both the lesser and greater flamingos which come to feed at the various soda lakes, especially when their more regular areas have dried up or the blue-green algae bloom has crashed (which happens occasionally when algae numbers become so great that they are, in fact, poisoned by the toxins which they themselves produce).

Right, a herd of Burchell's zebra graze the lush vegetation of the savannah, with the caldera wall behind them.

98

conservation area which makes it such an important place. Within the area are woodland, swamps, lakes, rivers and extensive grassland or savannah, part of the Serengeti ecosystem which extends into Kenya to include the adjacent Maasai Mara National Reserve.

The savannah grasslands support a remarkable diversity and great abundance of grazing animals, particularly during the dry season when there is ample food for over 2 million herbivores of all sizes. The list of animals in the area reads like a catalogue of African game, with wildebeest (gnu), zebra, gazelle, buffalo, eland and warthog, as well as giraffe, elephant and black rhino. Most of these animals range across the great extent of the Serengeti, while others such as the hippopotamus are confined to the lakes and swamps. Where there is prey on such a scale, inevitably there are predators, and the Ngorongoro Conservation Area supports populations of lion, spotted hyena, jackal, cheetah, leopard and serval.

The animal numbers might suggest great pressure on the area, but in fact it is a perfect demonstration of the intricate balance struck by

nature in such complex situations, with each of these grazing species filling its own specific niche and a degree of interdependency on others. Thus the zebras eat the tough parts of many plants, making the more succulent parts available for antelope. The wildebeest chew down the remaining sward stimulating the growth of new shoots essential to the gazelles. Without this grazing pressure much of the savannah would revert to woodland.

Above, the black rhinoceros, a shy herbivore, has been hunted to the brink of extinction for its horn.

The Scourge of Poaching

DESPITE the increased protection that many of the endangered large game species now receive in national reserves and other protected areas, poaching continues. Elephants have suffered badly across the entire African continent, with an estimated 50,000 killed each year out of an ever diminishing total of around 400,000 to 600,000. The black rhino has been eliminated from many areas and is now on the very brink of extinction. And despite the high risks involved the killing continues, with a single rhino horn worth as much as $30,000. With such rewards it is perhaps not surprising that the numbers of black rhino have plummeted from around 50,000 in 1976 to only 3,500 in 1990.

Extreme measures are now being taken to save this magnificent animal. Anti-poaching patrols protect certain areas and poachers may be shot dead on sight. In a desperate attempt to save the last of the black rhino the horn is even being removed by the conservationists to deny the poacher his prize and to deflect attempts to shoot them.

Zaire

THE ZAIRE RIVER, THE CONGO

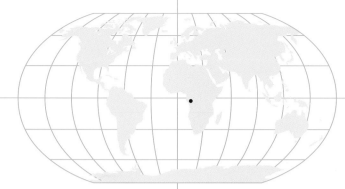

A powerful and mysterious river carves its way through the swamps and jungles of central Africa from its source in the savannah of Zambia.

The Zaire (Congo) River is 2,700 miles (4,344 km) in length from its headwaters to where it empties into the Atlantic Ocean at Banana Point. River trips can be taken from Kinshasa in Zaire, or from Brazzaville in the Congo. Precarious relations between the two countries prevents crossing the river from one city to the other.

PERHAPS no one has captured the terrifying essence of the Zaire River as well as the novelist Joseph Conrad, who, in *Heart of Darkness*, wrote that being on it, "was like travelling back to the earliest beginnings of the world, when vegetation rioted on the earth and the big trees were kings…It was the stillness of an implacable force brooding over

Right, the mighty Zaire River flows for more than 2,700 miles (4,344 km).

Facing page, a small settlement beside the river that acts as a highway to the most inhospitable regions.

an inscrutable intention. It looked at you with a vengeful aspect."

Although this river has been officially called the Zaire since 1971, its savage image is inextricably tied to its mysterious history, when it was known as the Congo, the Portuguese misinterpretation of a West African word meaning "the river that swallows all rivers". Indeed, it is an awe-inspiring natural force: more than 2,700 miles (4,344 km) long, with a basin that is 1.5 million square miles (3.9 million sq km), and a flow that is second only to the Amazon, pouring almost 1.5 million cubic feet (42,450 cu m) of water into the Atlantic every second.

The river rises in the highland savannah of northern Zambia, more than 5,000 feet (1,524 m) above sea level. Beginning life as the Chamber River, it wanders through Zambia into Zaire, where it joins the Lualaba and,

under that name, begins its slow descent toward the tropical rainforests of West Africa, which it reaches some 500 miles (805 km) later. The river flows northward more than 1,000 miles (1,609 km) before crossing the equator, becoming the Zaire and then turning westward in a magnificent arc that recrosses the equator going south. The equatorial rainforest is home to some of the densest growth on earth: oak, mahogany, rubber, ebony and walnut trees grow to heights of more than 200 feet (60 m), forming a canopy that creates a perpetual gloom beneath. Below this colossal ceiling is a nether world of intensely thick undergrowth, oppressive heat and humidity, deadly animals – crocodiles, pythons, cobras, hairy forest pigs and poisonous spiders – and debilitating and even fatal diseases such as malaria, bilharzia and black water fever. And nowhere is it more a maze of mystery than between the river and the fabled Mountains of the Moon – the Ruwenzori range that serves as the Zaire's easternmost watershed.

In the north-east of the great arc is the Stanley Falls, a series of cataracts and rapids that drop the river to an elevation of 1,500 feet (457 m) during a course of some 60 miles (97 km). This is followed by a 1,000-mile (1,609-km) stretch of navigable river, culminating in Malebo Pool (once called Stanley Pool), a 15-mile wide expanse that separates Kinshasa, the capital of Zaire, from Brazzaville, the capital of the Congo. Beyond Malebo Pool are the Livingstone Falls, a 220-mile (354-km) stretch that includes an entire series of rapids and 32 cataracts, the last of which, the Cauldron of Hell, takes the river out from the Crystal Mountains and down to sea level.

But even after rushing the final 100 miles (161 km) down to the Atlantic, the Zaire is not drained of power. Moving with a current of nine knots it sweeps its huge volume of water through a submarine canyon it has carved out to a depth of 4,000 feet (1,219 m), for another 100 miles (161 km) out to sea. There, in the waves of the Atlantic Ocean, it is still possible to see both the muddy red-brown stain of the rain forest and the bits of lighter vegetation that have been carried all the way down from the savannahs.

Stanley and the Congo

BY the 1870s the Congo was still shrouded in mystery to Westerners. Was it connected to the Nile, the Niger, the equally mysterious Lualaba in the heart of Africa, or was it a totally separate river? No one knew for sure, not even the Arab slavers who travelled to places in central Africa where no Europeans had ever been. All the major questions about the African watershed were resolved by Henry Morton Stanley between 1874 and 1877 when, with the backing of *The New York Herald* and *The Daily Telegraph* of London, he made a trans-Africa expedition from Zanzibar to the mouth of the Congo.

Stanley took with him 356 native labourers, 8 tons of stores, and a 40-foot (12 m) boat that had been built in sections so that it could be carried across as much of the continent as necessary. After assembling it first at Lake Victoria and then Lake Tanganyika, both of which he circumnavigated, he and his party marched to the Lualaba and turned north into areas completely unknown. His party sailed along the river, carrying their boats and canoes down at the rapids and falls. After 999 days, the expedition reached the Atlantic, with only 114 of Stanley's 356 followers still alive.

In less than three years, Stanley was back in the Congo, working for Leopold II, the King of Belgium. Between 1879 and 1884, Stanley supervised the building of a road around the cataracts and falls up to Stanley Pool; brought boats up to the pool, allowing easy penetration 1,000 miles (1,609 km) into the interior; and signed approximately 400 treaties with local chiefs, bringing them (without their full comprehension) under the hegemony of Leopold. By doing this Stanley built the foundation for what would become Leopold's private kingdom, the Congo Free State.

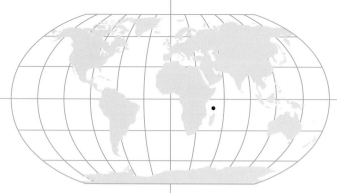

Seychelles
ALDABRA ATOLL

This isolated coral atoll in the Indian Ocean has escaped civilisation, and is now a nature reserve of unique richness.

Aldabra Atoll is in the Indian Ocean, 260 miles (420 km) north-west of Madagascar and 700 miles (1,100 km) south-west of the Seychelles. Access is very strictly controlled and human intrusion is kept to an absolute minimum.

ALDABRA Atoll is entirely encircled by a coral rim which is cut by three entrances; two deep ones divide the atoll into four main islands containing a large, shallow, mangrove-fringed lagoon covering 58 square miles (150 sq km) which itself contains several islets. The largest of the four islands is South Island, and together with West Island, Middle Island and Ile Polymnic they comprise around 72 square miles (186 sq km) of land.

Over the centuries most tropical islands have been heavily exploited by man, but Aldabra was considered inhospitable and was avoided by the sailors of old, and consequently has largely escaped the random destruction which has befallen many other isolated island groups. There has not been the usual guano mining, coconut cultivation or habitat degradation associated with modern day tourism. But Aldabra has not completely escaped exploitation, and for the last 100 years it has been a base for mangrove extraction and commercial fishing and turtling. As ever, with man has come his domesticated animals, but these introductions have been confined to South and West Islands. The Seychelles government has designated the whole area a Strict Nature Reserve, and it is also a World Heritage Site.

As with all the isolated oceanic island groups Aldabra has a high proportion of endemic species. But perhaps even more importantly in this case, in a world in which very little remains which is still in the strictest sense "natural", Aldabra comes very close.

There are two principal types of terrain: platin and champignon. Platin is much more restricted in distribution, confined to the eastern end of South Island, and consists of open scrub and trees with irregular turf and clumps of palms around the larger freshwater pools. Champignon is essentially everywhere else, and is an almost impenetrable scrub interspersed with tufts of coarse grass.

The relatively close proximity of Aldabra to both the African mainland and Madagascar has

Right, the platin country of Aldabra Atoll.

Facing page, top, fairy terns thrive on the island.

Facing page, bottom, the remarkable fruit of the coco de mer.

resulted in more species reaching these oceanic islands than might be expected. Aldabra has a remarkably rich flora, with 273 species of flowering plant and ferns of which 19 are endemic. It has a wonderful insect fauna with over 1,000 recorded species, including 127 species of butterfly and moth of which 36 are endemic. Adding to the list of endemic species, there is a land snail, some crustaceans, the Seychelles flying fox, the Aldabra giant tortoise, and freshwater fish which live exclusively in rainwater pools.

Because of its isolation it is favoured by many sea birds as a breeding area. It is the principal breeding ground in the western Indian Ocean for both the lesser and greater frigate birds, and also supports significant populations of red-tailed and white-tailed tropic birds, red-footed and masked boobies and fairy terns among many others.

Two of the most remarkable birds on Aldabra are the Aldabra warbler and the white-throated rail. The Aldabra warbler was discovered in 1968, and is believed to be confined to one tiny area of coastal scrub. It has only been sighted a handful of times, and is certainly one of the world's rarest birds. The white-throated rail is also endemic to Aldabra and is the only remaining species of the group of flightless birds which include the dodo (extinct).

Endemic Species of the Seychelles

THE Seychelles group is a collection of around 60 islands located in the middle of the Indian Ocean. Like Aldabra they have a large number of endemic species, but unlike Aldabra there have been numerous introductions of exotic species, and together with extensive coconut and cinnamon plantations this has resulted in changes to the native flora and fauna. The Seychelles support a number of endemic birds – most notably the paradise flycatcher and the Seychelles warbler. The islands are surrounded by extensive coral reefs and there are at least 45 endemic species of coral. The most famous endemic of all however is the coco de mer, *Lodoicera maldivica* which is endemic to just two small islands in the group. It produces a fruit with the appearance of two coconuts fused together, but on a massive scale. A single fruit can weigh up to 50 pounds (23 kg) and takes 10 years to mature. These great nuts have taken on mythical proportions, as they were found washed up on other islands around the Indian Ocean long before their origin was known.

THE

COELACANTH

A living fossil fish, rediscovered after 70 million years.

Fossils of this ancient fish are widespread, but live specimens have only been caught from the waters around the Comores Islands off the east coast of Africa. The area can be reached by boat from either Madagascar or the Comores. Nothing on the surface, however, distinguishes it from any other part of the Indian Ocean.

From Water to Land

IT is a matter of conjecture as to why animals that were clearly very successful and adapted to life in the aquatic environment should move on to land, but by the end of the Devonian period some 380 million years ago the first amphibians had indeed evolved.

The first pioneers of land were the lobe-fin fish. Various hurdles had to be overcome: gravity became a problem with the loss of the support of the water, and ways of breathing air and keeping respiratory surfaces moist, and of ending the dependence on water for breeding all had to evolve. Eventually many changes took place in the skeleton and musculature, and in the development of lungs. The lung fish of today, which are found mainly in rivers and lakes, breathe air using an adapted air bladder, and have remained unchanged for the last 150 million years.

Above, coelacanths were rediscovered by chance by local fishermen.

Facing page, the coelacanth shows the heavy, paired fins which enabled its ancient ancestors to take the first movements on land.

IN the Devonian period some 400 million years ago, a group of bony fish known as the lobe fins existed throughout the shallow oceans of the world. The fossil records show that the fish occurred in large numbers and was usually about 8 to 12 inches (20 to 30 cm) long. Indications are that they died out at the end of the Cret-aceous period around 70 million years ago – that is, at about the same time as the dinosaurs.

In 1938 however, a local fisherman from a small village on the Comores Islands, off the north-west tip of Madagascar hauled in his net to find it a strange fish which he had never seen before. The fish rapidly decayed in the heat and was in a rather poor state by the time it could be examined by a visiting scientist, Marjorie Courtenay-Latimer, who came across the catch by chance. On examination there was no doubt that this fish was a lobe fin or coelacanth, thought to have been extinct for the last 70 million years. In honour of its new discoverer the fish was named *Latimeria chalumnae*. After that initial specimen was caught, another appeared in a trawl in 1952, and there have been further specimens since, all caught in the same deep water off the east coast of South Africa between Mozambique and Madagascar.

The coelacanth is a large, deep bodied fish, covered in dull blue, heavy scales with characteristic paired, lobed fins and a triple-lobed tail. The living specimens which have been caught are typically over 6 feet (1.8 m) in length and can weigh anything up to 178 pounds (81 kg), quite unlike their fossil ancestors which were very much smaller. Like its ancestors, the coelacanth feeds on other fish – its jaws are lined with rows of small teeth adapted for catching its prey which it then swallows whole. All the specimens found so far have been in water between 230 and 1,300 feet (70 and 396 m) deep and restricted to the Mozambique channel. This apparently very restricted distribution is mysterious when compared to the widespread distribution of its ancestors, and raises the question why it should be only here, or whether it is in fact elsewhere still waiting to be discovered.

Other ancient animals exist, such as the pearly nautilus whose relatives were abundant in the seas of 500 million years ago. The horse-shoe crab is also thought of in terms of a living fossil, having hardly changed for over 300 million years. The coelacanth has, however, gained a higher status in evolutionary folklore for, like the prodigal son, it was thought dead and has now reappeared alive and well.

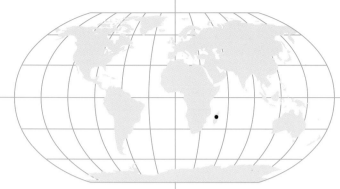

MADAGASCAR

A unique ecosystem has evolved on the world's fourth largest island, which parted from Africa 165 million years ago.

The capital of Madagascar is Antananarivo, which has a major airport. Lying in the Indian Ocean, Madagascar is half again as large as California, but not all the island is accessible by road. Some areas of outstanding natural beauty and biological importance have been set aside as national parks and reserves.

V AST rainforests once sprawled over much of this 1,000-mile (1,609-km) long island, but during the last 40 years the forest has been decimated for firewood and agriculture to support its ever-growing human population.

Despite this, Madagascar is still an island of staggering biological diversity. When the island ripped away from Africa at least 165 million years ago, the opportunity arose for the animals and plants to evolve without interference from

Madagascar's Primates

P RIMATES are a biologically similar animal group that includes apes – gorillas, chimpanzees, orangutans and humans, as well as gibbons and siamangs – and monkeys.

Fifty million years ago a squirrel-sized ancestor of all primates inhabited the subtropical forests of Africa. Through time, different species evolved from this creature: some became the ancestors of humans, apes, and monkeys, and others became lemurs, pottos, lorises and bushbabies. Lorises can be found in Asia, and pottos and bushbabies in Africa, while lemurs live exclusively in Madagascar and the nearby Comores Islands. Another primate unique to Madagascar is the aye-aye, a small, dark brown animal that lives in a nest of leaves, emerging only at night to feed.

Right, denuded of natural vegetation, in some areas of Madagascar the red earth is simply washing away.

outside: Madagascar became, in effect, a huge laboratory, and the plants and animals there are often unlike any others on earth. About 10,000 species of plant exist only in Madagascar, along with half the world's chameleons. One species of chameleon, the brookesia, is so tiny it sits easily on the tip of a human thumb, although Madagascar's islanders avoid it because they believe it is a harbinger of bad luck. Reptiles such as the radiated and ploughshare tortoises are other species unique to the island.

On the west of the island lies the forbidding Tsingy National Reserve of Bemaraha, where sharp fingers of limestone point 100 feet (30 m) into the air over an area of 60 square miles (155 sq km). The local people say that there is barely enough flat land in the area on which to place a foot, a factor that helps to protect at least some of Madagascar's plants and animals from human destruction.

South of Tsingy is Morondava, where rain falls for only four months of the year. In a unique habitat, six species of baobab trees grow here – that is, five more than survive today on mainland Africa. The trees are specially adapted to Madagascar's climate: they gorge themselves on water during the rainy season and then survive on the reserves for eight months until the rains come again. Like other areas in Madagascar, the baobab forests are under threat from human expansion, but baobab forests are particularly difficult to repair once the damage has been done. The trees live for hundreds of years, and often do not fruit annually; an extended period of drought might kill an entire year's seedlings. Animals also pose problems: the giant jumping rat, for example, lives exclusively in a very small area in west Madagascar and eats baobab seedlings. Conservationists face a difficult management problem here, torn

Above, a male panther chameleon, brightly coloured to blend into a leafy background.

Below, a watchful family group of the indigenous ring-tailed lemurs

between wanting to reinstate the baobab forests to allow other species to survive, and protecting the giant jumping rat.

The small Berenty Reserve lies in the south of the island. Some of the largest fruit bats in the world soar above the giant tamarind trees in which they roost, and the colony, which numbers several thousand, is believed to be one of the largest in existence so near human habitation. Ring-tailed lemurs also thrive at Berenty, strutting confidently in front of visitors and regarding them with their curious orange eyes.

Many of Madagascar's 1,000 unique species of orchid grow in the Montagne d'Ambre National Park on the northern tip of the island, but not all of Madagascar is rich and green, and years of deforestation and burning in some areas have taken their toll. When the earth is denuded of its natural vegetation, there is nothing to anchor the fertile soil to the land, and with each passing year, more and more is washed away by the rains. On the island's east coast in particular, rivers run red with the clay that is being swept off hills once richly carpeted with vegetation.

Lemurs

LEMURS are the best known of Madagascar's primates, and species include the ring-tailed, sifaka, black, sportive, ruffed and gentle lemurs. Primates are characterised by large brains, slender limbs, and hands and feet adapted for climbing. Lemurs are lower primates, and are less well adapted for walking on two legs, tending to be quadrupedal (four-footed) walkers.

Lemurs, like apes and monkeys, have opposable thumbs with flattened nails. This means that they have the manual dexterity common to all primates. While lemurs have developed certain monkey-like traits, there is considerable variation in behaviour patterns between the different species. For example, the rare and elusive Coquerel's lemur is monogamous, small, and golden-brown, while the more common ring-tailed lemur tends to live in groups.

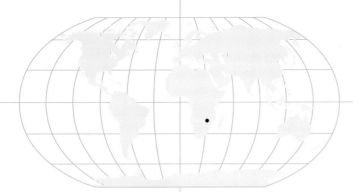

VICTORIA FALLS

The Zambezi River becomes a frothy cascade of water that thunders over sheer cliffs in one of the world's most magnificent waterfalls.

The Victoria Falls on the Zambezi River are located on the Zambia–Zimbabwe border. The nearest airport is at Livingstone (Maramba) which is only a short drive from the falls. The capital of Zambia, Lusaka, is about 300 miles (483 km) away by road.

West Africa's Waterfalls

WEST Africa also boasts stunning waterfalls. The Tagbaladougou Falls in Upper Volta is really three separate falls, including an elongated curtain of water flowing over a hard ridge, and a slender plume. The picturesque Tannogou Falls in Benin pour off a plateau into a large pool. In Guinea, the Tinkisso River tumbles across erosion-resistant rocks in a series of rapids, culminating in the Tinkisso Falls.

Right, a rainbow arches above a narrow gorge, to one side of the famous Victoria Falls.

WHEN the Zambezi River is in full flood, 270,000 cubic feet (7,560 cu m) of water surge over Victoria Falls every second. The volume of water is so immense, and the downward plunge so powerful, that the resulting spume of spray that rises into the air can be seen up to 25 miles (40 km) away. The local name for the Victoria Falls is "Mosi-oa-tunya", which translates as "the smoke that thunders". Rainbows often shimmer in the spray, which can rise to a height of 1,000 feet (305 m).

In November 1855, the Scottish missionary and explorer David Livingstone was the first European to reach Victoria Falls. He had first heard about the waterfall four years earlier when he and William Cotton Oswell had reached the banks of the Zambezi River 80 miles (129 km) to the west. Then, between 1853 and 1856, Livingstone made the first crossing of Africa by a European. Hoping to open the centre of Africa to Christian missionaries, Livingstone travelled north from southern Africa, through Bechuanaland (modern Botswana), and reached the Zambezi. He then headed west to the coast at Luanda in Angola. Deciding that this route to the interior was too difficult, he headed back east, following the Zambezi most of the way, and reaching Quelimane on the Mozambique coast in May 1856.

Surprisingly, the explorer was not happy with his discovery of Victoria Falls, despite his later description of it as providing "scenes so lovely [it] must have been gazed upon by angels in their flight". To Livingstone, the falls, which are a virtually unbroken wall of water some 5,500 feet (1,676 m) long and plunging 350 feet (107 m), were actually an impediment to Christian missionaries trying to reach the native peoples of the interior. To him, the highlight of the journey was the discovery of the Batoka Plateau east of the falls, a place that he saw as a potential settlement site if the Zambezi proved to be fully navigable (which it did not). Despite his disappointment at finding the falls in the way of his perceived "progress", Livingstone

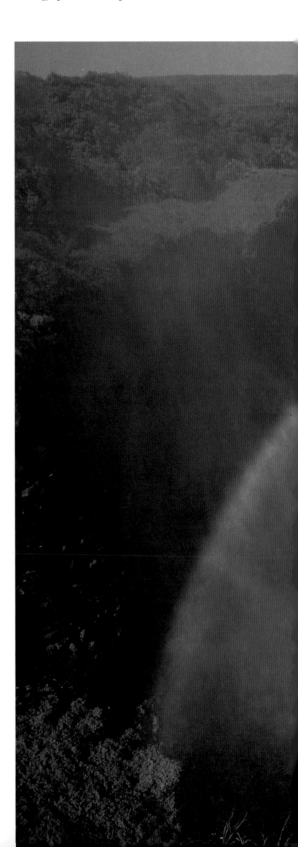

still acknowledged that they were so magnificent they could only be named after the British queen, Victoria.

The waterfall is only the start of a spectacular water course, for the spray-shrouded river immediately churns its way through a narrow chasm, which zig-zags back and forth for almost 45 miles (72 km). These hairpin bends were caused by faults in the rock that have been eroded by the sheer force of the water over thousands of years. The Zambezi River roams across a plateau formed of layers of sandstone and basalt, and it is at the points where these different rocks meet that the faults occur.

Above, up to 270,000 cubic feet of water per second pours over the lip of the main falls.

Southern Africa's Waterfalls

IN South Africa, the Orange River takes a 480-foot (146-m) plunge over the edge of a plateau at the Aughrabies Falls, before ripping its way through a gorge of granite. Granite is one of the hardest of rocks, and it is difficult to imagine the force of the water that allowed such a gorge to be eroded. In the dry season the Orange River is little more than a stream but, swollen with spring rain, the waterfalls are appropriately known as Aughrabies, a term which comes from the Hottentot word meaning "the place of great noise".

Another waterfall to vary seasonally is the Lofoi Falls in Zaire, although its 1,100-foot (335-m) drop is impressive at any time. South Africa also boasts the Tugela Falls, Africa's highest waterfall. This is really a series of five cascades, where the water falls a staggering 3,100 feet (945 m). The Maletsunyane Falls in Lesotho freeze in winter, and the eerie, contorted pillar of frozen water is matched only by its silence.

Namibia

THE NAMIB DESERT

The South Atlantic meets the undulating waves of sand of the Namib Desert, stretching 1,300 miles (2,092 km) along the coast of Africa.

The Namib Desert is a vast area in the south-west of Africa that begins near the Olifants River in the Cape province of South Africa and extends all along the Namibian coast to Angola in the north. International flights can be taken to Namibia's capital, Windhoek, and internal flights to Walvis Bay (Waalvisbaal) near the Namib Game Reserve in the desert itself.

Early Exploration of Namibia

THE first great European explorer to concentrate his efforts on Namibia was Charles John Andersson. An Anglo-Swedish naturalist, Andersson initially travelled to Namibia in 1850 as an assistant to Francis Galton, one of the great Victorian intellectuals. In the next two years, the two men travelled from Walvis Bay to the previously unknown Ovamboland. When Galton returned to England, Andersson remained in Africa, and in 1853–4 he trekked through Bechuanaland (modern Botswana) and reached Lake Ngami, which had been discovered by David Livingstone and William Cotton Oswell in 1849. In 1857–8 Andersson went north from Walvis Bay and reached a previously unexplored part of the Okavango River. Andersson's classic book *Birds of Damaraland* was published shortly after his death.

Right, low, scrubby trees and dry grasses survive the harsh conditions in this arid land.

AN apparently endless sea of sand dunes stretches inland to the Namib Desert's dry heart. At first sight, few animals or plants live in this arid environment, but when the merest sprinkling of rain falls, the desert awakens and life begins. Seeds and bulbs long buried in the sand suddenly sprout, the dry valleys turn into meadows, and with the plants come animals and birds. Finches and larks eat the seeds of grasses, and buzzards feast on the rich insect life. In places, the desert can even support oryx, large desert antelopes that graze the new grass. But the plant life is unpredictable, and the oryx often die of thirst or starvation. While one year might see an explosion of life in the desert, another will see little plant growth, and few animals bother to scour the sand for its scanty nourishment.

Recently, geologists have discovered that valuable minerals lie hidden under Namibia's hot sands. Uranium, copper, and even diamonds are thought to be present, and it is likely that even this uninviting land will soon fall prey to human exploitation and development.

The Namib Desert is so dry that its plants and animals have had to develop special biological mechanisms to deal with conditions here. One plant, the welwitschia, is found only in the Namib, mainly in the northern reaches of the desert where the sand dunes tumble down to meet the dry gravel beds. Welwitschias seem impervious to drought; during several years without water, the tips of their reddish-brown leathery leaves might wither, but at the first sight of rain, the water turns them green again and allows them to grow. They can survive for several years on reserves of water drawn from the earth during a wet year.

At the beginning of the day lizards and beetles emerge from their sandy burrows to stake out territory and to gather food before the temperatures rise, forcing them all back into the cool of the sand. Surface temperatures have been recorded at 150 degrees Fahrenheit (66 degrees C.), which is far too hot for most creatures to be active. For some animals there

is only a short time available between the chill of the night, which is too cold for them, and the searing heat of the day, when most must seek shelter. The desert plays host to totally

shelter. The desert plays host to totally different creatures by night, as nocturnal animals creep from their burrows and lairs into the cool air.

The coast near the Great Dune Sea is frequently swathed in mist, caused when the cold Benguela current sweeping northwards from the Antarctic meets the warmer, moist winds of the Atlantic. For about 60 days each year the mist is dense enough to be blown inland for a distance of around 50 miles (80 km). In a land where it rains rarely and lightly, these fogs are the main source of water for some desert creatures. Head-stander beetles drink the droplets of mist that collect on their bodies, while button beetles dig small furrows in the sand to collect the moisture. The body fluids of these creatures provide the necessary moisture for predators, such as the solifuge and the chameleon.

Above, a head-stander beetle makes the most of the moisture which collects on its own body.

Frozen Deserts

Deserts can be defined as areas where vegetation is supported only irregularly or sparsely. Deserts, however, are not onµly confined to the great sands of the Namib or the stony expanses of the Negev (HaNegev) in Israel. They also cover the vast tracts of the barren wildernesses of the Arctic and the Antarctic, where precipitation is low and little plant life survives.

In the interior of the great Antarctic continent, nothing grows, partly because there is no soil to support plant life, and partly because there is little moisture in the atmosphere. This is ironic considering that nine-tenths of the world's entire supply of fresh water is locked up in the great Antarctic ice sheet. However, some of the coastal regions of this massive continent and its islands support a variety of plant and animal life in the summer.

111

Botswana

THE OKAVANGO DELTA

The Okavango Delta in north-west Botswana is an oasis in one of the last remaining great wilderness areas of Africa.

Deep in the Kalahari desert the area is crossed by very few roads, often little more than dirt tracks. The nearest major airport is at Livingstone across the border in Zambia, some 200 miles (322 km) to the north-east of the centre of the delta area.

Makgadikgadi Pans

THIS is the largest salt pan in the world, covering 14,285 square miles (36,998 sq km). Like those in other areas such as the Camargue it attracts vast numbers of wildlife when in flood after the rains. At this time it bursts into life, providing an oasis of good grazing for the large nomadic herds of zebra and antelopes, and also a haven for spectacular flocks of flamingos and other waterfowl.

Right, with its intricate mosaic of open channels, reed swamps and thorn scrub, the Okavango Delta is a spectacular wilderness.

THE Okavango River rises in the highlands of Angola and flows to the south-east, but before it can reach the sea it disappears in the arid wastes of the Kalahari Desert in Botswana, one of the driest countries in southern Africa. The water moves very slowly, and forms a vast inland delta system covering a core area of some 6,175 square miles (15,993 sq km), but during periods of flood after the rains this can increase to 8,500 square miles (22,015 sq km). The slow-moving water passes through an intricate maze of channels where more than 95 per cent of it evaporates. The remainder travels either further south by way of the Boteti River for another 100 miles (161 km) before reaching the Makgadikgadi Pans (the largest salt pan in the world) where it eventually evaporates, or to the south-west where it finally enters Lake Ngami.

The Okavanga Delta represents not only one of the largest inland delta systems in the world, but also an area of unique character because of the juxtaposition of the highly productive wetlands and the extremely arid land of the Kalahari Desert. Even in such a vast continent as Africa the Okavanga Delta is one of the largest remaining wilderness areas.

The delta is a haven for a wide variety of both plants and animals. The upper reaches of the delta are covered by extensive, dense reed beds dominated by papyrus. These are inter-spersed with areas of permanent water supporting large stands of water lilies – popular with the pygmy goose, which feeds almost exclusively on lily fruit. This wetland habitat is ideal for a number of animals, including hip-popotamus, crocodile and a number of species of antelope. Most notable is the sitatunga, which is very specifically adapted to an aquatic lifestyle and is largely confined to the most impenetrable areas of the delta and other similar

areas in Africa. Other antelope adapted for this aquatic lifestyle and which are even more specific to southern Africa are the kobs which include the waterbuck, the puku and the lechwe. The Okavango Delta is home to the largest remaining concentration of red lechwe, with at least 20,000 animals living on the flooded grasslands.

The reed beds and open water areas are also home to a large number of different birds, including some of Africa's rarest species. The spectacular African fish eagle with its evocative, piercing cry hunts in these areas, along with other species such as the little bee-eater, malacite kingfisher, a number of species of heron and egret, and the African fishing owl.

In the lower reaches of the delta the reed beds give way to acacia thorn scrub and grassy flood plains which act as a magnet to the migrating herds of plains animals, including zebra, buffalo, elephant and antelope. The predators which follow these herds into the area include lion, leopard and hyena. The grassy plains are also inhabited by the local Tswana and Herero tribes who are cattle herders. In the past their livestock were confined to the margins of the delta because of attacks of the tsetse fly, carrier of sleeping sickness. Aerial spraying in recent years has all but eradicated the fly, allowing the cattle and the herdsmen to penetrate into the swamps, but the effect has been to reduce the range of the antelope, disturbing its habitats and making it compete with the cattle for the available grazing. The numbers of antelope are consequently in decline and the fragile integrity of this wilderness is threatened. This threat has been recognised by the local people and the Moremi Wildlife Reserve, covering 1,500 square miles (3,885 sq km), is the first wildlife sanctuary in southern Africa to be created and managed by the local people.

Above, red lechwe bounding throught the Okavango swampland.

Wetland Antelope

THE sitatunga is a shy animal, well adapted to the swamps of the Okavanga Delta. It feeds on a range of plants depending on the level of the water, which fluctuates with the seasons. This versatility contributes to its survival, along with other adaptations such as the extremely long hooves which spread out as it walks, giving it the support necessary to move over the soft, wet ground. It is the only large mammal to feed on the papyrus swamps, where it is fairly well protected from predators, although adults can be taken by crocodiles, lions and leopards, and the young may even fall victim to pythons.

The red lechwe are adapted more to the seasonally flooded grassland plains, and have also developed elongated hooves to help with movement over the flooded land. They favour the wet margins where there is good feeding from young green shoots.

TABLE MOUNTAIN

A great, flat-topped mountain mysteriously draped with cloud forms the magnificent backdrop to one of South Africa's most beautiful cities.

Table Mountain forms the backdrop to Cape Town and is a short drive from the city centre. Its flat summit is accessible by cable car.

The great slab top of Table Mountain is a landmark visible for many miles.

Towering over the city of Cape Town, Table Mountain is often shrouded in white clouds. But sometimes the clouds lift, or resettle so that only the "tablecloth" of mist remains draped over one end, revealing a splendid sight. The mountain is aptly named; viewed from the bay below it appears to have a perfectly flat top stretching 2 miles (3.2 km) from one end to the other. Its 3,500-foot (1,067-m) cliffs rise abruptly so that it totally dominates the bustling port of Cape Town.

From Cape Town harbour the mountain is a great, blue-green monolith shimmering slightly in the heat, and doubtless a welcome sight to many sailors braving the stormy seas of the

A closer view of the mountain (right) reveals steep, rugged cliffs. The point on the left is the Lion's Head.

Cape of Good Hope. From the Atlantic the broken skyline of the sandstone escarpment is known as the Twelve Apostles.

Table Mountain forms the northern end of a range of hills that lie between Cape Town and the Cape of Good Hope. The range is made up of sandstone and quartzite resting on older rocks of granite and shales. East of Table Mountain is Devils' Peak, 3,200 feet (975 m) high, while to the west are the smaller hills of Lion's Head and Signal Hill, which reach 2,100 feet (640 m) and 1,100 feet (335 m).

The tablecloth drapes itself over the summit of Table Mountain but never reaches the lower slopes. The clouds that form are blown in by south-east winds, constantly forced northwards down the slopes towards Cape Town, but they tend not to stay. On the summit clouds can form very suddenly, making the weather there unpredictable. The reputation for foul weather is borne out by figures for its rainfall: Cape Town's annual rainfall is 25.5 inches (65 cm), while precipitation on Table Mountain summit averages 72 inches (183 cm) per year.

Heavy rainfall on the summit has eroded a number of deep ravines running down the cliff face; the deepest of these, the Gorge, is also the shortest route to the top. On clear days the views from Table Mountain are breathtaking. Three great oceans meet at the tip of southern Africa – the Atlantic, the Indian, and the Southern. Cold currents from the south meeting the warmer waters of the Indian Ocean are responsible for some of the violent storms that pummel the region around the Cape of Good Hope.

The first European to reach the Cape Town area was the Portuguese explorer Bartholomew Dias in 1488, naming this the "Cape of Storms". After a massacre of Portuguese sailors 22 years later by native Hottentots, ships avoided the area, and it was not until 1652 that a settlement was established by the Dutch beside Table Bay, to supply passing East India Company ships with fresh vegetables. These early settlers built the fortress that can still be seen in Cape Town.

Famous Tablelands

Tablelands are formed in several different ways. The Jugurtha Tableland in Tunisia is an example of "inverted relief". It developed when softer rocks formed hills (upfold), and harder rocks formed the valley bottom (downfold). As the softer rocks eroded, the hard rocks of the valley bottom became a table-land. In the case of Jugurtha, the table is a natural fortress, with steep-sided cliffs of 2,000 feet (610 m) to protect it. It is named after the ancient African king who used it as a citadel to wage war on Rome.

Mesa Verde, Colorado in the United States, is also a flat table protected by 2,000-foot (610-m) cliffs, although it is far larger than Jugurtha. It is formed of sandstone, with layers of shale and coal. Successive uplifting of the land, combined with erosion of softer rocks by rivers, formed the tableland which is now covered with forests of juniper and pine. The area is famous for the Indian dwellings that nestle under the sandstone cliffs, some more than 1,000 years old.

In South America's inaccessible Guiana Highlands stands Mount Roraima, a red sandstone massif 9 miles (14 km) long, 3 miles (5 km) wide, and 9,000 feet (2,743 m) high. Erosion has scored deep gullies and chasms between the plateaux, seen in action on the barren top of Mount Roraima, where waterfalls plunge over its steep edges, wearing away the hard rock with the sheer force of the water.

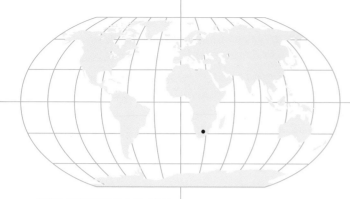

PLATINUM, GOLD AND DIAMONDS

The town of Rustenburg lies in the Transvaal about 50 miles (80 km) west of Pretoria, the national capital. Kimberley is some 280 miles (451 km) to the south-west in the Orange Free State. Both places are easily reached by road or rail from Pretoria.

Platinum

PLATINUM is the most valuable of all the precious metals. Some of the world's most expensive jewellery is made in platinum, but other properties that make it a highly valuable commodity in industry. It has a very high melting point, 3,216 degrees Fahrenheit (1,769 degrees C.), which is ideal for use in furnaces; it is almost inert and does not react easily with any other substances, and yet it is a well known catalyst, enabling other chemical reactions to take place while not being used itself. It is also used in pollution-free cells.

Right, the "Big Hole" at Kimberley is the remains of a 19th-century diamond mine.

South Africa's unique treasure-house of earthly riches.

SOUTH Africa is one of the most richly endowed countries in the world in terms of its mineral resources. It is world-renowned for the production of platinum, gold and diamonds, some of the most valuable of all the earth's natural riches, and the country has exploited them in enormous quantities.

Minerals such as these are formed when molten magmas intruded into the earth's crust in a sequence of pulses, creating layered intrusions. The composition changes slightly with each successive layer, until the residue of the source of the magma contains mostly those elements that do not occur in most rock-forming minerals. These elements and minerals are usually the rarest and most precious and, in the Merensky Reef in the Transvaal, platinum is one of them. Earth movements and erosion have now brought part of this layer to the surface where it can be mined. The reef is only from 3 to 6 feet (1 to 2 m) thick, but it continues for at least 150 miles (241 km). The Merensky Reef is mined by the Rustenburg Platinum Mines Group – the largest platinum producer in the world with an annual output of 28 tons.

Gold, like many other minerals, is found in some mineral veins, particularly those that are mined for copper. In fact, some copper mines have only been economic to work because a sufficient amount of gold could be extracted as a by-product to keep the mining operation solvent. Most South African gold, however, is found in placer deposits. These are sedimentary rocks deposited from the erosion products of other rocks, some of which included gold-bearing veins. Small flakes of gold, much heavier than the other grains of rock, have been naturally concentrated by the sedimentary process, making the mining operation comparatively easy.

The diamond mine at Kimberley is particularly spectacular. The original mine is located within the city limits and is now preserved as a museum. The mine is known locally as the "Big Hole", and that is precisely what it is – the largest man-made hole on earth, dug into a rock called Kimberlite that probably formed

the pipe or vent of a volcano between 70 and 130 million years ago. These volcanoes are very rare, and only a few others are known of elsewhere in the world. The source of the volcanic rock was at least 60 miles (97 km) below the earth's surface, where temperatures and pressure were sufficiently great to form diamonds – the hardest naturally occurring substance known.

At the Big Hole an observation platform built over the rim allows visitors to look some 1,300 feet (396 m) to the bottom of the hole, from where shafts lead even further, as far as 4,000 feet (1,219 m) down. The hole is nearly a mile (1.6 km) in circumference and covers an area of about 37 acres (15 hectares). During its operational years, about 14.5 million carats of diamonds were recovered from the mine, and most of the famous diamonds ever found were mined here in this region of South Africa.

Above, gem quality diamonds sparkle in brown gravel at the Oranjemund Mine, Namibia, the world's richest diamond mine. Below, miners sifting the dirt for elusive diamonds.

Uses of Gold and Diamonds

GOLD has been a prized metal since ancient times. Its early uses centred on jewellery and religious items, and its use for everyday items was an important indication of the wealth of the owner. Wars have been fought over it, and whole civilisations have disappeared in the greed for ownership by others. More recently, its industrial applications in many forms, including medical uses, has sustained the demand. Diamonds, like gold, have been similarly prized for jewellery, but its property as the hardest naturally occurring substance has also made it widely useful in industrial applications. The largest pure diamond, the Cullinan Diamond, was found in the Premier Mine at Pretoria. It weighed 3,106 metric carats (1.25 lb, 567g) and the largest cut stone in the world was taken from it; it is now in the Royal Sceptre of the British Crown Jewels.

117

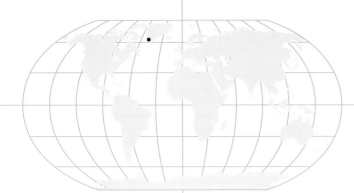

GREENLAND

Greenland lies 125 miles (200 km) west of Iceland. There are no major highways within Greenland, and internal transport is by plane and boat.

The world's largest island is covered almost completely by a huge ice cap.

GREENLAND is a land of towering mountains, great blue-green icebergs, spectacular fjords and barren rocks. Research has shown that the island possesses some of the oldest rocks in the world, estimated to be at least 3,700 million years old. From the air, it looks like a vast empty wilderness where jagged black mountain peaks occasionally puncture the endless expanse of dazzling white ice. But viewed from the land itself, Greenland is an island of great diversity: in the summer, the meadows near the coast burst into colour with

Right, brightly painted houses give a sense of the enormous scale of the frozen fjord at Angmassalik.

Facing page, despite the summer thaw, ice still litters the lonely inlet of Myggbukta Bay, in north-eastern Greenland.

purple saxifrage and yellow poppies, and there are thickets of mountain ash and birch trees. The middle of Greenland remains locked under the great ice cap, however, and neither a blade of grass nor a tiny flower can be found for hundreds of miles.

Greenland is about ten times as large as Britain and roughly a quarter the size of the United States. It covers about 845,500 square miles (2,189,837 sq km), is 1,600 miles (2,575 km) from Peary Land in the north to Kap Farvel in the south, and is around 800 miles (1,287 km) across at its widest point. The most impressive feature is its ice cap, more than 32,800 feet (10,000 m) thick in places, which covers 82 per cent of the island. The ice cap gives rise to huge glaciers: the Jakobshavn Glacier discharges millions of tons of ice into the sea daily, moving at a rate of about three feet (1 m) every hour. This produces enormous icebergs such as the one that sank the

Titanic in 1912. The ice cap was not successfully crossed until 1888, when the great Norwegian explorer Fridtjof Nansen made the journey on skis.

Greenland is a land of great beauty and enormous diversity. The east coast is choked with impenetrable pack ice for much of the year, and because it is so inhospitable and communications are so difficult, human settlements are few and far between. This has allowed a vast area to become a wildlife refuge for some the Arctic's endangered species of plants, birds and animals.

The west coast boasts some of the largest fjords in the world, cutting as much as 200 miles (322 km) into the land. Most human habitation is here, including the capital, Nuuk, which boasts a population of around 12,000 people. Greenland was a colony of Denmark for many years, but in 1979 the Danish government allowed the Greenlanders to govern themselves, a policy that became known as Greenland Home Rule.

Much of Greenland lies north of the Arctic Circle and therefore does not see the sun during the long winter months. However in the summer Greenland is host to a huge number of breeding birds and plants, all racing to make the best of the 24-hour daylight.

Although many birds only come to Greenland to breed and then fly south at the onset of winter, some stay all year round, including the ptarmigan and the tiny snow bunting. Greenland also is home to the world's largest predator, the polar bear, as well as to wolves, Arctic foxes, Arctic hares, reindeer, and lemmings. Northern Greenland supports large herds of musk-oxen, their thick shaggy coats protecting them against the icy Arctic winds. In the coastal waters several species of whales and seals may be seen.

The Greenland Vikings

ACCORDING to the Norse sagas, in the late 9th century a Norseman on his way from Ireland to Iceland was blown off course, and landed on islands off the east coast of Greenland. More than a century later, Eric the Red decided to sail west from Iceland to see if he could find these islands himself. Eric had already been banished from his native Norway, and was now banished from Iceland for murdering settlers.

Sailing around the coast Eric discovered the deep fjords on the west coast of Greenland. At this point, Greenland was experiencing one of its warmer periods, and the fjords contained rich vegetation that allowed Eric and his small band of followers to farm the land and graze their cattle. When news spread of Eric's success, other settlers made the dangerous journey from Iceland to Greenland, and the colony flourished for 400 years.

Archaeological excavations have uncovered about 300 different farms, along with Eric the Red's own house and a church, but so far no definite evidence has revealed the fate of the Vikings. Some scholars believe that the settlers may have died in skirmishes with the local Inuit tribes or raiding pirates, or that a series of epidemics killed them. Others believe that the climate became much colder so that the people were unable to grow their crops or feed their animals.

Canada

THE FOSSIL FOREST OF AXEL HEIBERG

A remarkable area of preserved trees in the Canadian High Arctic.

Travel in the Arctic is generally by light aircraft, and Axel Heiberg Island can be reached by plane from Resolute on Cornwallis Island, about 350 miles (563 km) to the south. Intending visitors should be prepared for severe weather, even in summer.

Right, the fossil forest ridge of Axel Heiberg island stands to the right of the picture, with the permanent ice cap in the distance beyond – note the white tents at the foot of the valley. The photograph was taken at 2am on a July morning.

Facing page, top, the mummified leaves and cones of a metasequoia (dawn redwood) that grew here 45 million years ago.

Facing page, bottom, a fossilised tree stump on top of the ridge, the remains of an ancient swamp forest.

ANYONE travelling north from Canada's border with the United States today will pass through temperate forests of mixed trees into coniferous forests, and then cross the tree line into the tundra. Here the climate is too severe for trees to grow, and the only woody plant is the Arctic willow, standing just a few inches high. In the islands of Arctic Canada very little grows apart from lichens and mosses, which eke their existence through the few months that the sun shines during the brief Arctic summer. Small wonder that surprise greeted US Army Sergeant David Brainard, a member of the Greely Arctic expedition, when he returned from Ellesmere Island in 1883 with tales and specimens of petrified wood from a fossil forest.

Since then several fossil forests have been found in the Canadian High Arctic. In some the wood has been mineralised by calcite solutions, but in others the wood has been effectively mummified. One of the most spectacular examples of the latter is on Axel Heiberg Island, just 680 miles (1,094 km) from the North Pole. Here tree stumps and roots, still in their growth positions, are just emerging from the ground. Geologists seeking specimens will need not a geological hammer, but just an ordinary saw, because the wood is still soft – even after 45 million years in this inhospitable environment. Removing the loose sand and silt around the stumps reveals their root systems, and, almost more importantly, the original leaf litter of the forest floor is exposed, complete with cones and fossilised remains of the beetles and other insects that once inhabited the forest. The fossils of other, larger forest animals have also been found in these Arctic fossil forests, indicating that the High Arctic was populated by alligators, crocodiles, turtles, snakes, salamanders, tapirs, cranes, giant land tortoises, flying lemurs, and coryphodons – tusked mammals resembling hippopotamuses. The fossil flora and fauna suggest that this was a swampy, ancient Arctic equivalent of the Florida Everglades – a dramatic contrast to their environment today.

How can a tropical swamp have existed in the polar regions? It is now well known that the continents have moved across the globe during the passage of geological time, but Axel Heiberg Island has moved hardly at all during

the last 45 million years. The climate was certainly warmer then, and there was probably no permanent ice in the polar regions, but the long winter darkness at these high latitudes would have been a serious obstacle for tree growth. Most of the fossil trees, recognised by the preponderance of their leaves, are a type of dawn redwood. These were known only from fossils and were believed extinct until 1946, when the last natural forest of dawn redwoods was found growing in central China. A study of the growth rings of the Axel Heiberg Island trees reveals that they had adapted very success-fully to a short summer growing season with 24-hour daylight, before rapidly becoming dormant for the winter.

These polar forests are unique; there are no large trees today which are capable of surviving in the Arctic, probably because of the present harsh polar climate.

Axel Heiberg Island in midsummer today, with the temperature hovering around 32 degrees Fahrenheit (0 degrees C.), is difficult to reconcile with the swamp forest of Eocene times. Ahead is the evidence of the tree stumps in the swamp where crocodiles swam and coryphodons grazed, and behind is the chill of the ice cap.

Fossilisation

ANY plant or animal that dies stands only the smallest chance of being fossilised and preserved. Most dead material is reworked in one way or another – scavengers eat animal corpses, and plant material usually rots as a natural compost to provide nutrients for other plants. To stand any chance of preservation an animal must have an internal skeleton of bones or an external skeleton of shell, or die and be buried in a stagnant pit, such as a tar pit, where bacteria cannot live and decompose the plant or animal carcass. Even then bones and shells can be crushed by the overlying sediment, dissolved by solutions percolating through the rock, and even completely destroyed by the heat and pressure of metamorphism and earth movements.

In some cases preservation takes place on a major scale where a rock, such as chalk, is almost entirely composed of the shells of minute inverte-brates. The rarest fossils are those where the soft parts of the body are preserved, like the feathers of Archaeopteryx, the famous flying reptile considered to be the link between the dinosaurs and modern birds. Equally rare are the delicate impressions of jellyfish found in fine-grained sediment.

121

LEMMINGS AND THE
ARCTIC ECOSYSTEM

*Thousands of these tiny animals race to find food
in one of nature's most curious events.*

Lemmings are found all over
the Arctic, from Russia and
North America to Greenland
and Norway, but it is
impossible to know exactly
when and where these strange
migrations will occur. The
most accessible locations to see
lemmings are probably Alaska
and Canada.

*Right, collared lemmings are widely
distributed across the far north, and
form a vital link in the Arctic food
chain.*

*Facing page, the grey, or timber
wolf is one of the predators to take
advantage of a lemming population
explosion.*

LEMMINGS are chiefly known in popular culture for their "mass suicides". However, recent research has shown that the lemming runs are not senseless suicides at all, but, ironically, a race for food which sometimes ends in tragedy. The resulting decrease in the lemming population serves to maintain the delicate balance between different animals in the Arctic ecosystem.

There are three species of lemming: the Norwegian lemming is found in Norway and parts of Russia; the Siberian or brown lemming lives in Russia, Alaska and Canada;

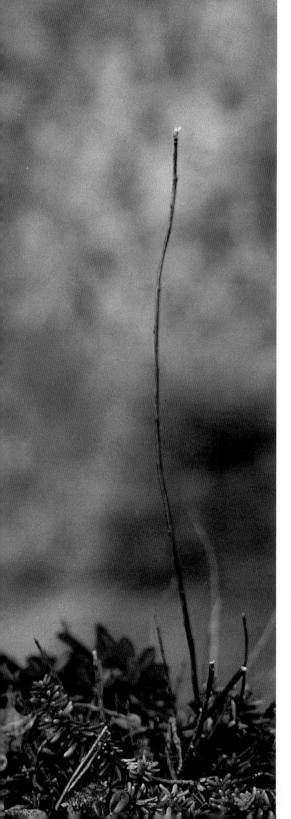

and the collared lemming that is widely distributed across the Arctic, including Greenland. Lemmings are appealing creatures, about 5 inches (13 cm) long and fat with bushy coats. They are mainly brown, although the Norwegian lemming has darker markings on its head and back. The collared lemming's coat changes from brown to white in winter, giving it camouflage against the snow.

These little rodents pass the winter beneath the snow, living in the gaps created by steam rising from the warmer earth after it has been covered in cold snow. Where there are no gaps lemmings burrow tunnels of their own, and they live and breed in this warm subterranean environment. A female can have up to six litters of five or six young each year, which means that she might have 36 babies a year. Young females can have their first litters when they are only two or three months old themselves, so a female born in March can have grandchildren by September of the same year.

The number of lemmings born depends on how much food is available, and on the weather. When the snow over their heads begins to melt, the lemmings must go out to find food for themselves. A shortage of vegetation keeps the numbers low, but every three or four years when there is an abundance of food, the lemming population explodes.

The Arctic tundra is unable to sustain the enormous population of lemmings, and the small animals become desperate for food. They sometimes eat poisonous plants, and occasionally become aggressive, even attacking larger animals. In their desperation to feed, the lemmings begin their mass migrations. Thousands of the tiny rodents scurry across the tundra in a great furry wave, seeking new territory. Wolves, foxes and even fish glut themselves on this easy prey that does not try to escape. When the lemmings reach rivers or the sea, the animals in front cannot stop because of the press of those behind. They try to swim on, but nearly all die.

The plentiful supply of lemmings also increases the populations of their predators, including polar foxes, ermines, snowy owls, peregrine falcons, buzzards, skuas and other birds of prey. When the lemming population is low, these birds and animals must look elsewhere for food. Snowy owls do not even breed if there are not enough lemmings to feed their chicks, and Russian foxes leave the tundra for hunting grounds in the great forests further south. Thus the life cycles of many polar animals depend on this little rodent, underlining the delicate balance between prey and predators in these lands of the frozen north.

Arctic Rodents

MANY small herbivores besides lemmings are able to eke a living from the vast, empty expanses of the tundra. These include species of vole, pikas, hoary marmots, muskrats, Arctic ground squirrels and hares. To deal with the intense cold of the polar winter each has evolved specific adaptations – some biological and some behavioural.

One of the simplest mechanisms by which small mammals can deal with the cold is to sleep through it. Arctic ground squirrels, which live in the North American Arctic, hibernate in communal burrows during the most severe winter months. Hoary marmots find themselves deep holes in scree slopes, and can hibernate for five or six months without food. Their layers of fat insulate them against the cold, and also provide nourishment during hibernation. Pikas, which live in western Canada, collect grass in the summer and dry it in the sun. This crop of hay is then taken into a burrow where it provides both food and bedding for the long winter months.

Voles, like lemmings, live underneath the cover of snow, eating seeds, plants and insects, and so neither hibernate nor need to go out for food. The Arctic hare has also made a remarkable adaptation to the environment. They have pure white winter coats that render them virtually invisible against the snow, affording them protection against predators so that they can go out to feed. All winter long they eat the plants that have been deep-frozen under the snow.

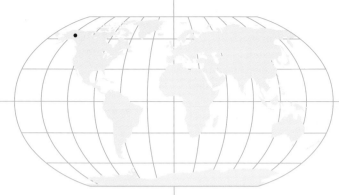

CARIBOU – THE GREAT MIGRATION

Vast herds of up to a million animals travel between the Arctic tundra and the Yukon.

The barren grounds caribou of northern Canada migrate from the Arctic tundra expanses north-west of the Hudson Bay to the taiga of the Yukon and Manitoba. Access to this great expanse of wilderness is limited to a few roads and the railway, or by seaplane or helicopter. Once leaving the roads there is little more than the migration trails of the caribou to follow, and the terrain is suitable for only the hardiest adventurers

Caribou are large herbivores, standing nearly 5 feet (1.5 m) tall at the shoulders and weighing up to 600 pounds (270 kg). They are perfectly adapted for life in the harsh climate of northern Canada with coarse, compact hair forming a dense covering up to

2 inches (5 cm) thick. Each hair is hollow, containing air cells which help insulate against the cold – probably the best windproof and insulating fur known among mammals. It is the only deer species in which both the males and the females have antlers, and they have broad, flat feet ideally designed for supporting such a large animal on the snow. Caribou are not fussy eaters, taking the leaves of almost any plant which, together with lichens, form about 30 per cent of their diet.

The caribou of the Canadian tundra, the barren grounds caribou, typically live in groups of around 100 individuals, spending the winter

The Caribou and Man

For many years the local Eskimos and Indians of the barren ground and taiga exploited the herds of caribou as they made their predictable journeys north and south. The balance was maintained until the subsistence hunting of old gave way to mindless slaughter, which resulted very quickly in a dearth of caribou. Their decline has now been halted, but care is necessary to ensure that numbers can recover.

Above, a herd of caribou on the run.

Right, migrating herds can number hundreds of thousands, and a herd may take days to pass a particular spot.

124

foraging for leaves, grass and lichens in the relative shelter of the coniferous forest or taiga. This area is dominated by white spruce with pine, tamarack and fir together with birch, aspen, beech, hemlock and maple. The taiga, like the tundra to the north, is under deep snow during the winter, but the forest provides enough shelter to prevent the snow from freezing hard, and consequently the caribou are still able to dig with their forefeet for green leaves and lichens buried below. Although there are animals that only over-winter in the others will spend their whole life here, foregoing the annual return migration.

Each year the caribou mass for a great migration north from their over-wintering grounds in the taiga to breeding areas in the far northern tundra. Sometime between February and April the small groups of caribou begin to assemble into vast herds, which can number anything between 500,000 and 1 million. These herds, made up of heavily pregnant females, juveniles and bulls begin to move north along routes which have been followed by generations of caribou. They travel at a rate of about 15 to 30 miles (24 to 48 km) per day; the 250 to 310-mile (400 to 500-km) journey can take anything up to 20 days. The herds that assemble are so vast that once on the move they can take days or even weeks to pass a particular point on the route.

The first females reach the tundra breeding grounds near the Arctic Circle towards the end of May, where they give birth almost immediately. The young caribou are able to run within a few hours of birth, and within a few weeks are independently foraging for food. While on the tundra the caribou feed voraciously, replacing the reserves used during the preceding winter and preparing for the next.

The tundra bursts into life in the early summer with a riot of colour and plentiful lush green growth. During this period of long days the temperature can rise dramatically, posing an overheating problem for the caribou. They seek out the high spots where they can take advantage of any cooling breezes or lingering snow pockets to help them cool down.

As the days shorten in September and the temperature drops, the caribou begin their migration south again to the relative shelter of the taiga. They tend to start south in small groups of two or three, converging into ever bigger groups before they reach the forest. The southward migration is faster, with the caribou able to travel at around 37 miles (60 km) per day.

Wolves and Warble Flies

CARIBOU suffer attacks from two main predators. Packs of timber wolves follow the herds, always ready to attack stragglers along the way. The wolves are no match for a healthy caribou, but any diseased animals or calves will be picked off. This level of predation on herds which number tens or hundreds of thousands has no serious effect on the overall stocks. A smaller scourge of the caribou is the warble fly. This noisy fly lays its eggs in the fur of the caribou, and when the larvae hatch they burrow under the skin where they spend the winter. In spring they emerge through the skin, drop to the ground and develop into adult flies, when the cycle begins again. Some animals can suffer such heavy infestation that they are seriously weakened and easy prey for the wolves.

Canada

DINOSAUR
PROVINCIAL PARK

*Badlands park famed for its wealth
of fossilised dinosaur remains.*

Dinosaur Provincial Park in southern Alberta is about 130 miles (210 km) east of Calgary and 84 miles (135 km) north-west of Medicine Hat. It is reached by leaving Highway 1 at Bassano and continuing along Highway 550, or leave at Brooks and continue along Highway 876.

*Right, the spectacular badlands
terrain of Southern Alberta has
been carved and eroded by rivers.*

*Facing page, careful chipping at the
soft rock has revealed one of the
most famous collections of dinosaur
fossils in the world.*

Dinosaur Provincial Park lies astride the Red Deer River in the heart of the Alberta prairie country. The rich soils of the underlying, flat-lying sedimentary rocks are ideal for extensive wheat farming. However, where rivers flow across these soft sedimentary rocks they cut deep channels and form typical "badlands" country, also found elsewhere in North America. In Alberta the badlands have yielded a crop of dinosaur fossils, just as valuable in scientific terms as the wheat crop is to the farmers and the economy of the province. The abundance and importance of the dinosaur fossils found in the park have led to its establishment as a World Heritage Site, one of the best in the world for dinosaur fossils.

The park is relatively small, covering just 23 square miles (60 sq km), but it is a fascinating place. This area has been geologically stable for about 75 million years – time enough for the forces of erosion to carve the spectacular cliffs and bluffs, gullies, canyons and ravines in the sands and clays of the area. During the Mesozoic era when these rocks were being deposited, the dinosaurs were plodding and paddling through the swamps of the region. The remains of some 35 species of dinosaur have been found here and more may yet be found. Many are displayed in the excellent Tyrrel Museum of Palaeontology Field Station,

the dinosaurs are a particular attraction for youngsters – and children are free to explore and climb on them. Access to much of the park is restricted, since the constant passage of visitors could easily accelerate the erosion before the area has been thoroughly assessed by scientists.

Further to the north-west along the Red Deer River lies Drumheller. From here there are two circular drives, the Dinosaur Trail and the East Coulee Drive. The East Coulee Drive goes through some of the best of the badlands scenery, where the "hoodoos" are a typical feature of the country. These are

Dinosaurs

DINOSAURS were reptiles that are, by definition, extinct, and the name simply means "terrible lizards". They evolved during the Triassic period (from about 240 million years ago) and became the dominant land animals during the Jurassic and Cretaceous periods, until about 65 million years ago.

The dinosaurs were truly colossal animals. The largest were herbivorous and slow-moving; the carnivorous dinosaurs were smaller and more athletic – adapted to catch prey. Calculating the sizes of dinosaurs is often difficult because skeletal remains are usually incomplete, but estimates of 128 to 170 feet (39 to 52 m) in length have been made for a specimen of *Seismosaurus halli*. The name of this dinosaur means "earthquake lizard", and with an estimated weight of over 50 tons its movements must indeed have made the earth tremble. It has been calculated that the maximum possible weight for a terrestrial animal is about 150 tons and some scientists believe certain dinosaurs might have approached this weight.

Probably the most famous of the carnivorous dinosaurs was *Tyrannosaurus rex*. In 1991, the largest specimen found so far was estimated to have been 19½ feet (6 m) tall, 36½ feet (11 m) long and to have weighed about 6 to 7½ tons. The most impressive part of the animal was undoubtedly the enormous mouth, lined with a fearsome set of teeth.

where there is also an audio-visual display about the environment of the park and showing some of the work that has been undertaken.

Self-guided hikes along some of the park trails reveal the sites at close quarters, and displays show how the fossil bones are excavated. Full-size replicas of some of

columns of rock that tend to resemble slim mushrooms, a cap of harder resistant sandstone protecting the softer clays and shales below. The land is very arid and many species of cacti flourish here. The area also contains the relics of abandoned coal mines and other mining settlements that present a fascinating history of human activity.

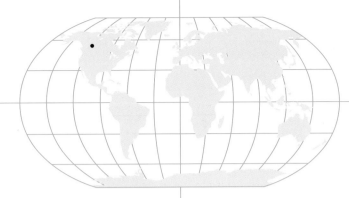

Canada

THE BURGESS SHALE

The Burgess shale is on Fossil Ridge, between Mount Field and Wapta Mountain in British Columbia, some 350 miles (563 km) north-east of Vancouver.

Fossil Formation

INFORMATION obtained from most fossil beds is incomplete, because typically only the hard parts of animals and plants are preserved. Very special conditions, which exclude the normal predators and scavengers of dead animals, are needed for the soft-bodied animals to be preserved. Thousands of fossil species are known, but they represent only around 0.001 per cent of all the species estimated to have lived on earth since life began. In this context the jewels contained within the Burgess shale are all the more remarkable.

Right, a party of palaeontologists camp high on the loose hillside near the site of a remarkable deposit of fossils.

The Burgess shale rock formation contains some of the most important fossil deposits ever found.

IN 1909, Charles Doolittle Walcott discovered the first relics from the fossil bed which has today become known as the Burgess shale. A rock unit some 200 feet (61 m) long and no more than 8 feet (2.4 m) thick on a ridge between two mountains in British Columbia, it has been described as the most important fossil deposit ever found. What is even more remarkable is that it gained such recognition despite containing only invertebrate fossils (albeit immaculately preserved) rather than the headline-catching dinosaur bones.

In the years immediately after the outcrop was discovered there were considerable numbers of specimens collected and meticulously studied, and this work is still continuing as new techniques enable palaeontologists to interpret more from these paper-thin imprints. The outcrop is now protected within the Yoho National Park.

The great antiquity of the Burgess shale find gives an insight into the surprisingly rich variety of marine invertebrates which inhabited the sea bed and overlying waters in Palaeozoic times, some 515 million years ago. What makes these shale deposits so important is the exceptional level of preservation of remains of animals with little or no hard parts, due to the unusual conditions under which the fossils were formed.

The abundance of marine invertebrates provides a unique insight into these creatures, many of whom would not normally appear in the fossil record. There are over 120 species belonging to a wide range of phyla, many of which have descendants living today such as sponges, coelenterates (which today include the jellyfish and corals), annelid worms (with modern day counterparts such as the lugworm and earthworm), echinoderms (sea cucumbers, crinoids and edrioasteroids), molluscs and arthropods. Once all these specimens have been accounted for, there still remain over 20 species for which no modern descendants are known. This discovery has revolutionised our vision of the marine life in Cambrian times, revealing new information about the scale and variety of animals which existed just after the explosion in

diversification of multi-celled life forms. The detective work to produce descriptions of many of these fossils is still going on, and new discoveries in other parts of the world are contributing to this work and our overall understanding.

Many remarkable creatures have been discovered, and scientists are attempting to piece together the clues. Sometimes this is not easy. For example, *Hallucigenia* was first described as an animal about 1 inch (2.5 cm) in length, standing on seven pairs of spiny stilts with a row of seven soft snorkels rising from its back. The question as to whether such an animal really existed persisted – until the discovery in China of another early Cambrian fossil with a caterpillar-like body, with short legs and protective spines on its back, prompted a re-examination of *Hallucigenia*. It transpired that the seven snorkels each had a hidden partner. The initial description had been upside down: the stilt-like legs were in fact protective spines and the snorkels were short legs.

Not all the animals in the Burgess shale were small like *Hallucigenia*. *Anomalocaris* at 2 feet (60 cm) was the largest – a voracious predator with

a streamlined body propelled by a beating pair of flaps. As parts of the *Anomalocaris* were discovered they were thought to be from different animals; only when a complete fossil was discovered was the puzzle solved.

Above, the Burgess Shale has revealed soft-bodied marine fossils in an exceptional state of preservation.

The Cambrian Underwater Scene

DESCRIBING the various animals from paper-thin fossil remains gives us an insight into the diversity of life 515 million years ago, but other studies have also produced a picture of what the sea bed would have looked like to a modern scuba diver.

The animals of the Burgess shale lived on or in a muddy bottom, banked up at the base of a gigantic submarine cliff at a depth of around 300 feet (100 m). The water at the very bottom of the sea was almost stagnant and very low in oxygen, but high in hydrogen sulphide, and unsuitable for animal life. Where the banked-up mud was high enough, the water had much more oxygen and a thriving animal community was present. Although the species were very different from today, various animals filled similar niches with many immobile species standing erect from the sea floor, and others living in burrows, while more mobile species crawled or walked over the sea bed or swam in the overlying waters.

129

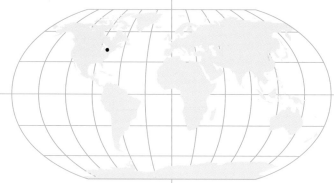

Canada

NIAGARA FALLS

Millions of tons of water plunge over the cliffs as the Niagara River flows from Lake Erie into Lake Ontario; the deafening roar can be heard for miles.

The Niagara River runs between Lake Ontario and Lake Erie, forming part of the border between Canada and the United States. The waterfalls are approximately halfway along the river's length, easily accessible by car from Buffalo in the United States and Toronto in Canada.

Canada's Other Waterfalls

ALTHOUGH most people would cite Niagara if asked to name a waterfall in Canada, the world's second largest country, not surprisingly, has many others. At Virginia Falls in the Northwest Territories the South Nahanni River thunders over a precipice almost twice the height of Niagara. The falls are not the only spectacular feature of this little known river: it descends 3,000 feet (915 m) over a distance of 370 miles (595 km) in a series of tumbling rapids and deep gorges.

The Hunlen Falls and the Helmcken Falls are both in British Columbia, set in provincial parks of outstanding natural beauty. At the Helmcken Falls, the Murtle River cascades over a cliff of ancient rock to a spray-filled basin 450 feet (137 m) below. The Hunlen Falls are seven times the height of Niagara, and drop mist-like in a curtain of spray 1,200 feet (366 m) to the rocks below.

Right, a cloud of spray hangs above the thunderous waters of the Horseshoe Falls.

A SPUME of spray lifts high into the air as the dark green waters of the Niagara River thunder into the frothing cauldron at the base of the falls. There are two parts to this famous waterfall: the American Falls, and the Horseshoe Falls. Between them is Goat Island, a tree-covered islet that sits in the middle of the river.

The Horseshoe Falls are perhaps the better known of the two, forming an arc about 2,600 feet (792 m) long on the Canadian side of the border. A road beside the river gives a good view of the falls at very close range, where the surface of the water has the appearance of dark green glass, turning to foaming white as it slides over the cliffs.

130

The American Falls are smaller and form a straight line about 1,000 feet (305 m) long. There are piles of broken rocks at the base of the American Falls, as opposed to the sheer plunge of the Horseshoe Falls. Both waterfalls are about 165 feet (50 m) high.

The Niagara Falls have only been in existence for around 10,000 years – a relatively short time in geological terms. As the last Ice Age ended, the massive glaciers began to retreat, leaving behind the Great Lakes. The drainage system is such that Lake Erie's outflow pours into Lake Ontario via the 35-mile (56-km) Niagara River down a drop of about 330 feet (100 m). In turn, Lake Ontario empties into the St Lawrence River.

Above the falls the river bedrock is hard dolomite, but underneath the dolomite are layers of softer rocks such as shale and sandstone. Originally the river dropped over an escarpment about 7 miles (11 km) north of the present falls, but as the softer rocks underneath the dolomite were eroded by the fast flowing water, the dolomite collapsed. Bit by bit the waterfall retreated, so that the falls today are a long way from where they were 10,000 years ago, and in their retreat they have left behind a deep gorge. The falls moved back at a rate of about 3 feet (1 m) per year, and are 1,000 feet (305 m) further upstream than they were when Louis Hennepin, the French explorer, saw them in 1678. However, Goat Island has divided the river in two, and this, coupled with the fact that at least half the water of the Niagara is channelled away from the falls to generate electricity, means that the falls are much more stable now than they were in the past.

Bridges and parks on both sides of the river provide good vantage points; one of the most popular is Rainbow Bridge, named after the rainbows that shimmer in the spray above the falls. The sheer power and size of Niagara is best seen from the boats that brave the churning waters beneath the falls.

Above, Bob Leech was one successful stuntman who came down Niagara in a barrel.

Over the Niagara Falls

SOME people have seen the sheer power and size of the Niagara Falls as a personal challenge. A number of people have gone over the falls in a variety of different vessels, including barrels, boats, and sealed capsules. One of the most famous death-defying escapades took place on 30 June 1859, when Jean François Gravelet, better known as Charles Blondin, crossed the falls on a tightrope. The rope was 1,100 feet (335 m) long, and suspended 160 feet (49 m) above the falls. A year later he made the crossing again with his agent on his back.

Below, on the American side of the falls the impact of the water is broken by fallen rocks

Canada
THE BAY
OF FUNDY

The long Bay of Fundy has the most extreme tidal ranges in the world.

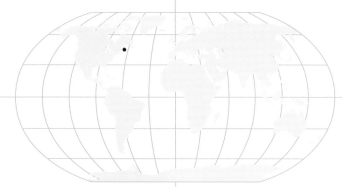

The Bay of Fundy lies between New Brunswick and Nova Scotia. St John lies on the northern New Brunswick shore about 110 miles (177 km) from the head of Chignecto Bay; Halifax lies on the Atlantic side of Nova Scotia about 80 miles (130 km) from the head of Cobequid Bay. The cliffs above Herring Cove, near Alma on the New Brunswick side of the bay, make an excellent and safe place from which to watch the incoming tide.

Tidal Forces

THE tides in the world's seas and oceans are caused by the gravitational pull of the moon and, to a much lesser extent, of the sun. The force that the moon exerts is too weak to move the earth, but is strong enough to move the water on the surface. The moon circles the earth in the same direction as the spin of the earth, and the water along the meridian closest to the moon at any given time is drawn towards the moon, creating an accumulation of water that is the high tide. On the opposite side of the earth the effect of the moon is least, so the water there also forms a high point – the opposite high tide. So, as the moon travels around the earth it draws the water with it like a bulge that continually processes round the globe, giving high tides as it passes.

Right, the tidal bore which races in across the wide Bay of Fundy also affects the local rivers.

Facing page, the speed and power of the tidal bore has eroded the local sandstone into fantastic shapes.

THE narrow and slightly tapering shape of the Bay of Fundy forces the mass of water rolling into the bay on the incoming tide into an ever decreasing space. This is rather like trying to squeeze the water from a large bottle into a much smaller bottle, except that in the bay the excess water is accommodated by becoming much deeper. The shape of the Bay of Fundy and its position on the the mainland coast of New Hampshire produces a very large variation in the mean tidal range from low tide to high tide – in fact the largest in the world.

(By contrast, the island of Tahiti, lying isolated in the middle of the Pacific Ocean, has hardly any tidal variation at all.)

The average spring tidal range at Burncoat Head, in Minas Basin at the head of the bay, is 47.5 feet (14.5 m), although the greatest range ever recorded was 54.5 feet (16.6 m) in Leaf Basin, Ungava Bay in Quebec. These figures are more than three times the average spring tidal range of 15 feet (4.6 m) for the British Isles, and about twice the height of a modern two-storey house. Where the coastline is a cliff edge, the tide simply rises and falls against it twice a day, but where there is a sloping beach the incoming tide is dramatic. It would be very dangerous to be on such a beach in the Bay of Fundy because the tide comes in faster than a person can run, and the penalty for being caught could well be drowning. When seen from a safe vantage point, the tide as it races in is very impressive.

The wind can also have a significant effect on the water and, when a gale is following the tide it pushes the water along, making the high tide run even higher than usual. When this occurs weather reports may refer to a surge tide, and severe tidal warnings advise people living close to the normal high tide mark to evacuate their homes. Sometimes the effect is so great that a small wall of water appears to move up the bay; this is a true tidal wave, sometimes called a tidal bore. Where this happens in a river mouth the opposing force of the river flowing into the sea causes the crest of the wave to break as it moves upstream, like a wave approaching a beach. A famous example of this is the bore of the River Severn above Bristol, in Britain, where the wave can be 3 to 4 feet (0.9 to 1.2 m) high, and can travel for several miles upstream. Other famous rivers around the world with bores include the Seine in France, and the Yangtze Kiang (Chang Jiang) in China.

HORSESHOE CRABS

Horseshoe, or king, crabs are found in the coastal waters of the western Atlantic and the Pacific Oceans where they wash on to the shores of North America and south-east Asia.

Unseen for much of the year in deep offshore water, the horseshoe crab appears on selected beaches on the Virginia and Maryland coast at very specific times of the year.

THE ancient lineage of the horseshoe crab dates back over 200 million years, making this creature one of the oldest animals still in existence. The five living species of horseshoe crab belong to the genus *Limulus*; the term crab is in fact a misnomer since these creatures are actually more closely related to scorpions or spiders than to crabs. Often referred to as living fossils, the species has changed little from the earliest fossil representatives, and their antiquity is reinforced by their prehistoric appearance. An abundance of horseshoe crab fossils indicate that the crabs were particularly numerous, but the hard shell is easily fossilised and it may be that other more numerous species are simply less well represented in the fossil record.

Right, a relative of modern-day scorpions and spiders, the extraordinary horseshoe crab is described as a living fossil.

Facing page, a mass-spawning of horseshoe crabs on the coast of New Jersey.

The body of the animal is protected by a large, domed head-shield which is hinged with a large body plate from which a long, spiked tail protrudes. An adult specimen can measure up to 2 feet (60 cm) in length and 1 foot (30 cm) in width. The heavy shell hides a segmented body with five pairs of walking legs and a pair of small pincers.

Horseshoe crabs live in relatively deep water offshore. Poor swimmers, they use a pair of body flaps to propel themselves through the water, and creep slowly over the sea bed. They are ideally adapted for soft mud, where they feed on small clams and worms which they burrow out of the mud using their head shield as a dredge.

For most of the year the crabs live offshore, but each spring the mature adults migrate en masse to selected beaches to spawn. The spawning sites are usually wave-exposed sandy beaches, and this preference is ultimately the downfall of many individuals. The trigger for this reproductive migration is not fully

understood, but it appears to be linked to full moon spring tides, when thousands of crabs migrate up the shore to dig pits in the sand at the extreme upper tidal limit. The female deposits 200 to 300 eggs into the pits, which are then fertilised by a male before they are buried and left to develop.

Spectacular Spawning Events

THE horseshoe crab is not the only animal to undertake synchronised spawning migrations. The most dramatic and inexplicable is that of the palolo worm, which lives in

On these exposed shores in the surf zone many are overturned by the waves, exposing their vulnerable soft bodies to the hot sun, and making easy prey for the gulls which congregate on the beaches at this time. The crabs are able to right themselves only with difficulty, using their long tail as a lever. Nevertheless the risk seems worthwhile, for although the crabs which spawn on less exposed beaches are themselves are more likely to survive, their eggs are less likely to hatch. The eggs hatch four weeks after they have been laid, just in time for the next set of spring tides to help wash the newly hatched larvae into the sea.

There are no obvious reasons for the survival of the ancient lineage of the horseshoe crab. Clearly, it is well adapted to its peculiar lifestyle, and robust enough to survive the considerable losses suffered during spawning. The design of the horseshoe crab – millions of years old – has never been bettered, giving modern observers a fascinating glimpse into the past.

the coral reefs off Fiji and Samoa in the western Pacific. The palolo is a burrowing worm which reaches about 1 foot (30 cm) in length. At dawn on the first three days of the moon's third quarter, every October and November, the billions of worms in the reefs all shed their tails which contain the eggs and sperm. These tails migrate to the surface of the sea, where the gametes are shed in vast numbers, ensuring maximum fertilisation. Lots of predators, including the local islanders, have also learned to congregate on these days. Although vast numbers are harvested as a great delicacy, even more survive to shed their gametes. How these numbers of worms achieve such precise synchronisation is not understood, especially since the movements of the moon do not coincide with those of the earth.

U.S.A.
THE DEVIL'S TOWER

A towering, fluted monolith of volcanic rock stands sentinel over the Belle Fourche River on the plains of north-east Wyoming.

Devil's Tower National Monument is in the far north-eastern corner of Wyoming, near the border with Montana and South Dakota. The nearest airport is at Rapid City, South Dakota, about 100 miles (160 km) from the monument by road.

Chimney Rock

ABOUT 25 million years ago, a deposit of sandy clay was laid down in western Nebraska, and then later covered with sandstone. Subsequent erosion has removed many of these deposits from the area, and only small, slightly more durable, segments remain. One such remnant is Chimney Rock, a dome topped with a sandstone pinnacle 325 feet (99 m) high. It was a landmark for pioneers on the Oregon Trail, heading west, who were able to see it from a distance of 30 miles (48 km). Although other geological formations on the route were also named, Chimney Rock is often regarded as the symbol for America's westward migration in the 19th century.

The gigantic columnar lava formation of the Devil's Tower was created some 50 million years ago.

136

A N Indian legend relates how seven maidens fled to the flat summit of the Devil's Tower's to escape a giant bear. The bear, desperate to catch the maidens, scored deep marks in the tower with his claws as he attempted to scramble to the top. When the bear finally succeeded in reaching the summit, the maidens jumped onto a low rock that saved them from the bear by soaring away into the sky. Another myth suggests that the tower gained its name because an evil demon pounded his drums on the summit, making thunder and generally terrifying anyone who heard him. More recently, Devil's Tower was

given international exposure when it featured as the backdrop for the landing site for aliens in the film *Close Encounters of the Third Kind*.

Devil's Tower is truly a giant, standing in the rolling plains of Wyoming near the pine forests of the Black Hills, rising majestically out of the trees at its base. It is the highest point for many miles, and on clear days it can be seen from 100 miles (160 km) away. From its base the tower is 865 feet (264 m) tall, although it rises 1,300 feet (396 m) above the Belle Fourche River. The Tower's base is 1,000 feet (305 m) in diameter, tapering to 275 feet (84 m) in diameter at the summit.

The Devil's Tower was formed about 50 million years ago when Wyoming was under the sea, and layers of sedimentary rock such as sandstone, limestone, shale, and gypsum were being deposited. At the same time, pressures from deep within the earth's crust forced a mass of magma to intrude into the sedimentary rock. The magma began to cool and crystallise, and as it did so, it contracted and cracked forming polygonal columns, much like those at the Giant's Causeway in Northern Ireland. A similar process is often seen in dried up streams and ponds, where water has evaporated from the crust, forming small polygonal saucers of mud with slightly upturned edges.

The igneous rock formed by the magma intrusion was much harder than the surrounding sedimentary rock, and over millions of years, as the sea bed rose from the water to become solid land, the forces of erosion began to eat away at the sedimentary rocks, leaving this great block of igneous rock standing proud. Even hard igneous rocks are not immune to erosion, however, and water seeped into the spaces between the columns, expanding and contracting with changes in temperature, and forcing some of the columns to fall away from the main body of rock. Broken columns litter the base of the tower, forming talus slopes. As this process of weathering continues, Devil's Tower will eventually collapse completely – but it's likely to be around for a good few million years yet.

The distinctive pair of rocks known as the Mittens are one of the great landmarks of Monument Valley.

Monument Valley

R ISING dramatically out of the flat desert floor in north-east Arizona are strangely shaped blocks of sandstone, standing up to 1,000 feet (305 m) high. These towering monoliths were sacred to the Navajo Indians, and watching them glow red in the setting sun in the empty expanses of desert it is easy to see how they have inspired a sense of awe for thousands of years.

The monuments were formed in a similar way to Devil's Tower, except that the rock here is sandstone. The entire area was once covered by sedimentary rocks, which were worn down over millions of years, leaving behind only the more resistant parts as free-standing towers and blocks. Many of the monuments have names. The Mittens are two formations with slender columns slightly apart from the main body of rock, like the thumbs on a pair of mittens. The Prioress looks like a kneeling figure wearing a gown with a cowl, and hands clasped.

DINOSAUR NATIONAL
MONUMENT

*A fossil cemetery
in the desert.*

Dinosaur National Monument
lies about 140 miles (225 km)
east of Salt Lake City along
U.S. Highway 40. The
entrance to the monument is
reached by turning north off
the highway at Jensen, Utah.

*Above, springtime in the badlands
scenery of Dinosaur National
Monument.*

*Facing page, fossilised dinosaur
bone are carefully excavated from
the bedrock.*

THE fossilised remains of dinosaurs are found
in many parts of the world, but they are
more common in the central parts of the
continents that have remained relatively stable
during the last 200 million years. Areas where
sediments accumulated during the Mesozoic
era (245–65 million years ago) and afterwards,
and that have undergone relatively little
folding or metamorphism since then, appear
to be ideal for the preservation of dinosaur
remains. One such place is Dinosaur National

Monument, on the Green and Yampa
Rivers where they cross the Colorado–Utah
state boundary.

Dinosaur bones were first found here in
1909 at Dinosaur Quarry, and since that time
more than 450 tons of bones have been
removed. The quarry is about 40 feet (12 m)
high, 40 feet (12 m) wide and 400 feet (122 m)
long – an immense dinosaur graveyard. Why
so many dead dinosaurs accumulated here is
uncertain, but their corpses appear to have

138

been washed on to an ancient river sandbank and left to be buried under the accumulating sands. A fossil find such as this represents a veritable bonanza for the palaeontologist, for the first fossil is always the most difficult to find, but where there is one there may be others. In this case nobody could have anticipated the wealth of material that would be uncovered, and research is still continuing on the site today.

The area is one of great scenic beauty. The two rivers have cut deep valleys and canyons through the horizontal sandstones, exposing excellent layered cliff sections along their

turns south, eventually joining the Colorado River about 200 miles (322 km) downstream. Access to the quarry is restricted because it is still a research site, but there is a fine museum at Monument Headquarters where many specimens are on display. It was here that a shoulder bone larger than a man, was found; a reconstruction based on the bone suggests that the original animal could have weighed 100 tons, about equivalent to a herd of 15 elephants. No wonder this animal has been given the nickname "Supersaurus". In addition to dinosaur fossils, the museum also has specimens of turtles and crocodiles. One part of

lengths. The best way to see the area is undoubtedly by boat along the rivers, but the flow is fast, and rapids make such a trip a serious undertaking. A look at the names on the map – Big Joe Rapids, Whirlpool Canyon and Hell's Half Mile – portends the dangers of the voyage. However there are good views from the plateau above and the descent in many places is not difficult.

Dinosaur Quarry is found at the western end of the monument, where the Green River

the museum is an active research site, with a building erected over a rock outcrop that is studded with hundreds of dinosaur bones. Visitors can watch technicians painstakingly chipping away the rock around the bones to release them for scientific study.

The debate about the lifestyles of the different dinosaurs, whether they were warm- or cold-blooded, or whether there were some of each, will continue to occupy scientists for years, and may never be resolved.

The Extinction of the Dinosaurs

THERE are various theories to explain why the dinosaurs became extinct, but none is completely satisfactory on its own. Mass extinctions of animal species are known to have occurred at other times during the geological past and it is important to remember that time is very condensed in the geological record. An abrupt change of any kind that can be determined across a few layers of sedimentary rock may actually represent a period of several million years. Many geologists now believe that dinosaur numbers dwindled relatively quickly to extinction over a period of 5 to 10 million years, until completed about 65 million years ago. Even then some smaller species were able to survive, such as the ancestors of modern crocodiles, possibly because they adapted to whatever environmental changes were overwhelming their larger cousins.

The presence of the element iridium in many of the sedimentary rocks of this age may be a significant clue. Its widespread occurrence may indicate a period of extensive volcanism that polluted the atmosphere with dust and poisonous gases to such a degree that the larger dinosaurs could not adapt. Another theory proposed that a major meteorite impact caused the increase in iridium levels, and in 1991 a potential candidate was found in a meteorite crater in the Yucatán region of Central America that has been dated at 65 million years.

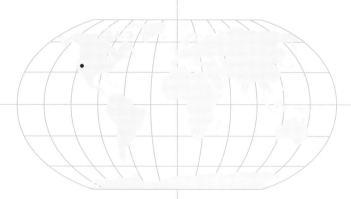

YOSEMITE NATIONAL PARK

Sheer granite rock faces rise thousands of feet above secluded lakes and meadows in one of the country's most popular national parks.

Yosemite National Park lies in the Sierra Nevada mountain range in central California, and is easily accessible by road.

F EW places in the world can have as many spectacular features in one small area as Yosemite Valley, a seven and a half mile (12 km) long natural masterpiece of such beauty and diversity that the great naturalist John Muir declared: "God himself seems to be always doing his best here."

Nestling in the heart of the Sierra Nevada mountain range of California, Yosemite Valley is home to many magnificent natural features. There is the Merced River, and waterfalls include Yosemite Falls – at 2,425 feet (739 m), the third-longest waterfall in the world. The landscape includes many splendid domes and peaks, with some of the largest and most majestic rock walls in the world – the most impressive of these is El Capitan, a granite buttress which rises almost straight up, 3,605 feet (1,099 m) from the valley floor.

The Yosemite valley is actually only a small part of the 1,189 square mile (3,080 sq km) Yosemite National Park. In 1864 the valley became the first state park in the United States, and in 1890 the area around it was designated a national park which, in 1906, incorporated the state park's area.

Near the southern entrance to the park, Mariposa Grove contains huge sequoia trees, some that are thousands of years old. To the east is the popular high country of Tuolumne Meadows, where huge rock domes tower over lush, green meadows, and lakes have a pristine clarity. Past Tuolomne Meadows is the 9,945-foot (3,031-m) Tioga Pass, the high point in the park, which leads down a steep road through the Inyo National Forest to the eastern side of the Sierra Nevada. To the north of all of this is the rarely visited High Sierra region of Yosemite, including the Grand Canyon of the Tuolumne River and the Hetch Hetchy Reservoir, created in 1913, and flooding a valley almost as beautiful as Yosemite Valley.

Yosemite lay unknown to Westerners until 1851, when the volunteers of the Mariposa Battalion entered the valley in pursuit of a

Right, the outstanding beauty of Yosemite is reflected in the glassy waters of the Merced River.

Facing page, the huge butress of El Capitan is one of the largest granite faces in the world.

number of Ahwahneechee Indians, whom they had been assigned to take to an Indian reservation. The park's name came from the corruption of the local Indian word for grizzly bear, "uzumati". Within a few years sightseeing parties were coming to admire the views down into the valley, and they are the same views that one sees today upon emerging from the Wawona Tunnel: to the left the awesome majesty of El Capitan; to the right, the elegant 620-foot (189-m) Bridalveil Falls pouring down from the back of the Cathedral Rocks, and then the seemingly unassailable Sentinel Rock; and, straight ahead,

the glacier-carved face of Half Dome.

It was John Muir who really made Yosemite a part of the American consciousness, however. Muir, who was a key figure in the establishment of a United States forest conservation policy, spent a great part of his life wandering in the Sierras – particularly in Yosemite – and writing about the wonders of nature there. He was succeeded in his role as prophet of the Sierra wilderness by the great American photographer Ansel Adams, whose black and white pictures caught Yosemite and its local surroundings in every season and mood.

Rock Climbing in Yosemite

F OR rock climbers from around the world, Yosemite National Park is the Mecca of their sport. The valley offers all types of climbing: cracks, chimneys, faces, overhangs, artificial aid, high angle, low angle – whatever a climber could desire. Yosemite's most spectacular climbs are its huge valley walls and routes that can require up to five days to climb: Half Dome, Sentinel Rock, Royal Arches, and the immense El Capitan – one of the largest granite faces in the world.

Yosemite became the centre for rock climbing in the United States in the 1950s and 1960s, when Royal Robbins, Yvon Chouinard, and Warren Harding first made ascents on climbs that had previously been thought impossible. Robbins, Jerry Galwas and Mike Sherrick were the first climbers to conquer the sheer, 2,000-foot (610-m) north-west face of Half Dome in 1957, and Harding, Wayne Merry, and George Whitwore made the first ascent of the 'Nose Route' of El Capitan the next year. The succeeding generation of climbers had a great many technical advantages, and the famous figures of Yosemite climbing in the 1970s and 80s included Bev Johnson, one of the greatest female climbers.

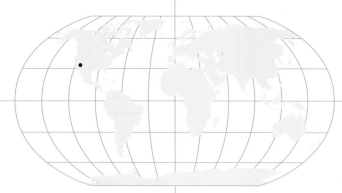

ZION NATIONAL PARK

Red sandstone rocks have been carved into strange formations in the small, but spectacular, Zion National Park.

Zion National Park is situated in the south-west corner of Utah, in the great desert region of the south-western United States. The closest major airport is at Las Vegas, 160 miles (257 km) away by road.

America's National Beauty

THE United States is home to a vast array of natural wonders, ranging from the Grand Canyon and the magnificence of Yosemite, to the preservation of plants and animals in the John Day Fossil Beds National Monument. Approximately 77 million acres (120,300 square miles; 310,000 sq km) in about 320 different sites are under the care of the National Park Service. Historical sites come under the Park Service's remit, as well as sites of natural wonder. These include battlefields (such as Saratoga and Gettysburg), early trading posts, and archaeological sites where evidence of Indian settlement or dwelling has been discovered. The first national park, founded in 1872 – and which remains one of America's favourites – was Yellowstone, home of Old Faithful geyser. Since then many other sites have been considered important parts of America's heritage, and their protection has been assured by their designation as national parks or national monuments.

Right, the curiously regular pattern of gullies on Checkerboard Mesa was carved by wind and rain.

M ANY thousands of years ago, a small stream meandered its way across the soft young rocks of a plateau on its way southwards. As the land rose, the stream began to cut itself a path, scouring the underlying rock with particles of grit and sand eroded from further upstream. The result of this was Zion Canyon, a winding gorge reaching a depth of 2,500 feet (762 m) in places, slicing through the Navajo sandstone to the older, underlying Kaibab limestone. Other canyons and gorges were formed at the same time, but it is the North Fork Virgin River's Zion Canyon that has attracted most attention.

The Mormons discovered and named Zion Canyon in the 1860s, though it was not surveyed until 1872. In 1919, 148 square miles (383 sq km) of the wilderness surrounding the canyon was designated as a national park; in 1956 this was enlarged to include an area of 230 square miles (596 sq km). Zion National Park is a fascinating array of rock formations, mainly carved out of the predominant stone – Navajo sandstone. The overwhelming image of the park is of towering cliffs, forbidding domes and deep chasms, ranging in colour from deep glowing red to a delicate rose-pink. Like the Grand Canyon, the sun and the seasons play with Zion's colours, changing them constantly.

Zion boasts many extraordinary natural features. Checkerboard Mesa is a great slab of sandstone looming over the road, its surface intricately carved into squares by the effects of wind and water. In Verkin Canyon, a natural arch spans between two cliff faces, while Great White Throne stands flat-topped and massive among towering red cliffs. The highest point in the park is the West Temple, towering 3,800 feet (1,158 m) above the canyon base. The Towers of the Virgin are a group of jagged sandstone peaks ranging along the west wall of the canyon, while the natural amphitheatre of the Temple of Sinawava provides splendid views of the surrounding cliffs and domes.

Another well known feature is the Weeping Rock, where water from springs higher up the rock trickles across its surface, dropping like tears from its overhangs. A similar phenomenon occurs at Hanging Gardens, but instead of dripping away, the water is absorbed by the plants that cling precariously to its slopes. The pale sides of Zion Canyon's west rim show clear lines where the Navajo sandstone has been laid in neat, regular layers. Fast-running water has scoured caves in the stone, which provide shelter for a variety of birds, small mammals and insects. Archaeologists have discovered artefacts from ancient Pueblo Indian settlements in some of the larger caves.

Above, the spectacular pinnacles of Bryce Canyon change colour dramatically in the sunlight.

Bryce Canyon

B RYCE Canyon National Park lies only a short distance from Zion. Water has raged across the sedimentary rocks, eroding them into a complex system of ravines and gullies, a process that is continuing today when flash floods cause walls to split and columns to collapse. Metallic minerals mixed in with the sediments have produced rocks coloured rich reds and oranges, and even pale mauve in places.

The Pink Cliffs escarpment is perhaps the best known area, containing a fantastic jumble of pinnacles, channels, ravines and oddly shaped pillars. As the first European pioneer to explore the area, Ebenezer Bryce, remarked, the area is "one heck of a place to lose a cow".

Zion Canyon

Z ION Canyon is only 15 miles (24 km) long, but it is very dramatic. At its northern end is a section known as the Narrows, where the towering cliffs begin to close in, so that in places, a mere 20 feet (6 m) separates them. It is possible to hike along the narrows in the dry season, although there is a danger from flash floods. In the spring,when the river becomes swollen with seasonal rains, travelling the gorge is difficult and dangerous, and it is easy to appreciate how the surging, frothing river has sliced its way 2,000 feet (610 m) through the rock.

U.S.A.
THE GRAND CANYON

"All these canyons unite to form one grand canyon, the most sublime spectacle on the earth." – Major John Wesley Powell

The Grand Canyon is in Arizona and lies between Lake Mead and Lake Powell. The nearest major city is Las Vegas, which is about 25 miles (40 km) from Lake Mead, although access to Grand Canyon Village, the main tourist centre, is easier from Flagstaff, which is about 80 miles (130 km) south by road.

Roosevelt and the Grand Canyon

ONE of the early visitors to the Grand Canyon was President Theodore Roosevelt, who first came in 1903, and made it a national monument in 1908. Even at the turn of the century, Roosevelt was aware of the delicate ecology of the region. He urged Americans to "leave it as it is. You cannot improve on it. The ages have been at work on it, and man can only mar it."

Right, remains found in caves here suggest that the Grand Canyon was first inhabited some 2000 years B.C.

No description can ever truly prepare the visitor for the sheer size and magnificence of this massive gorge, stretching as far as the eye can see in a vast, spectacular complex of canyons, waterfalls, caverns, towers, ledges and ravines. The Grand Canyon never seems to look the same twice, and the sun and the shadows of passing clouds constantly change the colours of the rocks through a delicate spectrum from black and purple-brown to pale pink and blue-grey.

Peering down at the bottom of the canyon from one of the many vantage points, it is difficult to imagine that the tiny brown stream of water far below was responsible for this huge gorge. However, viewed from the canyon floor

itself, the Colorado River is swift and powerful – the Lava Falls Rapids are said to be the fastest navigable rapids in the world – and it is easier to envisage how it was able to carve itself a path through the rocks.

Less than 10 million years ago the Colorado River meandered over a huge plain. Then movements in the earth's surface caused the land to rise, and the river began to cut a channel through the rocks. The soft 2-million-year-old limestones were the first rocks to be eroded, then the older shales and sandstones lying in layers underneath. The oldest rocks are the 2-billion-year-old granites and schists that form the bottom of the canyon today.

The main canyon is 227 miles (365 km) long and around 18 miles (29 km) across at its widest point. In places, it is a 1 mile (1.6 km) deep. No bridge spans the rift, and anyone wishing to get from the North Rim Headquarters to Grand Canyon Village on the south rim, less than 12 miles (19 km) across the canyon, will need to travel more than 200 miles (322 km) to get there.

The Grand Canyon is not just one gorge. Many other canyons run into it, each one different from the others, making up the Grand Canyon National Park. There are many things to see in the park. The Vulcan's Stone, a black cinder cone formed by volcanic activity about 10,000 years ago, stands high above the river; the Esplanade is a heavily eroded terrace of red sandstone that glows scarlet in the evening sun; and in many places, pinnacles of layered sandstone teeter at the edges of precipices affording the most incredible views.

Although millions of tourists visit the most famous parts of the Grand Canyon, such as Grand Canyon Village, there are many places where the visitor can find complete solitude. Fern Glen Canyon is famous for its micro-climate, and surprisingly, lush flowers and plants flourish there in the middle of the desert. North Canyon Wash has silent green pools of water that lie at the base of creamy-white canyon walls.

Above, in 1948 fewer than 100 people had travelled the entire length of the Colorado River; today the journey is a major industry and thousands of people make the trip each year. Several sets of rapids punctuate the journey, the most dangerous of which are the Lava Rapids.

The Grand Canyon Discovered

THE Indians knew about the Grand Canyon for thousands of years before it was discovered by Europeans. The caves and caverns in the park are rich in archaeological remains, and include rock paintings, pots and wooden figures. It was not until 1540 that a small group of Spanish adventurers came to the Grand Canyon looking for gold, but when they found none they moved on. The canyon was not fully explored until 1857, when an expedition was mounted to travel down the canyon by boat, but had to proceed on foot when the boats were wrecked almost before the trip had started. The most famous expedition was led by Major John Wesley Powell in 1869. Powell, a Civil War veteran and college professor, took nine frontiers-men with him to map and explore the huge canyon, but his account of the journey remained unpublished for more than 20 years.

REDWOODS AND GIANT SEQUOIAS

The largest living things on earth, the redwoods and giant sequoias form a lofty canopy over a silent carpet of centuries of leaf fall.

The Sequoia National Park is some 80 miles (130 km) by road from Fresno in central California, while the Redwood National Park lies in a coastal fringe between Crescent City and Eureka, where the scenic coastal highway runs along the edges of the park.

Exploitation of the Forest Giants

THE redwood and giant sequoia produce very high quality timber, prized as a multi-purpose wood suitable for a range of uses from house-building and furniture-making to railway sleepers and fence posts. It is straight-growing with very few knots and fine grain make it light but strong, and a combination of natural oils and resins makes it almost rot-proof and resistant to attack from termites and other insects. In the latter half of the 19th century these trees were heavily exploited, and because of their limited distribution were at risk of extinction. Exploitation continues today, although the U.S. National Parks Service continues in its efforts to annex remaining tracts of forest to the existing protected areas.

Above, a stand of giant sequoias known as "The Senate Group."

Right, giant sequoias, with their thick, fire-resistant bark, in the Sequoia National Park.

THE redwoods are now restricted to a narrow coastal strip stretching from the Klamath Mountains in southern Oregon to Monterey Bay in northern California, and giant sequoias inhabit the slopes of the Sierra Nevada mountains. The best redwood trees are in Redwood National Park on the north California coast, and the largest sequoias are in Sequoia National Park in central California.

Fossil records show that these giant trees were present in the Jurassic period, between 208 and 144 million years ago, when they were distributed over large areas of the northern hemisphere. Now they inhabit a relatively small area, confined to a region about 280 miles (450 km) long extending from the southern end of the Sierra Nevada in California northwards to the Klamath Mountains in southern Oregon. The extent of these forests is now very much reduced – the result of extensive exploitation. It is estimated that these woods originally covered as much as 2,367 square miles (6,131 sq km), but this is now much reduced, and largely confined to the two protected areas. Redwood National Park and World Heritage Site covers 164 square miles (425 sq km), and the Sequoia National Park and Biosphere Reserve contains 629 square miles (1,629 sq km).

The Redwood National Park is dominated by the redwood tree, *Sequoia sempervirens*, which is the tallest living tree. Specimens regularly reach heights of 300 feet (91m) and one tree has been measured at 367.7 feet (112.1 m). The trees are found on the seaward facing slopes and valleys of the mountains in the humid coastal belt, where they are engulfed almost daily in the warm sea fogs which drift in from the Pacific Ocean. The trunk is encased in a thick, fibrous, fire-resistant bark. The young saplings are branched along their entire length, but with age the lower branches are lost and a dense upper canopy is formed. This excludes almost all light from the ground, resulting in a relatively open forest floor where only ferns and other shade-loving plants can survive, together with the occasional redwood sapling. The redwood produces a prolific crop of seeds but only very few germinate successfully, and even when they do they have to struggle against the low light levels. Under natural circumstances this slow regeneration rate would be quite adequate, as the trees can live for more than 3,000 years, but with increased rates of exploitation, new trees to replace those felled are not produced quickly enough.

The Sequoia National Park is the main preserve of the giant sequoia, *Sequoiadendron giganteum*, a name taken in honour of the Cherokee Indian chief, Sequoyah. Whereas the redwood can claim the title of the *tallest* tree, the giant sequoia is the *largest* tree, and indeed the largest living organism. The giant sequoia can live for up to 4,000 years, second only in longevity to the bristlecone pine, which is found in the desert mountains of the Sierra Nevada – some are known to be over 4,900 years old. The giant sequoia grows to around 312 feet (95 m), and the trunk can have a diameter of 15 to 35 feet (5 to 11 m). The largest of these trees, the "General Sherman," is around 4,000 years old and weighs about 4,400,000 pounds (2,995,796 kg).

In addition to the majesty of the trees, the forests of the Redwood and Sequoia National Parks are also important for a wide range of animals including moose, elk, black bear, beaver, and white-tailed and mule deer.

MOJAVE AND
SONORAN DESERTS

*This hot and arid region has a silent, subtle beauty all its
own, with fleeting bursts colour after rain.*

The Mojave Desert lies in the
south-east corner of California,
extending across into Nevada,
with Las Vegas on its eastern
fringe. In the south it merges
with the Sonoran Desert which
extends down through Nevada
into Mexico.

A VAST tract of land extending southwards
from northern Oregon and encompassing
almost the entire states of Nevada and Utah
makes up the high mountain or cold, mid-
latitude desert of the Great Basin. At the
southern limits of this area it merges with the
high or hot mid-latitude Mojave Desert which
covers an area of around 25,000 square miles
(65,000 sq km), representing much of the
south-eastern part of California. Moving
further south into Arizona and Mexico, it
merges with the Sonoran Desert.

Much of this area is made up of relatively
recent geological deposits only 1.6 million years
old, although the various mountain ranges
thrust up across this area are of more ancient
lineage. Over many years, erosion by wind and
rain and long-dried rivers has produced a stark
and strikingly beautiful scenery which cannot
be matched anywhere else in the world.

The climate is extremely harsh; there is a
very high frequency of cloudless days, with
consequent intense solar radiation and very low
humidity. The Mojave and Sonoran Deserts
have an annual average temperature of around
73 degrees Fahrenheit (23 degrees C.) while in
Death Valley it is 77 degrees Fahrenheit (25
degrees C.). Temperatures range considerably
over a single 24-hour period, with highs of
over 104 degrees Fahrenheit (40 degrees C.)
during the day followed by a chilly 34 to 36
degrees Fahrenheit (1 to 2 degrees C.) at night.
Death Valley is one of the most inhospitable
places on earth, lying 282 feet (86 m) below

*Above, the extraordinary, bleak
terrain of Death Valley.*

*Right, a sudden blooming of
Californian poppies after a rainfall
transforms the Mojave Desert.*

sea level – the lowest point on the North American continent. It receives an annual rainfall of less than 2 inches (5 cm), and large areas are covered by salt flats which form an irregularly ridged mosaic of white crystallised salt which stretches for miles in all directions. In comparison the Mojave and Sonoran Deserts receive an average annual rainfall of 2 to 6 inches (5 to 15 cm) – although this comes only intermittently, and some areas may go for years with no rain at all.

The vegetation here is highly specialised to cope with the harsh conditions. The Mojave Desert is typified by a scrub vegetation of Joshua trees, creosote bush and burroweed, together with the occasional cactus. The Sonoran Desert supports extensive thorn scrub with species such as mesquite, paloverde, iron wood and burrowbrush together with a range of succulents. In addition to the perennial plants there are also many annual or ephemeral species such as poppies, rockroses and grasses. They spend most of their life as seeds waiting for the correct conditions – usually just after the rain – for them to burst into life for a brief period of time. When the rain comes the desert

plants react very quickly to take full advantage of the water. Germination, growth and flowering take just a short time, and the desert is transformed almost overnight with a fantastic and spectacular flush of colour, such as the bright orange carpet created by the Californian poppy.

The perennial cacti also conserve their energy and produce only an occasional spectacular bloom. The flowers are generally short lived, and flowering is synchronised to ensure maximum pollination and seed production. The brightly coloured flowers have a rather waxy appearance, and often open overnight only to shrivel the next morning under the intense heat of the sun. The seeds of all desert plants can lie dormant for months or even years, waiting for the right conditions so the cycle can be repeated with maximum chance of success.

As with the plants, the animals of the desert are highly specialised and adapted to the severe conditions. Various insects live here, with different sorts of reptiles, snakes and lizards, birds and some mammals, most of which are nocturnal, spending the heat of the day underground in burrows and emerging only at night.

The Desert Pupfish

REMARKABLY, even in the very harsh environment of Death Valley, fish are able to survive here. Many are isolated populations confined to a single river or individual water hole. These fish, the desert pupfish, are adapted to survive extremes of temperature from as high as 109 degrees Fahrenheit (43 degrees C.) to 34 to 36 degrees Fahrenheit (1 to 2 degrees C.) together with large variations in salt concentrations. This remarkable temperature tolerance has enabled these fish to survive in Death Valley for at least the last 30,000 years. One of these species, the Devil's Hole pupfish, faces destruction of its habitat, which consists of a single natural well. The drilling of boreholes nearby, and the consequent lowering of the water table threaten its very existence.

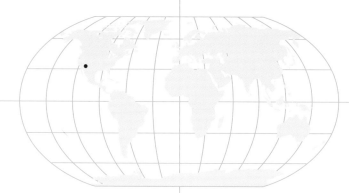

METEOR CRATER

A yawning depression in Arizona's desert marks the spot where a meteorite crashed into the earth.

Meteor Crater is just off U.S. Interstate 40, between Flagstaff and Winslow.

THOUSANDS of years ago, a bright trail flared in the sky over northern Arizona. The fireball came closer, travelling at an estimated 12 miles (19 km) per second, until it crashed into the earth with a great explosion, hurling millions of tons of rock into the air and creating Meteor Crater. The destructive energy of the explosion was a thousand times that of the atomic bomb dropped on Hiroshima.

Right, the great saucer-shaped depression left by the meteor measures some 4,000 feet across.

150

The crater is a great saucer-shaped hole 4,000 feet (1,220 m) in diameter and 600 feet (180 m) deep, with a rim around the edge that rises about 150 feet (46 m) above the flat plain. Debate still rages concerning the size of the meteorite that formed it, but a recent estimate is that this huge ball of iron and nickel was about 135 feet (41 m) across and weighed 300,000 tons. The meteor hit the ground with such force that it disintegrated on impact, and parts of it have been found up to 6 miles (10 km) away.

Fortunately, such enormous missiles from outer space do not often crash into the earth. However, it is estimated that about 50 tons of meteoroids penetrate the atmosphere each day. Most of these small particles of dust which are vaporised before they reach the surface by the heat generated by friction as the meteoroid hurtles through the outer atmosphere.

The edges of the crater rising 150 feet above the plain give the impression of a volcanic feature, and mean that the site can be seen for many miles.

Because meteoroids are often destroyed long before they reach the earth, few are ever found. Most of those that are found contain iron, which is better able to withstand the great heat generated as it plummets downwards. The world's largest single meteorite, Hoba, was discovered in 1920 near Grootfontein in Namibia. It is estimated to weigh about 66 tons, even though it is only 6 feet (2 m) by 6 feet (2 m) by 3 feet (1 m). The second largest meteorite was found at Cape York in western Greenland, where the local Inuit people had been using it as a source of iron for their tools for many years before the American explorer Robert E. Peary came and appropriated it for the American Museum of Natural History in New York in 1897. Many meteorites have been discovered in Antarctica, some of which are thought to have come from the moon and from Mars.

Although meteorites rarely crash to earth, there have been several documented cases. In 1908 there was an explosion about 6 miles (10 km) above the earth's surface at Tunguska in Siberia. The detonation could be heard 600 miles (965 km) away, and trees were flattened over 770 square miles (1,994 sq km). This huge explosion could have been caused by an asteroid or comet fragment.

Some scientists say that a meteorite may have been responsible for the mass extinction of dinosaurs that occurred 65 million years ago. The theory suggests that a huge piece of space debris tore through the earth's atmosphere to cut a crater 25 miles (40 km) deep and 125 miles (200 km) across under the ocean. Volcanic material and hot gases joined the millions of tons of dust and rock that were hurled into the air. The dust rose high into the atmosphere and blocked life-giving solar energy, causing a disruption in plant growth and a shortage of food, leading to the deaths of many animals and plants, including the dinosaurs. A large crater recently discovered off the coast of Mexico may provide the proof for this theory.

Meteorites

UNTIL the first rocks were collected from the moon, meteorites were the only samples scientists had of extra-terrestrial material – specimens are held in museums all over the world. Many meteorites date from the formation of the solar system about 4.6 billion years ago, and some contain particles from stars or planets that existed prior to the solar system.

There are two possible explanations for the source of these meteorites. They may come from the asteroid belt between Jupiter and Mars, which contains huge amounts of rock left over from a time when the planets were formed. Occasionally, chunks of that rock are pushed towards the earth by the gravitational pull of Jupiter. A second possibility is that they are knocked towards the earth after colliding with comets.

Meteorites fall into three different types: stones, stony-irons and irons, depending on their chemical and physical structure. The most common are stones, many of which contain round pieces of silicate that do not form on earth.

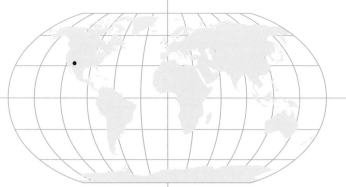

U.S.A.

THE PETRIFIED FOREST

*Monumental stone trees of an ancient swamp
are strewn over the land.*

The Petrified Forest National
Park lies beside U.S. Interstate
40. The nearest major airports
are at Albuquerque, New
Mexico about 200 miles (322
km) to the east, and at Phoenix,
Arizona, 230 miles (370 km) to
the south-west.

T HE Colorado Plateau in the south-western
United States straddles the Four Corners
meeting point of Utah, Colorado, Arizona and
New Mexico. This is desert country, trapped
between the coastal range of California to the
west and the main Rocky Mountain chain to

the east, and provides a wealth of particularly
spectacular scenery. Within a radius of 200
miles (322 km) of Four Corners there are no
fewer than 27 national parks and monuments,
most of them related to the desert. One of
these is the Petrified Forest National Park.

*Sections of a fossilised tree trunk at
Blue Mesa, in the Petrified Forest.*

Many of the rocks in the region are sandstones deposited during the Mesozoic era, from about 230 to 70 million years ago, when the climate was markedly different to that of today. Much of the region was once a low-lying, swampy flood plain that was heavily forested with conifers, some of them as high as 200 feet (61 m). Geologists have been able to determine this from the fossil tree trunks that now litter the area. Not all the trees actually grew where they fell; many were growing on hills to the south, and were toppled by storms and washed into the area by the ensuing floods. Sand and silt were washed off the hills by the rains, and the trees were gradually buried in the swamps.

Under normal conditions the fallen trees would have decomposed, but rapid burial by the sediments helped to preserve them. Layers of volcanic ash are mixed with the sediments, indicating volcanic activity. Ground water

The wood in this fossil log has been replaced by agate, but the original growth rings are still clearly visible.

percolating through the sediments dissolved some of the minerals present, and then re-deposited the silica minerals in the cells of the trees, gradually replacing the woody material. In this way the trees were petrified – literally turned to stone – and they survived intact as they were buried deeper by the accumulating sediments. Eventually the area was invaded by a shallow sea, when thick deposits of other sediments pressurised and hardened the sands and silts until they became sandstones and shales.

Towards the end of the Mesozoic era, about 70 million years ago, major geological changes were taking place to the west and beginning to form the Rocky Mountains to the east. The waters of the shallow sea gradually drained away and the forces of erosion began to work on the emerging sea floor. The sedimentary rocks deposited during the previous millions of years were gradually removed, until the petrified tree trunks were uncovered again.

Today the petrified trees within the national park are protected from would-be collectors. Their enormous range of colours depends on the composition of the replacing mineral. Jasper gives an opaque, brick-red colour, amethyst a clear purple, and agate can display a great variety of colours. Some of the trees are enormous, up to 100 feet (30 m) long, although the largest normally occur in several sections, which can be matched, like some giant puzzle.

The contrast of the once swampy conditions with the arid desert climate of today is a reminder that the earth is very much a living planet, where conditions are constantly changing.

Treasures of the Desert

MANY other outstanding natural features of the desert landscape are within reach of the Petrified Forest The Painted Desert, one of the most colourful geological features, lies between the Petrified Forest and the Grand Canyon to the north-west. Further upstream on the Colorado River, Utah, are Rainbow Bridge and Natural Bridges National Monuments and Arches National Park, where streams have eroded huge arches through the rocks. Rainbow Bridge is the largest natural arch in the world, 270 feet (82 m) long and more than 22 feet (6.5 m) wide, but Landscape Arch in Arches National Park is the longest, 291 feet (89 m) long by 6 feet (1.8 m) wide. West from there is the extraordinary Bryce Canyon.

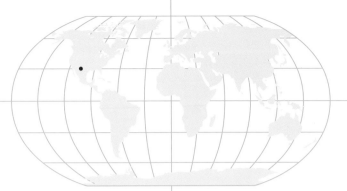

CARLSBAD CAVERNS

Miles of exquisite chambers and tunnels run through the Guadalupe Mountains in New Mexico, also home to enormous colonies of bats.

The nearest major city to the Carlsbad Caverns National Park is El Paso, Texas, about 120 miles (193 km) south-west. U.S. Highway 180 leads directly from the city to the national park.

Above, thousands of bats inhabit the cave system, roosting there during the heat of the day and only coming out in the evening cool to feed.

Facing page, floodlighting enhances the spectacular dripstone formations.

A⊤ dusk, the entrance to the Carlsbad Caverns is blackened by an incredible sight. Millions of bats flutter from their daytime resting places in the cool darkness of Bat Cave to hunt insects in the night. Despite their vast numbers, bats are sure fliers, and have a complex echo-location ability so that they never collide. Although the whirring of their wings and some squeaks can be heard by visitors watching this spectacle, the sounds made by the bats' natural sonar systems are well above the sound frequencies audible to man.

The Carlsbad bats are only one remarkable feature of this enormous underground cave system. The deepest cave explored to date is about 1,000 feet (305 m) below the surface, while the largest of the 60 or so caverns, the Big Room, is larger than 14 football fields.

The story of Carlsbad Caverns began 250 million years ago when a thick layer of limestone was deposited. Cracks and fissures developed in the limestone, and water seeped into them, dissolving softer rock and carving out the tunnels and caves. The limestone deposits were later lifted, forming the Guadalupe Mountains. The Guadalupe Ridge, under which the caverns lie, is about 6,300 feet (1,920 m) high. The water drained from the caves, but continued to drip, leaving traces of minerals to form stalactites, stalagmites and other dripstone formations.

Today, 3 miles (4.8 km) of paved trails meander through Carlsbad's most famous caverns, although there are at least another 20 miles (32 km) of passages and tunnels that are less frequently visited. A series of switchbacks begins the passage down the 830-foot (253-m) drop along the Main Corridor. The first major chamber, and one of the deepest, is the Green Lake Room, named after the emerald pool at the centre of the cavern. The cave is full of delicate stalactites, including an impressive cascade that has joined with stalagmites to form a column in the aptly named Veiled Statue.

The Queen's Chamber houses fantastic draperies, where stalactites have grown together to form curtains of stone through which light can shine, while the Temple of the Sun has dripstone formations that are shaded pastel hues of yellow, pink and blue. Throughout the caverns, fantastic shapes abound – the Bashful Elephant looks like an elephant with its back to the trail, while the famous Rock of Ages is a gigantic stalagmite standing aloof and majestic in its own dark alcove. In the Hall of Giants three great domed stalagmites stand sentinel, while the ceiling of the King's Palace drips a dazzling array of stalactites. Other curious features include the Big Room draperies, so fine that they ring when struck (although the practice is seldom allowed in case it damages the formations), and cave pearls. Cave pearls are formed when small grains of sand pick up extra coats of calcium carbonate – rather as snowballs grow larger as they roll down a hill. The result is shiny balls of stone that lie together in hollows, looking very much like nests of birds' eggs.

Mammoth – the Longest Cave System in the World

THE 200 miles (320 km) of winding passageways and tunnels of Mammoth Cave, Kentucky, make it the longest cavern system in the world. Although lacking stalactite and stalagmite formations on the scale of Carlsbad, the sheer size of the Mammoth system is overwhelming. One cavern, the Temple, is 540 by 290 feet (165 by 88 m) and 125 feet (38 m) high, while the largest river, Echo River, is up to 40 feet (12 m) across in places and occasionally runs 25 feet (8 m) deep. One of its largest dripstone formations is called Frozen Niagara, for its startling resemblance to a motionless cascade of water.

Ice Caves

HIGH in the Austrian Alps lies Eisriesenwelt, a system of caverns estimated to be about 26 miles (42 km) long. Like other limestone caves, it is filled with stalactites, stalagmites and elegant fluted columns. The main difference is that while in other caves these formations are made of calcium carbonate, in Eisriesenwelt they are made of ice. Eisriesenwelt means "world of the ice giants", an appropriate name for the largest permanent ice-filled caves in the world.

The caves were formed millions of years ago when water seeped into flaws and cracks in the limestone. Because the temperature of the caves is always at or slightly below freezing, water dripping through the rocks freezes into enormous icicles, sometimes forming thick white pillars, and sometimes delicate curtains of colour. The ice caves have stalactites, stalagmites, draperies, columns, needles, and domes – all looking surprisingly like their mineral counterparts.

THE EVERGLADES

*A vast expanse of freshwater wetland
at the southern tip of Florida.*

The Everglades are on the end of the Florida peninsula, bounded on the west by the Gulf of Mexico and by the islands of the Florida Keys to the south. The area is crossed by various roads, and large areas can also be explored by boat.

The Florida Manatee

THIS gentle, plant-eating mammal is a member of the group of animals known as the Sirenia, which were once believed by sailors to be mermaids. The manatee feeds on the seagrass beds in the shallow waters fringing the mangrove forests. These delightful, harmless creatures face a threat from marina developments and the like, which decrease their feeding area, and bring with them pollution and the increased danger of death or injury from being hit by boats.

Above, the population of the manatee, or sea cow, is vulnerable to the increasing loss of its habitat, and to the dangers posed by boat traffic.

Facing page, part of the lush swamp vegetation which covers large areas of the Everglades.

THIS unique sub-tropical wilderness, which the American Indians called "pa-hay-okee", or grassy waters, includes an area of some 2,700 square miles (7,000 sq km). Though it once covered around 4,000 square miles (10,360 sq km), it still represents one of the largest remaining freshwater marshlands in the world. The Everglades National Park covers 2,188 square miles (5,687 sq km) which is classed as protected wilderness, and along with the 73 square miles (189 sq km) of Fort Jefferson National Monument,

holds international status as a World Heritage Site, Biosphere Reserve and Ramsar site.

This great swampland is fed by water from Lake Okeechobee, the largest lake in North America after the Great Lakes. The water from the lake seeps into the underlying limestone, and from there feeds this vast wetland area through a series of aquifers. The Everglades are dominated by dense, and in places impenetrable stands of sawgrass that grow up to 13 feet (4 m)

high, covering vast areas. The region is criss-crossed by channels and small lakes of open water, where other plants such as water lilies and bladderworts thrive. The bladderworts are specially adapted for living in these nutrient-poor waters: they have small air bladders that trap insects and larvae which the plant then absorbs to obtain vital nutrients.

The small islands, or hammocks, where the underlying limestone rises above the water table, support a variety of hardwoods together with many species of orchids, ferns and animals. At the coast, the freshwater marsh, or glade, gives way to a fringing strip of red mangroves, the only forested marine wetland in North America.

Despite a variety of human pressures on the area it is still relatively unspoiled, and the large range of habitats is reflected in the highly diverse flora and fauna of the area. There are over 1,000 seed-bearing plants, including 25

varieties of orchid and 120 species of trees which range from tropical palm and mangrove, through temperate forest species such as oak and ash to desert plants such as yucca and cactus.

Many of the creatures depend on more than one element in this mosaic of habitats – for example, colonial birds use the cypress and mangrove forests as nest sites, while feeding in the sawgrass marshes. The Everglades are an exceptionally important area for birds, with over 320 different species recorded. These include such rarities as the wood stork, the reddish egret and the southern race of the bald eagle. The Everglades kite feeds exclusively on snails, using its specially adapted, long, curved and sharply pointed bill to extract the flesh of the snail from the shell. Many species of fish-eating birds also frequent the freshwater swamps, and the coastal mangrove fringe ii home to anhingos, roseate spoonbills, pelicans, wood ibis, herons and egrets.

Over 150 fish species are found in the coastal waters, providing good feeding for the many birds, reptiles and mammals. These include twelve species of turtle, such as the giant loggerhead turtle, the green turtle, and the Florida manatee. The American alligator is the main predator in the swamp, but there are others such as the American crocodile, the rare Florida Panther and various otters.

Encroachment on a Wilderness

PROTECTING an area as complex as the Everglades is never simple, and the national park faces threats from drainage works and flood defences which cut off the life waters to the swamps. With less water and reduced flooding the area of swamp has decreased, and so have the numbers of wildlife. In the 1930s an estimated 1½ million birds nested here; now that number is less than 50,000, and the alligator population has declined by over 90 per cent in the same period.

THE SARGASSO SEA

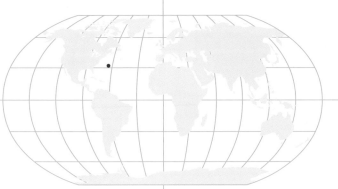

A strange and mysterious area of near-stagnant, warm water in the North Atlantic.

The Sargasso Sea lies in the south-west of the North Atlantic Ocean between Bermuda and the West Indies. The area is only accessible by boat. There are no organised cruises, and the journey involves a considerable voyage from the West Indies or Bermuda.

Why Such a Migration?

THE European eel is not alone in undertaking this remarkable journey. Its American cousin also returns to the Sargasso Sea to spawn. But why make such a journey in the first place and why commit your young to the rigours of the return trip? It seems the reasons lie in the past, 100 million years ago when the continents of Europe and North America were very much closer together and the Atlantic was only a narrow strip of water between the two. It may be that the eels from the sea discovered the rich feeding in the estuaries and fresh waters and started to migrate between the two, and even now after the continents have drifted so far apart it is a habit they cannot break.

Above, the urge to return to the sea is so strong that eels will wriggle across damp meadowland to reach a main waterway.

Facing page, top, sargassum weed floats freely on the ocean surface.

Facing page, below, transparent elvers nearing the end of a 2½ year journey from the Sargasso to Europe.

THE Sargasso Sea is bounded by a clockwise rotating warm water current system – the Gulf Stream – which starts in the Florida Straits. In its progress up the east coast of North America, recirculation gyres are set up and it is one of these which creates the area of the Sargasso Sea. Remnants of the Gulf Stream continue across the North Atlantic as part of the North Atlantic Drift, eventually passing up the west side of the British Isles before finally disappearing in the Arctic Ocean currents.

The Sargasso Sea is a strange place, and the almost stagnant conditions combined with clear warm water support a floating habitat of sargassum weed, kept afloat by numerous small air bladders. This seaweed provides an environment more similar to inter-tidal areas than mid-ocean, and it supports a range of animals that reflect this, with some of the species endemic to the area.

While the Sargasso Sea is renowned for its floating habitat, it is as the beginning and end of an unusual journey for the European eel that it is even more remarkable. The Sargasso Sea is the spawning area for the eel, which has a life cycle so amazing that it was not understood until the early part of the 20th century.

The adult eels normally inhabit European freshwater streams and lakes, where they can

remain for years, feeding, growing and laying down fat reserves. The urge to spawn arrives in the autumn after the males have reached up to 16 inches (41 cm), and the females 24 inches (61 cm) in length. They begin to change in appearance, turning from yellow to black in colour and their eyes enlarge. Moving mainly at night, they begin to descend the streams and rivers. The urge to return to the sea can be so great that if they find themselves in a pond with no direct route to the sea they will wriggle out of the water and cross damp meadows to find a stream which will take them to salt water. Once they reach the sea the eels swim in a roughly south-westerly direction at a depth of about 200 feet (60 m) until they reach the edge of the continental shelf, where they dive to around 1,400 feet (427 m). The journey takes around 80 days, covering a distance of some 3,500 miles (5,630 km). When they reach the Sargasso Sea they dive to depths of around 4,000 feet (1,220 m) where they spawn and then die.

The eggs develop into tiny, transparent, leaf-like creatures, so unlike their parents that the connection between the two states was not realised until the end of the 19th century. These *leptocephalus* larvae rise from the sea bed to depths of around 700 feet (213 m), where they are caught up in the Gulf Stream currents and transported eastwards. This return journey

takes some two and a half years. As they near the European coast they begin to change to resemble the adult, although at this stage they are still transparent. Some swim through the Strait of Gibraltar and into the Mediterranean, and even on to the Black Sea. Others pass along the north coast of Europe entering the many estuaries of western Europe, with some even passing through the Kattegat into the Baltic. Only after they have been in the fresh water for a few months do they begin to feed, changing colour to the usual opaque yellow. After a number of years the urge leads these animals to embark on their final amazing journey to spawn another generation in the depths of the Sargasso Sea.

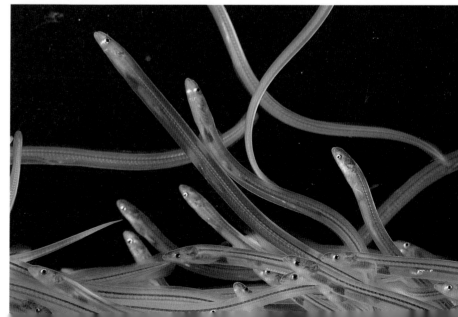

The Hawaiian Islands are in
the north Pacific. Honolulu,
on the island of Oahu, has an
international airport and has
regular daily flight connections
with mainland North America
and other places. To see the
eruptions at Kilaeua take an
onward flight to Hilo or Kona,
on Hawaii, to join a tour.

U.S.A.
THE HAWAIIAN ISLANDS

*Volcanic hot-spot
of the north Pacific Ocean.*

*Above, red-hot basaltic lava boils
the sea water where it flows into the
Pacific Ocean, at Kalapana on
Hawaii's south-east coast.*

*Facing page, a fountain of molten
lava explodes from a vent on the
side of a volcano.*

THE Hawaiian Islands stretch about 1,500
miles (2,415 km) across the north Pacific
Ocean between latitudes 19 degrees and 29
degrees North, from Kure and Midway Island
in the west to the island of Hawaii itself in the
east. They seem to be unrelated to any of the
other volcanoes that lie around the margins of
the Pacific – the "Ring of Fire". Most of the
other volcanoes are associated with deep sea
trenches where the oceanic crust is being
dragged back into the mantle below the

continental margin. This process, called
subduction, creates frictional heat as the slab of
oceanic crust descends, and this in turn
provides the heat source for the volcanoes
beyond the trench.

Conversely, the Hawaiian Islands occur
where they do because they lie above a hot-
spot in the earth's mantle, a point source of
heat. Geologists believe there are about 30 such
hot-spots that are stationary relative to the
earth's interior, and are long-lived features

through geological time. This means that a hot-spot beneath the moving crust of the ocean will produce a line of volcanoes as the crust passes over it.

That is exactly what has happened with the Hawaiian Islands. The crust of the western part of the Pacific is moving steadily westward, and seems to have moved about 1,500 miles (2,414 km) during the life of this hot-spot. All the islands in the Hawaiian chain are volcanic; the oldest are at the western end, and the most active – and hence the youngest – are on the island of Hawaii itself, at the eastern end of the chain.

Most of the current volcanic activity in Hawaii is at Kilauea, a subsidiary vent on the flanks of Mauna Loa, the second highest mountain, about 20 miles (32 km) east of the summit (13,680 feet, 4,170 m). This volcano has been in continuous eruption since 1983, continually producing lava at an average of 7 cubic yards (5 cu m) per second. The caldera, Mokuaweoweo, is 500 to 600 feet (152 to 183 m) deep and covers an area of 4 square miles (10.4 sq km). The best known features of this eruption are the spectacular lava fountains that hurl red-hot lava up to 300 feet (90 m) into the air, with occasional fountains as high as 1,650 feet (503 m).

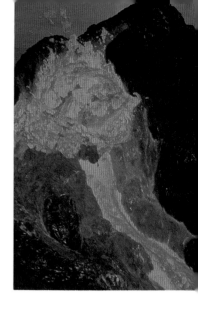

Hawaii is a roughly triangular-shaped island about 80 miles (130 km) by 95 miles (153 km). The highest point is the summit of Mauna Kea at 13,796 feet (4,205 m), making it the tallest mountain in the world when measured from its base on the ocean floor, some 19,680 feet (5,998 m) below sea level. The height of Mauna Kea, together with its clear, unpolluted atmosphere in the middle of the ocean, has made it an ideal place to locate several of the most powerful astronomical telescopes in the world.

Lava leaving the crater flows downhill like a crimson river of basalt at temperatures as high as 2,012 to 2,192 degrees Fahrenheit (1,100 to 1,200 degrees C.). The lava is very fluid and can travel at a speed of 20 miles (32 km) per hour or more. Everything in the path of the lava is burned, roads are blocked, and if the flow enters the sea it cools explosively. Eruptions such as these provide spectacular excitement for the tourist in this tropical paradise.

Predicting Volcanic Eruptions

THERE are no universally applicable features that indicate a volcanic eruption because all volcanoes are different. However volcanoes that erupt frequently, such as those in Hawaii, tend to show similar symptoms before each eruption. Seismometers measure earthquakes and can detect minor tremors that may presage an eruption, particularly the increasing frequency and magnitude of the tremors. The build-up of pressure within the volcano before an eruption causes the mountain to swell; after the eruption and the emptying of the magma chamber, the mountain will shrink again, so sensitive tilt-meters are also used on the flanks of the volcano.

Some Hawaiian eruptions are preceded by a low-pitched humming or roaring noise, the origin of which is unknown. This noise is known locally as "hearing Pele", after the legendary goddess of the Hawaiian volcanoes. Another detectable sign is a change in the local magnetic and electrical fields: magma heated above about 1,100 degrees Fahrenheit (600 degrees C.) loses its natural magnetism, implying that a large body of molten rock has developed within the volcano. Other indications include sudden changes in the temperature, gas composition and general activity of fumaroles and hot springs in the vicinity of the vent.

Predicting eruptions is still an uncertain art, but it is generally more reliable than predicting earthquakes. However some eruptions do come without any warning at all, and these are especially dangerous when the volcano has been considered extinct, and therefore safe.

KAUAI: HAWAII'S EMERALD ISLAND

This emerald island is the lushest and most beautiful of the Hawaiian Islands, with dense green vegetation, golden beaches, and turquoise seas.

The Hawaiian Islands lie far out in the north Pacific. Flights are usually to the capital, Honolulu, from which there are connecting flights to the other islands. The administrative centre of Kauai is Lihue; roads run around most of the edge of the island, except for the Na Pali Coast.

G REAT blue-green waves crash onto the sunny palm-fringed beaches, while inland, steep hillsides densely covered with thick, green vegetation disappear into mysterious white clouds at their summits. Kauai is an island of stunning beauty, no doubt enhanced by the fact that the greater part of it has remained relatively free from development. In September 1992, Cyclone Iniki swept through the Hawaiian islands, and 10,000 homes and 70 hotels were

Captain Cook and the Hawaiian Islands

I N a sun-drenched clearing in the small Kauaian village of Waimea, a lone statue gazes out across the Pacific. Like other statues that are as far afield as North Yorkshire and Australia, it is of Captain James Cook, the 18th-century explorer who made three great voyages of science and discovery. The statue on Kauai marks the point where, on 18 January 1778, Cook became the first European to set foot on the Sandwich Islands, now known as the Hawaiian Islands. A plaque on the beach at Kealakekua Bay on the island of Hawaii commemorates the place where, a year later, he was killed following a dispute over the theft of a boat.

Right, steep green cliffs and a sharp reef protect the Na Pali coastline.

Facing page, the Banzai Pipeline is a spectacular natural tunnel of water much favoured by surfers.

destroyed in 175 mile (282 km) per hour winds. This has been a major setback for the tourist industry, although rebuilding began immediately.

Kauai was formed about 5 million years ago by volcanic activity. The centre of the island is an extinct volcano, Mount Waialeale, that stands a mile (1.6 km) high. It is the wettest place on earth with an average of 460 inches (1170 cm) of rain every year. The high precipitation means that Kauai is fantastically green, and more than 70 per cent of the island is devoted to plantations, national parks and open space.

The island's main industry was traditionally the growing of sugar cane. In 1835 the first sugar cane mill opened, and workers were recruited from China, Japan and the Philippines, as well as from the local people. Many migrants settled in Kauai permanently, which accounts for the island's richly multicultural background.

There are many diverse and beautiful sites on Kauai. One of the most spectacular is the Na Pali Coast, where sheer cliffs plummet into the sea. The coast is home to a large number of birds and exotic plants. Archaeologists have discovered temples tucked away in some of the valleys of this mysterious land, suggesting that early Hawaiians made this their home.

In the centre of the island, the slopes of Mount Waialeale are home to tiny plants clinging precariously to the steep hillsides, while ribbons of gushing water stream from the rain-drenched upper reaches. Nearby is Waimea Canyon, 14 miles (23 km) of steep green-tinted volcanic rock with a fast-running, muddy river swirling along its base. The Fern Grotto on the Wailua River is a more gentle sight, with fronds of vegetation hanging like curtains from the roof of an enormous cavern. Kauai is indeed an island of contrasts, with miles of empty beaches, huge waves in the surf, bright colours of the exotic plants or birds, and chilly mountain tops.

Much of the musical *South Pacific* was filmed along the north coast, immortalising such place names as Bali Hai. Another popular song tells of "Puff the Magic Dragon," who lived at Hanalei, a verdant valley on the northern coast.

The Banzai Pipeline

WAVES are born far out in the world's great oceans, and are caused by a combination of winds, currents, and the gravitational pull of the earth. As the waves roll towards the land, other factors begin to determine their size and shape, such as the shape of the sea bed over which they travel. A gently sloping sandy beach will give rise to waves very different from those where the beach rises sharply.

The sea bed on the northwest coast of the Hawaiian island of Oahu gives rise to the famous wave known as the Banzai Pipeline. Huge Pacific waves roll towards the shore, growing taller as they reach shallower waters, eventually toppling over themselves. The Banzai Pipeline is so called because the toppling effect occurs at a slight angle, forming a blue-green tunnel. It is a popular venue for surfers, who skim along the inside, surrounded by its translucent walls.

Trinidad

THE PITCH LAKE

A gently bubbling cauldron of grey-black slime forms one of the world's largest deposits of asphalt.

The pitch lake is at La Brea, which is in the south-west of Trinidad, about 50 miles (80 km) from Port of Spain, on the main coastal road to Bonasse in the south.

Above, a natural stream of hot black asphalt.

Facing page, at one time the tar pits formed an important part of Trinidad's economy.

S ET among Trinidad's feathery-leafed palms and verdant foliage is an oily expanse of sticky grey-black mud that is its most famous, although not most beautiful, feature. However, the steady stream of visitors to the Trinidad pitch lake attest that it is a phenomenon that holds a certain curious fascination.

The lake, on the south-western coast of the island, is said to be the largest deposit of asphalt in the world, and is made of about 40 per cent bitumen, 30 per cent clays, and 30 per cent salt water. The lake has been estimated at 270 feet (82 m) deep, covering 110 acres (45 hectares) of land. Surprisingly there are small islands of vegetation dotted about the lake, where dead leaves and other rotting plant matter has become trapped in pockets on the surface forming a rich compost that allows scrubby trees to grow.

The lake has been quarried on an industrial scale for pitch and tar for at least 100 years, and new asphalt soon oozes into any trenches dug, obliterating evidence of human interference. Trinidad was discovered by Columbus in 1498; almost a century later, the English adventurer Sir Walter Raleigh visited the island and used some of the pitch on his ships, reporting that it was of a far better quality

though it is formed of folds of the thick, viscous pitch. Rainwater collects in the dips between the folds and oil from the bitumen spreads across the pools, turning them different shimmering rainbow colours in the changing light. According to local legend, the pitch lake fills the site of a Chaima Indian settlement, cursed by the gods when the villagers dared to make a meal of sacred humming birds.

According to the scientists, the Pitch Lake was once under the sea. Some 50 million years ago, the bodies of small marine creatures fell to the sea bed and decomposed into oils that were

La Brea Tar Pits, Los Angeles

THE Trinidad pitch lake is not unique: there is a tar lake in nearby Venezuela, and asphalt deposits at the La Brea Tar Pits in the centre of bustling Los Angeles (*brea* is simply the Spanish word for tar). The tar pits here are surrounded by fences to stop people from falling in and becoming trapped – a fate which befell hundreds of animals long before the city was founded by the Spanish two hundred years ago. In 1875, geologists speculated that the tar pits might contain preserved animal bones, but it was not until 30 years later that archaeologists began to explore the contents of the bubbling pits. More than half a million animal bones have been excavated, including sabre-toothed tigers, mammoths, a type of bear which is now extinct, huge vultures with wingspans of 12 feet (4 m), and many species of rodents, lizards, and insects. The La Brea skeletons, forming the world's largest collection of animals from 15,000 years ago, are housed in the Los Angeles County Museum.

than pitch obtained from Norway. Today the pitch is more likely to be used for surfacing the local roads.

The tarry surface of the lake is firm enough to walk on, although there are always bubbles plopping and bursting as sulphurous gases are forced out. The surface looks as

able to sink through permeable rocks. Upheavals in the earth's crust forced the oil back to the surface, where it was baked into a hard layer by the sun.

The lake is not a static thing: new pitch is constantly oozing to the surface and forced to the edges by slow-moving currents.

ANGEL FALLS –
SALTO ANGEL

*The highest waterfall
in the world.*

South-eastern Venezuela is still a remote area, but it can be reached without too much difficulty. The river journey from Porto Ordaz on the Orinoco is about 150 miles (240 km); flights from El Dorado and Santa Elena are about 75 miles (120 km) and 150 miles (240 km).

Waterfalls

EVEN the smallest waterfalls create a sense of excitement; there is something compelling about watching water crashing into a pool. Little wonder that ancient and primitive peoples have stood in awe of waterfalls, marvelling at their power and regarding them as something special, homes of gods and spirits that should be respected. Larger falls that have undercut their supporting cliffs to create a passageway behind the curtain of water have a particular fascination. Modern man has a more practical and less superstitious viewpoint, seeing possible uses in economic terms. Falls are indicators of water power, and that power can now be harnessed to provide electrical energy for many applications.

Right, the edge of the Auyán Tepuy plateau towers above the jungle.

Facing page, the remarkable drop of the Angel Falls.

IN the remote south-eastern corner of Venezuela, close to the borders with Guyana and Brazil, is the highland area of La Gran Sabana. Roraima, the highest mountain in Venezuela at 9,270 feet (2,825 m), sits astride the border, and on its southern flank is the source of the Caroní River that eventually flows into the Orinoco. To the north-west lies Auyán Tepuy, the high point of a high plateau at around 8,250 feet (2,515 m), which towers above the surrounding luxuriant jungle. The rock of the plateau is a horizontal pale red sandstone, cut by innumerable fractures and vertical joints that provide drainage channels for the torrential tropical rains frequently deluging the area. Some of the rain also supplies the Rio Churún, a tributary of the Caroní River, that winds slowly over the

plateau until it reaches the cliff on the northern edge. At that point a spectacular transformation takes place.

The river gathers pace down a short incline and then rushes suicidally into empty space. The first drop over the cliff edge is a sheer 2,648 feet (807 m) to an obstruction, and then a second plunge for a further 564 feet (172 m) into a tremendous pool in the jungle at the foot of the cliffs – a total fall of 3,212 feet (979 m). From a distance the thin white line at the cliff edge gradually broadens into a wide white blur of spray as the water crashes downward, until it is lost to sight in the green carpet of jungle. In wet weather, this king of waterfalls is attended by numerous smaller jets of water issuing from the crevices in the sandstone below the cliff edge. It is a sight of both elegant simplicity and immense grandeur, worthy of its status as the tallest waterfall in the world.

The falls have long been known to the local American Indians as Churún-Meru, and their name for the plateau, Auyán Tepuy, means "Devil's Mountain," an apt description when the cliffs are shrouded in mist. In 1910 the falls were reported by Ernesto Sánchez la Cruz, but it was an American pilot who brought them to the attention of the world. Jimmy Angel was flying in the area exploring for gold when he noted the falls in his logbook on 14 November 1933. After this they were named in his honour: "Salto Angel" in Spanish, Angel Falls in English. Jimmy Angel never found gold, but he achieved lasting fame.

For a long time the entire area was virtually inaccessible to all but the most determined jungle explorers, but now fame has led to exploitation by the tourist trade. Today it is possible to take a tourist trip to the falls in a motorised dugout canoe or in a light aircraft. The falls are also visited by adventure tourists, those eager for the added adventure of leaping off the plateau in a hang-glider or under a para-glider – to the enthusiast, an essential opportunity for a "first" that cannot be missed.

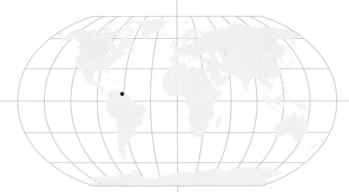

Venezuela

THE ORINOCO FLOOD PLAIN AND DELTA

Rivers tumble off the foothills of the Andes into one of the largest wetlands in South America.

This massive area stretches from the Cordillera de Merida in the west of Venezuela to the Guyana Shield and the Orinoco River in the south and east.

Above, the Orinoco River meanders through Venezuela, flanked by vast areas of swamp forest and savannah which are periodically flooded.

Facing page, the distinctive blunt nose and watchful eye of a capybara.

THE flood plain, or llanos, of the Orinoco and Apure rivers together with their major tributaries forms a large area of wetlands, in Venezuela alone covering a total area of around 92,640 square miles (239,9437 sq km). This is made up of 69,480 square miles (179,953 sq km) of savanna and 23,160 square miles (59,984 sq km) of semi–deciduous forest and cultivated land in the Orinoco basin.

The swift flowing, silt–laden rivers flow down off the foothills of the Andes, slowing as the gradient decreases, dropping their load of rich alluvial sediment in the process. During the rainy season between June and October large areas of the llanos flood, creating around 39,000 square miles (101,010 sq km) of wetlands – an intricate mosaic of slow, meandering rivers and streams, oxbow lakes, riverine marshes, swamp forests, freshwater lakes and inundated palm savannah. By the end of the dry season in late April the floodwater has retreated and vast expanses of dry savannah appear, with many of the smaller rivers reduced to a series of stagnant pools.

168

As the Orinoco reaches the coast the main river channel divides into a complex network of smaller channels separating innumerable islands. The Orinoco Delta dominates the Atlantic coast of Venezuela, covering an area of some 14,000 square miles (36,260 sq km). It supports a diverse range of habitats with fringing mangroves, permanent freshwater swamps with groves of palms, seasonally flooded palm savannah, swamp forest and tropical evergreen forest on the higher ground.

The Orinoco Delta and the llanos are extremely important areas for many different species of wading birds, with over 100 breeding

characteristic bird fauna with rheas, tinamous, seriemas and a wide variety of smaller warblers, as well as a large number of hawks, kites, falcons and vultures.

Much of the llanos is used for cattle ranching, but there is an increasing business in rearing capybara for their meat. The semi-aquatic capybara is the largest living rodent in the world, growing to 175 pounds (79 kg). It is much more productive than cattle, yielding more than four times the weight of meat for a given area of land. The white tailed deer is also common on the savannah, and feline predators, including cougar, ocelot and jaguar, are all widespread.

Tio Tigre – Uncle Tiger

THE jaguar, or Tio Tigre as it is known by the local people, is a highly adaptable big cat, as much at home climbing trees as swimming in the lakes and rivers of the llanos. It is a majestic animal with an exquisitely patterned coat, and has suffered very badly at the hands of hunters and poachers who kill it for its highly prized pelt. Numbers have been drastically reduced to such levels that the jaguar is now classified as a threatened species. It has largely retreated to the more inaccessible forest regions. Solitary animasl, jaguars are active mainly at night, and an adult male will range over an area of 30 to 50 square miles. They feed on a variety of prey including tapir, caiman and capybara.

Tree Frogs of the Llanos

THE moist conditions of the marshes and the tropical rainforest are ideal for amphibians, and a wide variety of frog species have evolved here. The tree frog is superbly adapted for its life in the canopy of the forest with the development of specialised toes and fingers with pads from which a sticky material is secreted. This, together with a highly developed sense of balance, helps them to cling on to the foliage of the trees. They are nocturnal, feeding mainly on insects, and typically are coloured bright green for camouflage against predatory birds.

colonies of various species. The spectacular scarlet ibis nests in the clumps of trees scattered across the llanos, with a breeding population of over 65,000 pairs representing a significant proportion of the world population. Large numbers of wood storks – some 5,500 pairs – also breed in the area, together with significant numbers of jabiru, various species of herons, egrets and ducks. In particular the llanos is important for two species of tree duck, the white-faced tree duck and the black-bellied tree duck. The savannah also has a

The freshwater lakes and the rivers of the delta support many different creatures, including the largest snake in the world, the anaconda. Spectacled caiman still occur in reasonable numbers, despite extensive hunting, but the Orinoco crocodile has not fared so well and the species is now classified as endangered and on the verge of extinction. Similarly, the numbers of manatee and giant otter have declined dramatically in recent years as a result of hunting and continued destruction of their native habitat .

Brazil

THE AMAZON BASIN

The best way to appreciate the grandeur of this vast area is to fly over it and simply marvel at the scale.

The Amazon basin in northern Brazil extends from the heights of the Andes to the Atlantic coast, and includes a vast area drained by the many tributaries of this mighty river. The area has only limited road access, although there are numerous small air fields.

The Giant Otter

THIS gentle, curious creature is now one of the rarest animals on earth, because of over-hunting and pressures imposed by the destruction and pollution of its habitat. The giant otter pairs for life, living in an extended family group of as many as 30 individuals. An adult male may be up to 6 feet (1.8m) long and weigh 71 pounds (32 kg). It feeds almost exclusively on fish, mainly taking fish around 10 inches (25 cm) long although they have been recorded tackling specimens as large as 2 feet (60 cm) in length.

Right, the upper canopy of the rainforest emerges through the mist.

THE Amazon River flows for 4,080 miles (6,565 km) – the second longest river in the world after the Nile at 4,132 miles (6,648 km). The Amazon Basin contains the world's largest tropical rainforest covering a staggering 2.3 million square miles (nearly 6 million sq km), and extending into nine different countries. The lifeblood of this vast expanse of rainforest is the mighty Amazon and its tributaries, which together contain about 25 per cent of all the water carried by the world's rivers.

This vast expanse of tropical rainforest contains over a million species of plant and animal life and is the repository of the genetic inheritance of the world. Even within a relatively small area the diversity is enormous, and just a 3.9 square mile (10 sq km) patch of rainforest can contain as many as 1,500 species of flowering plants, 750 different trees, 125 mammals, 400 different birds and countless insects and other invertebrates. Many of the species remain unrecorded and unidentified. Scientists can only speculate about the true wealth and diversity of the natural resources of this rainforest.

The Amazon and its tributaries support over 2,000 species of fish, and many unusual mammals and reptiles, including the Amazonian manatee, the Pink River dolphin, the giant otter and the spectacled caiman. The diversity of fish is extra-ordinary, ranging from the small but infamous red-bellied piranha – a feared and voracious carnivore that occurs in large shoals – to other closely related species which eat seeds and fruits that fall into the water from the fringing trees. The arowana, which can grow up to 3 feet (1 m) in length, leaps out of the water to pick off beetles from low-hanging branches of trees.

The recent exploitation of the rainforest is continuing at an alarming rate, with over 1½ square miles (4 sq km) of irreplaceable forest disappearing every hour. The indiscriminate destruction of this complex and diverse eco-system has global implications, threatening the survival of the wildlife, the way of life of the native American Indians who have lived in the forest for centuries, and the opportunities for

future generations to enjoy and unlock the mysteries that these forests hold.

The local American Indian tribes live in harmony with the forest, exploiting it in a sustainable way by mimicking nature. One

gleam of hope is offered by the Colombian government, with recognition that the Indians are the best custodians of the forest. In 1989 Chiribiquete National Park was created, an area of 3,900 square miles (10,000 sq km) where all external exploitation is banned, and the management is to be left to the Indians. Large as this is, it represents only 0.17 per cent of the total area of rainforest. The traditional Indian custom involves clearing small areas known as *chagra*, or "garden in the forest", to cultivate yuccas, peppers, mangoes and other crops. After a short period of fertility the tribe moves on to clear another *chagra*, leaving the old one to revert to rainforest. A natural clearing which may have been caused by fire will revert to mature natural forest in as little as 40 years; a *chagra* may take as long as 200 years, still far preferable to the complete, irreversible destruction caused by clear felling.

Above, sharp teeth and strong jaws are characteristics of the fearsome red piranha.

Not Enough Trees

EXPLOITATION of the forests has resulted in the loss of many species, and others are now on the brink of extinction. The Brazilian rosewood has long been in demand for its beautiful timber, used in making furniture. It is now used only as a very thin veneer over other woods, but this tree has been so exploited that there are not enough left even to supply this market, and it has been placed on the endangered species list. The Rio Palenque mahogany is on the list of the ten most endangered plants in the world. Only twelve mature trees are known to survive, though many young seedlings are now sprouting. These are just two examples of what is a much larger problem, and only an indication of many other unknown species under the same threat of extinction.

171

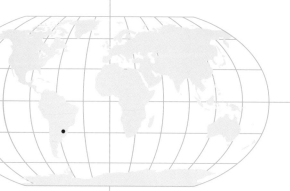

IGUASSU FALLS, CATARATAS DO IGUASSU

Spectacular white-water falls in an emerald green jungle.

Iguassu Falls lie on the Argentina–Brazil border about 200 miles (322 km) east of Asunción in Paraguay. From the airport at Asunción a main highway leads across Paraguay to the Brazilian side of the falls, and a turning off this road leads across a bridge to the Argentine side.

Right, an aerial view of the Parana River between Brazil (left) and Argentina (right) as it plunges over the falls of Iguassu.

Facing page, flood waters cascade past islands of jungle into the torrent below, on the Brazilian side of the falls.

THE River Iguassu rises in the Serro do Mar, close to the Brazilian coast south of São Paulo, and flows inland (westward) for about 820 miles (1,320 km). It follows a winding course across the Paraná Plateau until, swollen by tributaries, it makes its way downwards via some 70 waterfalls that punctuate its path. The largest of these, Ñacunday Falls, has a drop of 130 feet (40 m) – almost as great as Niagara. Where the river eventually reaches the edge of the plateau it plunges over the Iguassu Falls, shortly before joining the Paranã River.

The river here is about 2.5 miles (4 km) wide, and the water tumbles down across the full width of the river in a magnificent crescent-shaped cliff. There are as many as 275 separate cascades, some plunging directly 270 feet (82 m) into the cauldron below, others crashing over a series of smaller cataracts to the river. These smaller cataracts are broken by ledges of resistant rock that disperse the tumbling water into clouds of mist and spray; sunlight then completes the display with brilliant ever-changing rainbows. Between the cascades the rock outcrops are covered in dense stands of trees and foliage: palms, bamboo and lacy tree ferns form outposts of the surrounding jungle. Beneath the trees, wild tropical flowers – begonias, bromeliads and orchids – splash brilliant colours through the undergrowth. This riot of colour is completed by the birds, as parrots, macaws and other gaudily feathered species fly through the canopy.

National parks in both Brazil and Argentina flank the falls on either side, and access to the falls is normally through one of these. Perhaps the best view is achieved from a helicopter, when the whole breathtaking panorama is spread out below. But the most thrilling way to experience the falls is from the catwalk that extends over the river, passing the falls at close range and crossing to the far side. The catwalk has occasionally been swept away by the river in full spate, and at these close quarters one can almost feel the immense power of the water as it plunges into the abyss below.

The falls are at their most spectacular during the rainy season, from November to March, but there is usually a good show at any time of the year. Yet despite the impression of permanence given by the constant rush of water, the falls have been known to fail. In May and June 1978, during a period of particularly dry weather the river gradually ceased to flow, and for 28 days not a drop of water passed over the lip – a serious blow to visitors at the time but a good demonstration of the perfidy of nature. This was the first time that the falls had dried up since 1934.

On the Alto Paraná River, about 100 miles (160 km) upstream of the confluence with the Iguassu, is the Salto dos Sete Quedas or Guairá. This waterfall, with an average height of only 110 feet (34 m), is the greatest in the world when measured on its average annual flow. The lip of the falls is 3 miles (5 km) wide and the estimated flow is 470,000 cubic feet (13,300 cu m) per second – equivalent to filling the dome of London's St Paul's Cathedral in 0.6 seconds.

The World's Largest Dam

THE Paranã River, the fifth largest in the world, has been successfully dammed to produce hydroelectric power. Itaipu, on the border between Paraguay and Brazil, was the site selected. A channel was dug and the main stream of the river diverted into it by specially built barrages, which then formed coffer dams to allow work to begin on the main dam. A barrage dam was built on the eastern (Brazilian) side to hold back the water in the new reservoir, and a spillway channel was constructed on the western (Paraguayan) side. The main dam housed the hydro-electric power station with its 18 generators. Once the construction work had been completed, the coffer dams were demolished and the sluice gates closed for 40 days to allow the reservoir to fill, creating a new lake 100 miles (161 km) long, and covering an area of 600 square miles (1,554 sq km). After 14 years of labour, during which 28 million tons of concrete were poured, the world's largest dam and hydro-electric scheme was completed in 1988. Its generators have a capacity of 12,600 megawatts – sufficient to power the whole of Paraguay and the industrial cities of Rio de Janeiro and São Paulo in Brazil.

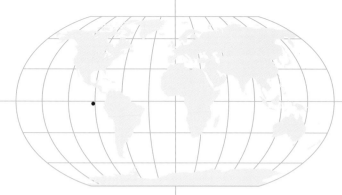

THE GALAPAGOS ISLANDS

One of the most isolated and beautiful archipelagos in the world.

The Galapagos Islands lie on the equator in the eastern Pacific Ocean between 500 and 620 miles (800 and 1,000 km) from the nearest mainland.

Darwin's Finches

CHARLES Darwin formulated his theory of evolution based on observations made during the entire voyage of H.M.S. *Beagle*, but undoubtedly one of the most fertile grounds for inspiration was the Galapagos finches. All these birds are descended from common ancestral stock which arrived by chance from South America. They found a large number of vacant niches in habitats throughout the islands, and have evolved into 13 species, distinguishable in size, shape of bill, colour of plumage, song, diet and behaviour. This adaptive radiation is best illustrated by the differences in the beaks of the various species. Some have the typical seed-eating bill, others that feed on cacti have developed a long, pointed bill, while yet others have a small tit-like bill for feeding primarily on insects. The woodpecker finch has not only developed a specialised bill, but also a complex behaviour pattern which includes using a cactus spine to prize larvae out of cracks and crevices.

Above, a Galapagos hawk hitches a ride on a giant tortoise, Isabela Island.

Right, seven different species of marine iguana – the only sea-going lizard – have evolved in this remarkable group of islands.

VISITORS to the Galapagos Islands are always impressed by their beauty, variety and uniqueness. So it was for Charles Darwin when he came to the islands in 1835 during his epic voyage of discovery on the *Beagle*. He saw much here which would inspire his great thesis, *The Origin of Species*.

The Galapagos are a group of oceanic islands formed from accumulations of lava rising from the sea bed. The archipelago extends 186 miles (300 km) from north to south, and is made up of 15 main islands, 42 islets and a further 26 rocks or reefs. In all they cover some 3,012 square miles (7,800 sq km), of which 96.6 per cent is now a national park surrounded by a marine reserve of some 30,850 square miles (79,900 sq km). They are islands of contrast. The lowland coastal fringes are arid and dry, the vegetation here dominated by cacti. The humidity increases with altitude, and the hillsides between 650 and 1,600 feet (200 and 500m) are covered by lush evergreen forest, while on the highest regions there is an open area dominated by sedges and ferns.

The flora and fauna of these islands, as with all oceanic archipelagos, depends on chance arrivals by sea or air, although recently humans have also played their part. Many of the animal species found on the islands are unique, not only to the archipelago, but to specific islands in the group. For example, the Galapagos Islands are the only place on earth where marine iguanas occur. These lizards feed exclusively on seaweed,

and have adapted to their marine way of life by developing partially webbed feet. Seven different races of marine iguana, each showing marked variations, have evolved on the different islands. On six of the islands there is also a species of land iguana peculiar to the Galapagos.

The islands are also famous for another reptile, the giant tortoise. Mature individuals can weigh 300 to 400 pounds (135 to 180 kg). Fifteen distinctive races have evolved to fill various niches for which there are no other competitors – but four races are extinct and a fifth is now represented by a single male.

Two species of seals are found in the waters around the Galapagos Islands, both of which are endemic. The Galapagos fur seal is the only tropical representative of a sub-Antarctic genus and is active by night, while the other, the Galapagos sea lion, is active by day. Even more remarkably there are two species of bat which are also endemic to the islands, together with three races of native rat, including a recently discovered giant race, previously known only from fossil remains.

The bird populations include both migratory sea birds, such as the waved albatross which visit the islands to breed, and 28 endemic species of land birds. Over 750,000 pairs of breeding sea birds are found on the islands, including the largest known colony of masked booby in the world, as well as endemic species such as the Galapagos penguin and the Galapagos dark-rumped petrel.

Chile

THE ATACAMA DESERT

*The cold, dry coastal strip
of northern Chile and southern Peru.*

The Atacama Desert lies in northern Chile between the Andes and the Pacific Ocean. Access is from Iquique, Tocopilla or Antofagasta, all of which are served by airports. The southern end of the desert is about 500 miles (805 km) north of Santiago.

THE Atacama Desert stretches for about 600 to 700 miles (965 to 1,126 km) along the coastal strip of northern Chile, lying between the Pacific Ocean to the west and the Andes to the east. The mountains of the Cordillera de la Costa are about 5,000 feet (1,525 m) high with the highest peaks rising to 6,560 feet (2,000 m). On their western side they slope steeply to the coast, frequently ending in abrupt cliffs up to 1,600 feet (488 m) high. The desert itself is a high-altitude depression on the eastern side of the Cordillera de la Costa that extends to the foot of the Precordillera of the Andes in the east.

The typical surface of the desert is a salt pan, with its eastern margin formed of alluvial fans skirting the Precordillera ranges. These alluvial fans are frequently accumulations of pebbles, although some are sandy, and even with sand dunes. The whole region is extremely dry, and what little water does reach the desert soon evaporates or sinks underground. The area is much colder than other areas in the same latitudes, with average summer temperatures of about 66 degrees Fahrenheit (19 degrees C.) on the coast; the desert, at a higher altitude, is colder still.

The coastline of Chile is washed by the Humboldt Current, a cold current flowing north from the Antarctic which causes a temperature inversion of cold air over the sea with warmer air higher in the atmosphere. This inversion produces frequent fogs and stratus clouds but no rain. Meteorological records show that the coastal towns of Iquique and Antofagasta have heavy rain only two to four times in a century.

Two extraordinary natural features are combined, to create one of the driest places on earth. On the eastern side of the Andes, in the Amazonian basin of Brazil, rain is plentiful, but the moist air from this region is blocked by the mountains so that no rain reaches the Atacama. Artesian water is known to exist in several places, but its very high boron content makes it unsuitable for irrigation. Nevertheless, large areas have been planted

with tamarugoes, an acacia-like plant that quickly sends roots downward into the water table. Once established, this plant is used as a feed for sheep.

Right, a herd of llama grazing a rare patch of scrub vegetation on the edge of the Atacama Desert.

176

Relatively few people live in the region – apart from the direct drawbacks of such a harsh climate there is only a little agriculture, and the main industry of the region is mining. In the early years of this century, the nitrate mines in the north of the region produced as much as 3 million tons and were the focus of territorial disputes with Peru and Bolivia. Today, the territorial disputes are over and barely 780,000 tons of nitrates are produced each year, for synthetic fertilisers have largely secured the market.

Copper is abundant in the region, and mines have been developed at Chuquicamata in the Andes and at Paposo on the coast. In many places the rocks are coated with a green veneer caused by the oxidation of copper minerals. The veneer is a hydrated copper chloride called Atacamite, first described from this region, that is typical of copper oxidation in an arid climate.

Above, evaporite deposits form where the mineral-rich streams flow from the Andes onto the eastern margin of the desert.

Desert Conditions

THE formation of a desert depends on a combination of factors. High atmospheric pressure results in the deserts in the polar regions, the Kalahari, Sahara and Arabian deserts; mid-continental position controls the Gobi and other deserts of central Asia. The Mohave desert in the western United States and the Patagonian desert in South America are caused by the rain shadow of the Rocky Mountains and the Andes, and up-welling cold currents on the western coasts of Africa and South America play an important factor here.

On the whole, the world's deserts lie in the latitudinal belts of 20 to 50 degrees north and south of the equator. The criterion for desert status is an average annual rainfall of less than 10 inches (25 cm) per year. This usually means that vegetation is minimal. It is a popular misconception that all deserts are sandy; they may be rocky where the wind removes nearly all the loose products of erosion, or stony where the surface is covered with rock fragments broken by temperature changes. Some deserts are poor grassland and only the Antarctic ice sheet is effectively devoid of life.

177

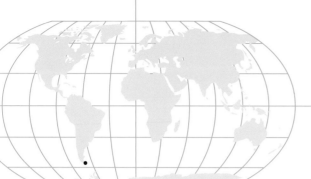

Chile / Argentina

TIERRA DEL FUEGO

This wild and desolate land thrusts southward to a point where three powerful oceans battle.

Tierra del Fuego is an archipelago at the very tip of South America. Flights go from large airports at Buenos Aires or Santiago to smaller ones in Ushuaia, Porvenir or Rio Grande, from where Tierra del Fuego can be explored.

Above, the impressive Martial Mountains (Cerro Martial), behind Ushuaia in the Argentine section of Tierra del Fuego, are part of a spectacular national park.

Facing page, autumn colour at Lago Alto, in the national park.

I N winter fierce storms lash the desolate coast at the southern tip of South America, driven by the freezing, snow-laden winds from the Antarctic seas. In the summer the land near the coast is balmy and mild, though sudden squalls are a threatening reminder that Tierra del Fuego is not far from the wild shores of the Antarctic. The total area of the archipelago is 28,000 square miles (72,520 sq km), of which 70 per cent belongs to Chile, and the rest to Argentina.

Tierra del Fuego forms part of the hook at the tip of the South American continent, a finger of land reaching towards the vast icy wastes of Antarctica just 600 miles (965 km) away. Tierra del Feugo and the Antarctic Peninsula once formed a continuous stretch of land, but the continents began to move apart some 25 million years ago. The similarity in the structure and type of rocks provides strong evidence of how they were once joined.

The fossil record also suggests that many animals and plants that lived in South America also lived in Antarctica.

The archipelago that forms Tierra del Fuego was discovered in 1520 by the Portuguese navigator Fernando de Magellan, who gave the land its name because of the fires lit by the Indians along the coast as he sailed down what is now known as the Strait of Magellan. In 1578 Sir Francis Drake sighted the small group of islands later named by Dutch explorers as Cape Hoorn (Cape Horn). A full survey of Tierra del Fuego was not undertaken until the 19th

in December 1832, when Darwin disembarked and remarked of the mountains and glaciers that it was "scarcely possible to imagine anything more beautiful." Fitzroy named the snow-dusted mountains that range down the Beagle Channel after Darwin. As the tiny ship edged its way down the channel, Darwin looked for native American Indians. It is estimated that there were about 3,000 Yahgan Indians in the 1830s, but Western diseases, the destruction of their hunting grounds and other changes forced on them by European settlers decimated the population.

Patagonia

TIERRA del Fuego is sometimes counted as part of the region of Patagonia, an area that covers the southern part of South America. Patagonia as a whole is noted for its rugged beauty, and has spectacular mountains with two little-known ice fields and desolate plains. Geographically, the region is roughly divided into two: the Andes and the tablelands. The tablelands rise from the coast to the foothills of the Andes in a series of steps, and the overlay of soft sedimentary rocks is deeply incised by a number of gorges that run from west to east. Only a few of these gorges still carry permanent rivers, and most canyons are dry. In some gorges, saltwater lakes have formed. The Chilean part of Patagonia has magnificent fjords, carved out by the glaciers that once covered the region.

The Andes

THE Andes, which form the western part of Patagonia, make a rocky spine that runs the entire length of South America. The range is about 5,500 miles (8,850 km) long, and 400 miles (644 km) across at the widest part in Bolivia. The highest peak is Aconcagua, which, at 22,800 feet (6950 m), is the tallest mountain in the western hemisphere. The Andes are still growing – movements in the earth's crust are forcing the mountains up at an estimated rate of 4 inches (10 cm) every 100 years. Glaciers from the last Ice Age also remain, and are still shaping peaks and scraping out U-shaped valleys in some parts of this magnificent mountain range.

century, when the British Admiralty sent two expeditions to explore it. The second of these voyages was undertaken by Captain Robert Fitzroy in a small barque named H.M.S. *Beagle*. Fitzroy wanted to take a naturalist with him when he charted these little-known coasts, and he chose the 22-year-old Charles Darwin.

On 27 December 1831, the *Beagle* set sail from Plymouth on a journey that was to last almost five years. Tierra del Fuego was reached

Darwin noted the harsh lifestyles of the people, scraping a living from meagre plant life and taking fragile canoes into the mountainous seas. For the Yahgans, the prospect of starvation was never far away. The American Indians were not the only people to have suffered from the harsh climate and sparse food supply. In the 1580s, a group of 300 Spanish settlers founded a colony 40 miles (64 km) from Punta Arenas; all but one died of starvation.

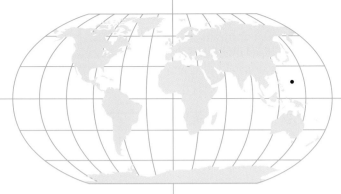

THE MARIANA TRENCH

A cleft in the deep ocean bed on the edge of the Philippine Sea in the Pacific Ocean.

The Mariana Trench is centred on 15 degrees North, 147 degrees 30 minutes East. However, on the surface of the ocean there is nothing to indicate the great depth below. Vessels of all shapes and sizes pass over the area, particularly merchant shipping between the Philippines and North America, and between Japan and Australia.

Right, the pale forms of crabs, molluscs and anemones can be identified living on the edge of the Mariana Trench.

Facing page, the extraordinary gape of the deep-sea Pseudoscopalus, a fish which can eat prey larger than itself.

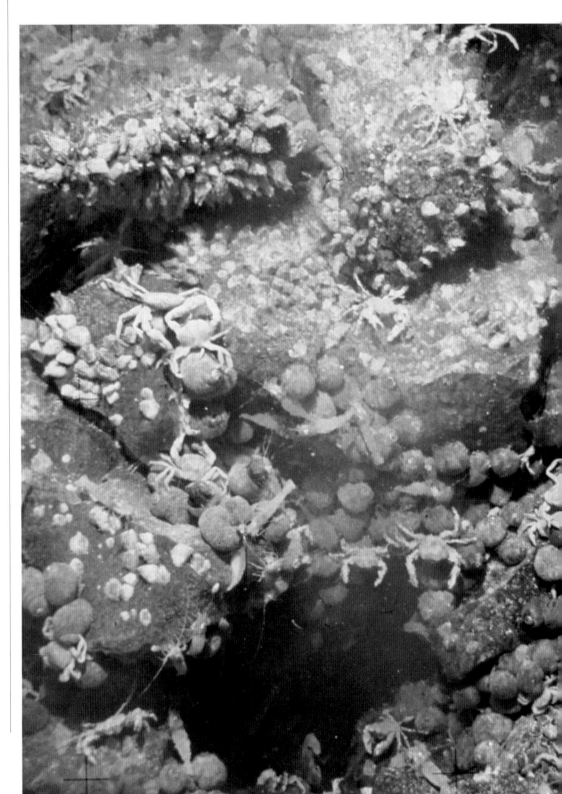

MANKIND has never been able to resist the challenge of exploring the unknown, and remarkable technological advances have made it possible to probe the mysteries that lie in the most inhospitable environment on earth – the deep ocean plains and trenches. There is much still to explore, with 141 million square miles (365 million sq km) of the world's surface covered with ocean at an average depth of 2.3 miles (3.7 km), compared to the land mass of 39 million square miles (63 million sq km). The abyssal plain sea bed lying between 1.2 and 3.7 miles (2 and 6 km) deep has only recently become accessible, and even then it requires specialised, sophisticated equipment. Where there is significant geological activity such as

submarine volcanoes there are even deeper areas known as trenches, which are at depths in excess of 3.7 miles (6 km). Trenches occur in all the major oceans of the world but are best represented in the Pacific; the Mariana Trench to the east of the Philippines is the deepest of all.

The challenge of exploring and understanding what lives at these amazing depths is enormous. Even to take samples using a vertical grab would require more than 7 miles (11 km) of wire of immense strength. The pressure at these depths is more than 1,100 atmospheres, and so far human ingenuity has only succeeded as far as being able to send a manned submersible, made from titanium, to depths of 3.7 miles (6 km), which is just to the edge of the trench.

In the quest for knowledge, however, these hadal regions have been explored remotely by grabs, sensors and most recently with video cameras, and a flourishing, specialised animal community made up of examples from both familiar and less familiar marine groups has been discovered. The variety of species in the trench is reduced in comparison to the abyssal plains, with only a few starfish and brittlestars and other groups such as sipunculids and echiuroids, but there are many species of crabs and other crustaceans, polychaete worms, bivalve molluscs and sea cucumbers. No light penetrates to these depths, and yet when these creatures are illuminated by artificial light they prove just as colourful as their counterparts in the waters above.

Many of the animals appear to grow to a much greater size than their equivalents even in the abyssal depths. Around some of the hydrothermal vents in the more active regions, sea anemones which are elsewhere no more than a few inches in length may grow up to 4 or 5 feet (1.2 or 1.5 m), with tentacles over 3 feet (.9 m) long, and tube worms normally inches in length measuring up to 4 feet (1.2 m) long.

Hydrothermal Vents

THE existence of hydrothermal vents was only discovered in 1976. Springs heated by molten rock below the sea bed can raise the temperature of these very deep waters from their normal 36 degrees Fahrenheit (2 degrees C.) to temperatures as high as 716 degrees Fahrenheit (380 degrees C.). A unique fauna including "giant" creatures – clams, mussels, brightly coloured tube worms and anemones – are associated with these vents.

These hydrothermal waters appear either as diffuse emissions at temperatures between 41 and 482 degrees Fahrenheit (5 and 250 degrees C.), or as very high temperature emissions at between 518 and 716 degrees Fahrenheit (270 and 380 degrees C.). The high temperature emissions appear as black smoker chimneys formed by the precipitation of minerals, or as white smokers from which a cloudy plume of heated fluid escapes rapidly. Despite the enormously high temperature of the escaping liquid it soon dissipates and falls to the ambient temperature of 36 degrees Fahrenheit (2 degrees C.).

Some animals that live on the walls of the black smokers are able to tolerate temperatures as high as 662 degrees Fahrenheit (350 degrees C.), notably some tube-dwelling polychaete worms, and certain species of limpet-like molluscs which graze the bacteria growing on the walls of the black smokers. Studies so far have only identified one or two species of fish in connection with such warm-water vents.

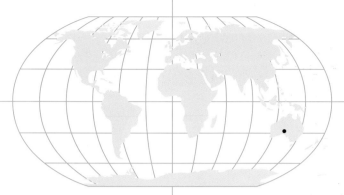

Australia

OPALS AT COOBER PEDY

Precious stones with a unique "fire".

Coober Pedy lies in the Stuart Range of South Australia at the eastern edge of the Great Victoria Desert. It is about 500 miles (805 km) by road from Adelaide along the Stuart Highway, and the railway from Adelaide to Alice Springs passes near by.

AUSTRALIA is well known for its mineral production and it is one of the richest countries in the world in terms of its mineral

Coober Pedy. Subsequent finds were made at Andamooka in 1930 and at Mintabie in 1931, and these discoveries have developed into

Above, a particularly fine example of a boulder opal shows the firey colours for which this stone is so highly valued.

Facing page, a miner holds up a raw opal, just visible as a flash of blue in the stone.

reserves. But there is one mineral more than any other that identifies Australia: opal. As much as 90 per cent of the world's gem-quality opal is mined in Australia, and about three-quarters of that comes from the state of South Australia. And just as opal is something peculiarly Australian, so is the method of mining and the lifestyle of the mining community.

Common opal was first found in Australia in 1849, but in 1915 precious opal was found at

major fields. Although opal mining remains a relatively small-scale operation, it nevertheless contributes some $30 million to Australia's economy every year.

At first sight, Coober Pedy looks much like many other remote mining areas. Dirt roads cross the area and there are spoil tips of waste rock, but there are no drill rigs, no winding gear over shafts and virtually no buildings. But strange circular mounds with a central hole create the appearance of a volcanic area studded

with small ash volcanoes. To discover the
mines and miners at Coober Pedy you must,
quite literally, go beneath the surface. Each of
these small mounds has an access shaft to a
separate underground world. The soft
sandstone rock of the desert can often be dug
quite easily by hand with shovel and pick-axe,
although explosives are also used. Most opals
occur in the first 80 feet (24 m) below ground,
but many workings are much shallower. Some
opal is found in discreet pockets within the
rock but much occurs in veins. Each miner has
a small area that he can work; the technique is
largely serendipitous, with the miner
excavating his given area of ground in the hope
of finding a major vein that will make his
fortune. Stories abound of men who have
come to Coober Pedy to dig their patch of

ground, only to give up after months of hard
work when they have found nothing and
their money has run out. In some cases,
another miner arriving to work the same area
subsequently "strikes it rich". Such miners are
the lucky ones, for although most make a
reasonable living, relatively few make fortunes.

Below about 20 feet (6 m) the overlying rock
has absorbed much of the searing heat of the
desert sun and conditions are comparatively
cool. The early opal miners quickly realised

that it would be possible to live in relative
comfort underground in dwellings that would
cost little to build. So today's miners and their
families live in modern subterranean comfort.
Many of these homes are very large and quite
luxurious – some even have swimming pools
underground – while just a short distance
above the sun beats down relentlessly.
However, life in the opal fields it is still hard,
and many miners and their families eventually
return to an easier life elsewhere.

Formation of Opal

PERCOLATING ground water is
often rich in minerals; the
waters saturated with calcium
carbonate that seep through
limestone to form stalactites and
stalagmites are perhaps the best
known example. In the right
circumstance such waters,
instead of simply and indiscrim-
inately depositing their mineral
content from solution, will
concentrate deposition in
pockets and veins.

Geologists know opal as
hydrated amorphous silica
($SiO_2.nH_2O$), where the water
content is generally less than 10
per cent. It forms by deposits
from silica-rich water and is
probably derived from silica gel;
in other words it is like a solid
jelly, and it is considerably
softer than quartz. During the
solidification process many
extremely thin films are caught
in the gel, and it is these that
provide the fiery slices of light
and colour in precious opal.
Silica-rich water may occur in
many ways and is very common
in siliceous hot springs, so many
deposits around such clear,
non-sulphurous springs are
opaline in character. But there
is a world of difference between
an opaline deposit and gem-
quality precious opal. The
colour of opal varies from the
rare black opal through to
white but perhaps the most
famous are the red or orange-
tinted fire opals. As a good
quality opal turns in the light, a
myriad of reflections and
refractions from within make it
appear alive inside; a good
orange-red opal seems to be full
of flickering flames. Such stones
can command high prices in the
jewellery markets, where they
are normally cut into rounded
cabochon shapes.

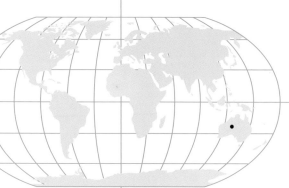

Australia
AYERS ROCK
AND MOUNT OLGA

The largest monolith in the world in the midst of the Australian desert.

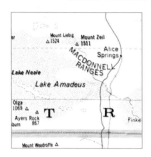

Alice Springs, in central Australia, is accessible by road, rail and air from Adelaide; the Uluru National Park is some 250 miles (400 km) to the south. It is also possible to drive or fly direct to Ayers Rock.

AYERS Rock lies near the south-western corner of Northern Territory in the dry red heart of Australia. This enormous, orange-brown rock is 1½ miles (2.4 km) long, 1 mile (1.6 km) wide and towers 1,143 feet (348 m) high above the surrounding desert plain – the largest exposed monolith in the world. Dusty outback roads lead from Alice Springs to the motels near the rock, allowing spectators time to climb up and experience the spectacle of the rock in the changing light of morning and evening. As the sun sets the rock appears to

glow from an inner fire as it changes from the dry brown of the day to an intense fiery red, before becoming a black silhouette in the fading light. To those rising for an early vigil, the dawn light reveals the rock in even more beautiful pastel shades. Climbing the rock is not difficult, but the blistering heat of the Australian desert makes the ascent a serious undertaking. The most important item to carry with you is water, for without it dehydration, sunstroke and heat exhaustion are certain dangers, as well as the risks from prolonged

Right, sunset paints the extraordinary tillite formation of Ayers Rock a deep, glowing shade of orange.

184

exposure to excess ultra-violet (U.V.) radiation.

Ayers Rock was first seen by a European in 1872 when the Australian explorer, Ernest Giles, was crossing this part of the desert. However, long before Europeans came to Australia, and the British began settling and transporting convicts there, the Aborigines had known the rock as Uluru. There are many Aboriginal paintings around the foot of the rock, and the place is an important feature in their culture. Equally, the rock has inspired Western artists, poets and photographers.

Ayers Rock is impressive mainly for its size. Some 16 miles (24 km) away to the west, Mount Olga is famed because of its beauty. Here the original single monolith has been sculpted by nature into an inselberg group – a fascinating landscape of miniature monoliths jumbled together. Mount Olga itself stands 1,500 feet (457 m) above the surrounding plain, some 3,507 feet (1,069 m) above sea level. There are about 30 rounded hills in the groups that are called collectively, the Olgas. Ernest Giles named the hills after the Queen of Spain, but the Aborigines have known these hills for centuries as Katajuta, aptly describing the hills as "the mountain with many heads".

In this small group of hills covering an area of 11 square miles (28 sq km), determined travellers encounter deep gorges and ravines carved over millions of years by rare torrential rains. Precipitous cliffs flank these cuttings, providing shady walks that offer a cool retreat from the searing heat of the desert. Here it is possible to relax and enjoy nature's handiwork without the threat of being burned alive by the sun.

The spectacular steep-sided domes of Australia's second most famous rock formation, the Olgas.

Geological History

AYERS Rock and the Olgas are formed of tillite, an ancient glacial deposit that seems at odds with its present location in the middle of a hot desert. However, the rock was formed about 680 million years ago when Australia was located in much higher latitudes. Similarly, ancient glacial rocks are found at many places in countries of the Southern Hemisphere, and indicate that ice ages have occurred at several times in the geological past. Such rocks are valuable climatic indicators, helping to confirm the former positions of the continents that have been determined by other means, such as palaeomagnetism.

The strata at Ayers Rock are approximately vertical, while those at Mount Olga are close to horizontal, a contrast that may explain the difference in patterns of erosion between the two outcrops. Two main types of erosion have affected both areas: rain and thermal erosion. Despite their desert locations they do have a measurable rainfall of a few inches per year, but this tends to fall in one or two major storms every few years, when raging torrents of water flood down the sides of the rocks, washing away all loose particles in their path. Thermal erosion is caused by the extreme temperature variation between very hot days and very cold nights, when the constant expansion and contraction of the rock eventually causes fragments to break away.

THE GREAT
BARRIER REEF

*The largest complex of coral reefs and islands
anywhere in the world.*

The Great Barrier Reef extends
from Lady Elliot Island in the
south to the tip of Cape York
in the north. Access is generally
unrestricted, and organised boat
trips visit the reefs and cays.
There are a few areas which are
designated as highly vulnerable,
and where there is strict
protection.

The Discovery of the Great Barrier Reef

CAPTAIN Cook discovered
the Great Barrier Reef
during his epic voyage in 1770,
which involved charting the
waters off the east coast of
Australia. The reef was very
nearly the downfall of the
expedition, for Cook had in
ignorance sailed northwards for
over 620 miles (998 km) inside
the reef. It was only when he
reached Cape Tribulation that
he became aware of the
labyrinth of reefs which lay to
his seaward side and the
consequent danger to him and
his crew. Their ship *Endeavour*
eventually grounded on a
small reef not far from Cape
Tribulation, and only after
jettisoning many provisions and
much equipment could she be
pulled off and the voyage
continued.

*Above, many of the sea creatures
which live on the reef are brilliantly
coloured, like this coral or red
grouper fish.*

*Facing page, the little jewel of
Green Island is an atoll emerging
from the reef, off Cairns.*

THE Great Barrier Reef extends along the
east coast of Australia for a distance of more
than 1,250 miles (2,011 km) – biologically,
geologically and scenically one of the greatest
natural wonders of the world. It is a major
natural feature which justifiably arouses
superlatives, but its recognition as a World
Heritage Site, a Biosphere Reserve and a
marine park reflect the importance of the
area in global terms.

The Great Barrier Reef comprises around
2,900 reefs, ranging in size from 0.004 square
miles (0.01 sq km) to 38.6 square miles (100 sq
km), over 300 reef shingle islands or cays, of
which around 100 are permanently vegetated;
and a further 600 high islands, many of which
have their own fringing reefs. The total area is
134,633 square miles (348,698 sq km) – greater
than the land area of Great Britain.

The reef, a major geological feature in its
own right, is essentially made up of living
animals or coral polyps, similar in design to the
sea anemones found on the shore. These tiny,
primitive animals live in vast colonies, each of
which was derived from an individual polyp
which has undergone innumerable divisions.
The coral comprises a soft body surrounded
by an exoskeleton of limestone, which creates
the fabric of the reef. A living reef is the

product of thousands of years of life and
death: the bulk of the reef is made up of the
empty skeletons of past generations of polyps
which are covered by a thin veneer of
living organisms.

Coral reefs are restricted to waters which
maintain a temperature of between 72 and
82 degrees Fahrenheit (22 and 28 degrees C.)
throughout the year, resulting in a habitat
capable of supporting a very complex ecology –
the most diverse ecosystem known on earth.
The Great Barrier Reef contains over 400
species of hard and soft coral. The hard,
reef-forming corals occur in many different
shapes and sizes, and include mushroom corals,
brain corals and staghorn corals, in colours
ranging from red and yellow to black. In
addition, over 4,000 species of molluscs ranging
from chitons and snails to giant clams and
octopus have been identified, together with
countless numbers of sponges, anemones,
worms, crustaceans and echinoderms.

Coral reefs throughout the world are famous
for the variety of fish which frequent them.
Over 1,500 species of fish are known to live in
and around the Great Barrier Reef, presenting
a kaleidoscope of colour and pattern as shoals
dart one way and then another. The reef is also
important for a number of species of whale,
including minke, killer and humpback. These
waters are an important breeding area for the
humpback whales; mothers and suckling
calves are sighted regularly. It is also home to
six of the seven species of sea turtle in the
world, all of which are endangered, and which
depend on the remote islands of the reef for
safe nesting sites. The mysterious dugong also
finds a safe haven in the sea grass beds that
lie in the shallow waters off many of the
reef islands.

The islands are also important to many
species of waders and sea birds. Over 240
species nest on the low islands of sand and
coral, with shearwaters, tropicbirds, frigatebirds,
six species of terns including the roseate tern,
noddies, white-bellied sea eagle and osprey.

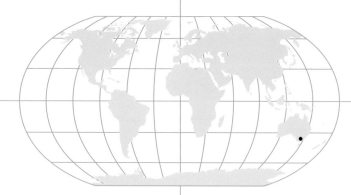

Australia
DUCK-BILLED
PLATYPUS

The elusive duck-billed platypus inhabits the banks of rivers and streams in east and south Australia and Tasmania.

From either Adelaide or Melbourne, the habitat of the duck-billed platypus needs to be investigated with the help of local knowledge. This elusive animal is seldom encountered by accident.

The Spiny Anteater –Echidna

ONLY two species of spiny anteater survive, and together with the duck-billed platypus, they are the only surviving monotremes. The long-beaked spiny anteater is endemic to New Guinea, while the short-beaked spiny anteater is found only in Australia. It is widespread and numerous, surviving on a specialised diet of ants and termites. Although it is found in the hot, arid interior of Australia, the short-beaked echidna lacks sweat glands, and avoids the scorching heat of the day by digging itself into deep burrows, emerging only at night. Like its close relative the duck-billed platypus, it detects its prey using highly sensitive electromagnetic receptors on the tip of its snout. In the hot desert conditions of the interior, the echidna prefers to feed on termites rather than ants, as the termites have a higher water content.

Right, the strange duck-billed platypus is a vital link in the evolutionary chain.

Facing page, the short-beaked spiny anteater is another egg-laying mammal.

THE duck-billed platypus is a highly specialised animal which has adapted to fill a very specific niche in the marine environment. It has a sleek, streamlined body covered in short brown fur. The front paws are fan-shaped and webbed to help propel it through the water, suiting its aquatic and burrowing life style. The back feet act as a rudder and it has a large flattened tail, similar to a beaver, which it uses as a stabiliser. Its small eyes and nostrils can close when under water, and it has no external ears. The most characteristic and striking feature however, is its large, flat, leathery, duck-like bill – very sensitive to touch and able to detect the weak electromagnetic fields made by its invertebrate prey. It feeds by disturbing the sediments in the bottom of the rivers and streams where it lives, and then picking up the loosened crustaceans and molluscs. Although it lacks teeth, it does have hardened patches in its mouth which it uses to crush the shells of the molluscs.

The platypus together with the two species of spiny anteaters, or echidna, are the only remaining living members of one of the earliest groups of mammals to evolve – the monotremes. The earliest mammals discovered so far in the fossil records, some 210 million years old, are thought to have been small rodent-like creatures with a nocturnal habit, probably giving birth to very immature young rather than laying eggs. The ancestors of the living monotremes appeared around 140 million years ago, before the vast ancient continent of Gondwana divided. Fossils of monotremes have been discovered in South America, but here the evolution and rapid diversification of placental mammals resulted in them losing the battle for survival. The early separation of Australia from the main continental land mass meant that there was less competition, and although recent discoveries show that placental mammals had reached Australia before it separated, they did not survive here. The duck-billed platypus and the short beaked spiny anteater are living examples of a vital evolutionary stage,

providing an invaluable insight into the process of evolution from reptile to placental mammal.

An egg-laying mammal, the female platypus produces two or three yolky, white, leathery,

188

soft-shelled eggs, which it lays in a nest deep in a burrow in the side of a river. The eggs are incubated for around 10 days until they hatch, at which time the young feed off milk produced by specialised sweat glands of the mother, which, in the absence of nipples, oozes onto the fur from where is it lapped up by the young.

The other monotremes and marsupials, which do not lay eggs but give birth to very undeveloped young, all have a pouch in which they carry their babies. This ensures the developing animal is maintained at the correct temperature and is well fed without confining the parent to the nest or den. Progressive steps in evolutionary development proceed from the mother duck-billed platypus, with no pouch or nipples, to the spiny anteater with a pouch but no nipples, to the marsupials with both a pouch and nipples.

TASMANIA

Some of the finest remnants of a vast, ancient rainforest are found in Tasmania where over a quarter of the island is still a true wilderness.

Tasmania lies off the south-east coast of Australia, separated from the continent by the Bass Strait. It is a short onward hop from the mainland of Australia with flights to Devonport, Hobart or Launceston, or via an overnight ferry ride from Melbourne to Devonport.

Extinct or Not?

THE Thylacine, or Tasmanian tiger, is extinct according to the official records. Although it once roamed the forests of the Australian continent, it was exterminated around 3,000 years ago by competition from the dingo, introduced by the Aborigines. Afterwards it was confined to Tasmania, but even here it was declared extinct in 1936. Since then there have been periodic reported sightings of what are believed to be the Thylacine in the more remote parts of the Tasmanian wilderness. It is slightly smaller than a wolf, with a massive wolf-like head and jaws with an exceptional gape. The tail is that of a kangaroo, broad at the base and so stiff it cannot even be wagged. To compound the mystery and legends surrounding the Thylacine, sightings have recently been reported in Western Australia, where it is supposed to have been extinct for over 3,000 years.

Right, cushion plants like green velvet grow in the remote and mountainous South West National Park.

Facing page, the Tasmanian devil is a carnivorous marsupial endemic to the island.

SOME 250 million years ago, Tasmania – along with the rest of Australia, New Zealand, Antarctica, South America, Africa and India – was part of the great southern continent of Gondwana. This massive continent extended over half the globe and much of it was covered in temperate rainforest. Some of the best remaining areas of this rainforest are found today in Tasmania. A large part of this is contained within the 4,175 square miles (10,813 sq km) which make up the Tasmanian Wilderness World Heritage Site, incorporating four national parks, two state reserves, two conservation areas and a number of state forests. True wilderness of any sort is an increasingly rare commodity, and this great expanse of rainforest is a unique and invaluable resource to be carefully protected and treasured.

This wilderness area extends from the coast into the heart of Tasmania, rising from sea level to altitudes over 5,300 feet (1,615 m). The coastal margins of the temperate coastal rainforest support both evergreen and deciduous trees. In this damp yet mild climate many species thrive, reaching tremendous heights and producing timber of the very highest quality prized the world over, and subject to the ever-present threat of commercial over-exploitation.

The temperate rainforest of Tasmania contrasts markedly with tropical rainforests in having only a very small number of tree species – rarely more than eight – although there is a luxuriant growth of understorey plants and epiphytes such as mosses, ferns and lichens, all jostling for a foothold. The characteristic tree is the myrtle beech, and with the Huon pine, of which some ancient specimens over 2,000 years old still survive, and the King Billy pine, they represent a true relic of the Gondwanaland rainforest. In some areas stands of eucalypts, the tallest flowering plants in the world, form a towering canopy reaching heights of 300 feet (91 m). In the higher regions alpine plants fight for survival, the trees stunted and knurled by the cold and the wind.

The timing of the separation of Australia from Gondwanaland resulted in the unique fauna of marsupial and monotreme mammals, and the subsequent separation of Tasmania has resulted in a number of species of animals, birds and plants being endemic to the island. The fauna includes four endemic marsupials: the Tasmanian devil, the pale Tasmanian bettong, the rufous wallaby and the thylacine or Tasmanian wolf, which once ranged widely but is now thought to be extinct even here. Among 150 recorded bird species is Australia's rarest, the budgie-sized, brilliantly coloured orange-bellied parrot.

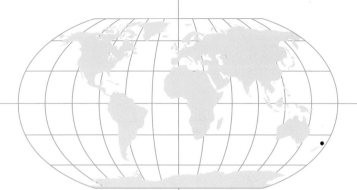

New Zealand

ROTORUA

Rotorua lies about 120 miles (193 km) south-east of Auckland and around 260 miles (418 km) north of Wellington. It is easily accessible by road, or by air to Rotokawa, 5 miles (8 km) north-east of the town. Once in Rotorua the hot springs are everywhere.

A volcanic centre with geysers, mud pools, hot springs and multi-coloured lakes.

Above: steam rises from Waiotapu, the "champagne lake", which has a constant water temperature of 75 degrees C.

Facing page: geysers of naturally hot water shoot from the sulphurous rocks at Rotorua.

Geothermal activity at Rotorua, near the centre of New Zealand's north island, has attracted tourists here for many years. More recently the Maori settlement and the Maori Arts and Crafts Institute have opened up to give an insight into the tribal customs of the earliest New Zealand settlers. The Maoris have traditionally used the hot springs for cooking, washing and heating, but the springs are also reputed to have healing properties, particularly for arthritis and rheumatism, and the Queen Elizabeth Hospital still uses the sulphurous waters in its treatment regime.

Nowhere in Rotorua is far from thermal activity of some sort. The many spas in the town include the Bath House, founded in 1908, with its aura of Edwardian sophistication. A popular boat trip is to Mokoia Island, in the middle of Lake Rotorua, with a dip in Hinemoa's hot pool. On the edge of the town is the Whakarewarewa thermal area and Geyser Flat, where Pohutu, the "splashing" geyser, can be seen. It is the greatest geyser in New Zealand, although somewhat erratic, usually spouting about every 20 minutes to a height of 100 feet (30 m). Normally the smaller "Prince of Wales Feathers" geyser close by provides a display shortly before Pohutu erupts, like a prelude to the main act to ensure that the audience is attending. There are bubbling, sulphurous mud pools near by, and the rock is hot beneath your feet.

About 6 miles (10 km) south-east of Rotorua along Highway 5 are the famous blue and green lakes of Waimangu – hot water lakes in an extinct volcano crater. The water is heated at depth, and dissolves different minerals in its upward passage that colour the water. The source of the water in each lake is probably different, and each has separate routes to the surface, leaching various minerals from the rocks to make the different colours. Iron oxides in the low cliffs surrounding the lakes produce a contrasting red colour; in some places a yellow colour is the result of sulphurous deposits. Throughout most of the 19th century famous White and Pink Terraces graced Waimangu, covering an area of more than 12 acres (5 hectares). The dazzling White Terraces looked like a giant marble staircase. Unfortunately, an eruption of nearby Tarawera Mountains destroyed this famous landmark on 10 June 1886, along with several villages, burying everything under a huge shower of incandescent ash and debris. However, hot springs continued to bubble in the area, and in 1900 a new geyser, the Waimangu Geyser, appeared. At the time it was the most powerful geyser in the world, firing an explosive mixture of mud, steam and water as high as 1,500 feet (457 m) into the air. In four years its power had decreased, and by 1908 the geyser had become extinct once more.

How Hot Springs and Geysers Work

THERE are three basic criteria for hot springs: a good supply of ground water, a source of heat, and a suitable vent from the underground reservoir to the surface. New Zealand's wet climate ensures plentiful ground water, and the molten rock below ground provides a steady supply of heat. After a volcanic eruption residual lava frequently slips back into the magma chamber, leaving voids in the rocks above that can be filled with water, providing reservoirs for hot springs. If there is no obstruction in the passage from the reservoir to the surface, a hot spring will form, gently bubbling as the hot water continually rises towards the surface.

Geysers work on a similar principle, but they erupt scalding hot water fountains – some every few minutes, some with hours or days between eruptions – and they are not always regular. The essential factor that changes a hot spring into a geyser is an obstruction in the passage leading to the surface. As the water in the reservoir heats it expands: if that expansion is confined by an obstruction the pressure increases and so does the boiling point of water. The water becomes super-heated until the pressure can no longer be contained and the water rushes upwards. The reduction in pressure promotes instant boiling and an explosive release of steam in the reservoir that forces the water upwards ever faster. The result is a spurting, steaming column of super-heated water – a geyser.

New Zealand

GLACIERS OF THE SOUTHERN ALPS

Tongues of ice reach down into the rain forests.

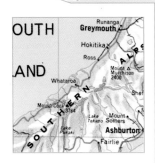

The snout of the Tasman Glacier is some 160 miles by road from Christchurch, on New Zealand's South Island. Westland National Park is about 140 miles from Westport, and accessible by air from Christchurch.

T HE Southern Alps form a high mountain barrier along the western side of the South Island of New Zealand. The highest point is Mount Cook at 12,349 feet (3,764 m), the highest mountain in New Zealand, and a mere 20 miles (32 km) from the summit westward across the coastal strip to the Pacific Ocean. To the east the land descends more slowly for some 80 miles (129 km) across the Canterbury Plains to the coast. The westerly winds that blow in from the Tasman Sea are laden with moisture, and as the damp air rises against the mountains it drops heavy snowfalls along the range that feed the glaciers – the three most

Right, a party of tourists negotiates the hazzards at the edge of the Franz Josef Glacier.

Facing page, the long snout of the Fox Glacier pours down into the forest.

194

famous are the Tasman, Fox and Franz Josef glaciers.

The glaciers on the western side of the mountains are short and steep, tumbling downward like frozen cataracts that reach into the dense, subtropical evergreen rain forests. The juxtaposition of ice and trees is extraordinary, and it is indeed rare to see these features of contrasting climates so close together. Elsewhere in the world the two keep their own company and do not mix. On the eastern side of the range the glaciers are quite different in character, with the higher reaches typically steep and rugged, patterned by networks of crevasses that make travel difficult. Lower down these glaciers flow to low altitudes, and the Tasman Glacier reaches almost as far as the central plain.

The Fox and Franz Josef glaciers flow to the west, the latter reaches 7 miles (11 km) in length, although both have receded in recent years. Only 15 miles (24 km) apart, both are located within the Westland National Park, an area which covers 217,000 acres (87,817 hectares) and includes alpine peaks, snow fields, glaciers, forests, rivers and lakes. Lake Mathieson provides a famous view of the three major peaks – Cook, Tasman and La Perouse – reflected in its calm waters.

The Tasman Glacier, which flows down from Mount Cook, has been described as its crowning glory and is an an impressive sight. The glacier forms a narrow tongue of ice 17 miles (27 km) long that widens in places to as much as 2 miles (3 km) and covers a total area of about 20 square miles (52 sq km). In places it is 2,000 feet (610 m) thick, and is the largest glacier in New Zealand. This is also a very active glacier, flowing as fast as 20 to 25 inches (51 to 64 cm) per day. Despite its high speed the glacier is gradually retreating: its snout is only 2,500 feet (762 m) above sea level, where temperatures are relatively high, and the rate of melting and evaporation is greater than its flow.

The Changing Climate of New Zealand

THE climate of New Zealand, like many other continents, has gone through change over time. Apart from the natural variation in the climate of the earth as a whole, the continents continually move and change latitude under the influence of plate tectonics, or continental drift.

More than 500 million years ago, New Zealand was a part of the ancient super-continent of Gondwana. New Zealand lay on the eastern edge, between Australia, Tasmania and Antarctica, and at that time lay about 35 degrees north of the equator. During the next 250 million years Gondwana drifted southward until Australia and New Zealand lay close to the South Pole, where they experienced widespread glaciation. Continuing rotation of Gondwana over the next 120 million years took New Zealand northward again into warmer temperate or sub-tropical regions, and the ice sheets disappeared. At about this time Gondwana began to break apart to form the different continents that we know today, but first New Zealand made another voyage southwards, still attached to Antarctica.

Some 80 million years ago the Tasman Sea began to open between Australia and New Zealand, and some 20 million years later, as that opening ceased, Australia and then New Zealand also began to separate from Antarctica. While New Zealand moved north, Antarctica moved south into its present polar position. New Zealand was again glaciated in the last Ice Age, until the earth began to warm again about 10,000 years ago. Today, New Zealand's glaciers continue to retreat, and the long-term effects of current global warming may be to melt them completely.

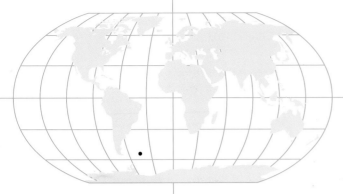

BLUE
WHALE

The blue whale ranges over the vast tracts of the world's oceans, migrating between the icy polar oceans and the subtropical Indian, Pacific and Atlantic oceans.

There is an increasing traffic in wildlife cruises to the Southern Ocean, on which there is always the chance of seeing one of these mighty animals.

THE blue whale is by far the largest animal ever to have lived on this planet. An adult blue whale will grow to over twice the weight of the Brachiosaurus, the largest dinosaur which ever lived, and about 30 times the weight of an African bull elephant.

It is truly a leviathan; averaging 85 feet (26 m) in length and a recorded maximum of 110 feet (33.5 m), the average weight is a massive 150 tons – equivalent to around 2,400 people. A creature of these gargantuan proportions requires vast amounts of food. An adult blue whale will consume around a million calories a day, equivalent to 1 ton of krill – a small shrimp-like animal – which is its staple diet. The whales feed on the krill by swimming into a shoal and taking enormous mouthfuls of water and krill. The krill are filtered out by

the tongue, which acts as a sort of piston, forcing the water through massive sieve-like structures (baleen) which hang suspended from either side of the roof of the mouth. The tongue of a blue whale is over 10 feet (3 m) thick and heavier than an elephant.

Blue whales once ranged throughout all the oceans of the world, and it is estimated that there were once as many as 250,000 of

these creatures in the Southern Oceans alone. Over recent years, relentless whaling has reduced the numbers to less than 1 per cent of this total. Determining total numbers of the great whales is very difficult, and current estimates of the blue whale population of Antarctica vary from a few hundred to 11,000. Whatever the correct figure, it is dangerously low in comparison to the numbers there once were.

Blue whales migrate over very great distances. In the summer they inhabit polar waters, feeding on the vast shoals of krill near the edges of the pack ice, and as winter approaches they migrate to the warm equatorial waters, undertaking journeys of thousands of miles. One whale is known to have travelled over 1,900 miles (3,055 km) in only 47 days. Such epic journeys take them away from their feeding grounds, and for periods as long as four months they do not feed at all, surviving on reserves they have built up.

The gestation period of the blue whale is 11 months, but a new-born calf is around 23 feet (7m) in length and weighs 2 tons or more, consuming over half a ton of milk per day and doubling in weight in just one week. By the time it is weaned, at about six months old, the calf will have doubled in length, but it will be another four and a half years before it is sexually mature and more or less fully grown.

The blue whale evolved to range throughout the oceans of the world, journeying in solitude or sometimes in pairs, and can live to be 120 years old. Despite this solitary existence they have developed ways of communicating over unimaginable distances producing a note of very low frequency but high intensity. Recorded at 188 decibels, it is the loudest noise known to be produced by a living organism and exceeds that made by a passing jet aircraft. The notes may last for up to 30 seconds, and can be heard by other blue whales over 1,000 miles (1,610 km) away.

Above left, by far the largest of the world's mammals, the blue whale must surface to breathe.

Above right, tiny krill form the bulk of the whale's food.

Facing page, the vast bulk of a blue whale surfaces from the deep, in winter feeding grounds off Mexico.

Sense at Last

BLUE whales have suffered the ravages of ever more efficient commercial hunting, and their numbers have declined from an initial population of 250,000 to an estimated 2,250, of which around 500 to 700 are in the Southern Ocean. Despite restrictions over the last 50 years, and a total ban on catching blue whales imposed in 1967, commercial whaling for other species has continued under the guise of scientific research. In 1994 some sense was seen to prevail with the declaration of a vast whale sanctuary around Antarctica.

Krill – Food for Giants

THE waters of the Antarctic Ocean support a very high concentration of zooplankton. One species, the krill (*Euphausia superba*), a small shrimp-like animal, represents around half the total biomass. The blue whales of the Southern Ocean feed almost exclusively on *Euphausia* while those of the northern oceans rely on closely related genera, primarily *Meganyctiphanes* and *Thysanoessa*. Vast shoals of krill form, turning the surface layers of the ocean into a reddish-brown soup. With the decline in the numbers of great whales feeding on the krill, there is now an imbalance – and man is now looking to exploit this, having already over-exploited its biggest natural predator.

Antarctica

THE ROSS ICE SHELF

The largest ice shelf in Antarctica.

The Ross Ice Shelf is normally reached by ship or aircraft from New Zealand, with the transport of personnel and supplies to the U.S. McMurdo Station and the New Zealand Scott Base. Tourist ships also visit the area, but passengers rarely see little more than the cliffs of the ice front.

Barrier and Highway

WHEN Captain Scott and Ernest Shackleton went to the Antarctic at the turn of the century they still referred to the ice shelf as "The Barrier", but to them it was the highway to the south. During the 1901–3 *Discovery* expedition, Scott marched 400 miles south across the shelf to make a new "farthest south" record. Shackleton passed Scott's farthest south during his own 1907–9 *Nimrod* expedition, and discovered the Beardmore Glacier that leads up and through the Transantarctic Mountains to the polar plateau. Shackleton did not reach the pole; that honour went to the Norwegian Roald Amundsen four years later when he found another route from the shelf to the plateau via the Axel Heiberg Glacier.

Right, the Ross Ice Shelf forms an impenetrable barrier at the edge of the sea ice.

Facing page, early discoverers likened the ice cliffs to the White Cliffs of Dover.

DURING his second great voyage of 1772–75, Captain James Cook became the first man to circumnavigate Antarctica in high latitudes, but he never saw the continent; every attempt he made to sail farther south was thwarted by pack ice. It was not until 1840 that Captain James Clark Ross, already the most experienced Arctic seaman in Britain, sailed south and successfully broke through the belt of pack ice into what is now called the Ross Sea. He discovered Ross

Island, and to the east of it, what he called the Victoria Barrier, of which he wrote "…we might with equal chance of success try to sail through the cliffs of Dover, as to penetrate such a mass."

Ross, like any visitor, was impressed. Ice cliffs 150 to 200 feet (46 to 61 m) high towered over his ships so that he could not see to the south, but the view is one of an unending plain of ice. In fact the Ross Ice Shelf is a sheet of ice approximately triangular in shape, which varies

198

in thickness from about 600 feet (183 m) at its seaward face, the ice front, to more than 4,264 feet (1,300 m) at its landward edge. It covers an area of 209,400 square miles (542,344 sq km), larger than Spain and almost as large as France, and because it is afloat, it rises and falls with the tide. Large sections of the ice shelf break off as tabular icebergs, and the largest ever recorded, 208 by 60 miles (335 by 97 km), had an area of 12,000 square miles (31,080 sq km) – larger than Belgium.

The Ross Ice Shelf is fed by glaciers. Many, such as the Beardmore Glacier, flow through the Transantarctic Mountains, but the ice streams draining Marie Byrd Land may

contribute more ice. A ship sailing in the Ross Sea during the 1950s encountered an iceberg with the corner of a hut protruding from its side, identified as part of a hut from one of Admiral Byrd's Little America stations built some 30 years earlier.

Most of the ice shelf is uncrevassed and makes good travelling country. It is relatively flat, but the state of the surface will dictate the progress of a sledging party. Soft snow surfaces are heavy going, whether the sledges are being pulled by people, dogs or tractors. Sastrugi – hard, wind-blown ridges of snow – are common, and when more than a foot (30 cm) high they can make travelling difficult. It is particularly frustrating when the troughs between the ridges are filled with soft snow, when the surface appears deceptively flat but men and tractors will still flounder.

Ice Shelves

AN ice shelf usually forms where glaciers and ice streams draining the continental ice sheet flow into a bay. As the glaciers flow across the grounding line, typically 1,000 or more feet (305 m) below sea level, the ice begins to float and the different glaciers will coalesce into a single sheet. This sheet will continue to grow until it fills the bay. When it expands outside the confines of the bay, however large the bay may be, the forward part of the ice shelf beyond the "anchor" points at the mouth of the bay becomes unstable and susceptible to the forces of the open ocean. The shelf will then eventually break back to a line connecting the anchor points, and icebergs will be calved. An ice shelf also loses ice by melting from its underside, and this is the source of the cold bottom water that flows north across the floor of the oceans, eventually to rise and oxygenate tropical waters. Although the shelf also gains snowfall over its surface, the net result is a general thinning of the shelf as it extends towards the open sea. The ice front, the seaward edge of the shelf, is about 600 feet (183 m) thick and the ice cliffs are about 60 to 100 feet (18 to 30 m) high. An object left on the surface of the ice shelf will describe a slow downward path as it moves towards the sea.

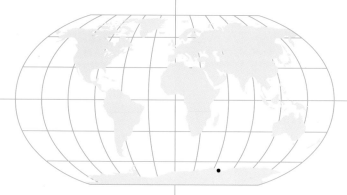

THE LAMBERT GLACIER

The largest and longest glacier in the world.

The Lambert Glacier in Greater Antarctica flows approximately north along the 90 degrees East meridian through the Prince Charles Mountains and into Prydz Bay. Some tour ships sail past the area, but to see the glacier it is necessary to travel inland, best done by helicopter.

THE Lambert Glacier in Greater Antarctica is probably the world's largest glacier. It is up to 40 miles (64 km) wide as it passes through the Prince Charles Mountains, and about 440 miles (708 km) long when its seaward extension, the Amery Ice Shelf, is included. It drains about a fifth of the ice sheet of Greater Antarctica; when the figures are extrapolated, it means that about 12 per cent of all the fresh water on earth passes through the Lambert Glacier. This staggering figure is almost as difficult to comprehend as the glacier itself is to appreciate when standing in the Antarctic. The popular image of an Alpine or Himalayan glacier flowing down the mountains as a river of ice does not really apply to the Lambert Glacier because the scale of it is so huge. A satellite image is the best way to see enough of it to realise that it is a glacier.

Glaciers move slowly. The fastest in the world, Jakobshavn Isbrae in Greenland, flows at 4.3 miles (7 km) per year, whereas the Lambert Glacier slides through the Prince Charles Mountains at about 0.14 (0.23 km) miles per year, eventually accelerating to 0.62 miles (1 km) per year at the Amery Ice Front. Though not a rapid mover, a great mover it certainly is, with about 8.4 cubic miles (35 cu km) of ice

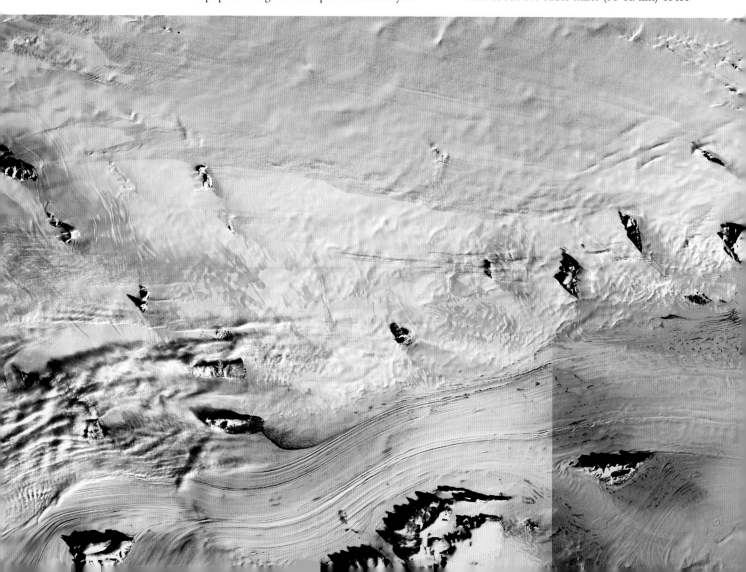

Antarctic Glaciers

ANTARCTIC glaciers are the largest in the world simply because they are the drainage system for the largest ice sheet in the world. Many of the glaciers are more correctly termed ice streams because they do not have well-defined margins. Where a glacier reaches the coast at the head of a bay it starts to float and usually forms an ice shelf. However, a glacier that flows across a straight stretch of coast will not form an ice shelf but will simply flow forward into the sea as it starts to float. Such a projection is called a glacier tongue and is usually very unstable, although the Erebus Glacier tongue that flows into McMurdo Sound frequently projects more than 6 miles (10 km) into the sea before it breaks away. The major ice shelves in Antarctica – the Ross Ice Shelf and the Filchner Ice Shelf – are so large that they are fed by several glaciers and ice streams. The Rutford Glacier, flowing past the Ellsworth Mountains into the south-west corner of the Ronne Ice Shelf, is about 1 mile (1.6 km) thick where it starts to float, the thickest floating ice known anywhere in the world.

passing through the Lambert Glacier every year.

The surface of a glacier such as this, when viewed from the high vantage point of an aircraft, is marked by flow lines – natural ridges in the ice that mark its direction of movement, like the brush strokes of a giant painting in oils on a panoramic canvas. On the surface the ridges are imperceptible, but they may be marked by zones of en échelon crevasses. These are created by differential flow rates in the glacier, but other crevasses may be formed by irregularities in the glacier bed or obstacles in its path. In this case an area of chaotic crevassing may be formed as the surface

gradient changes rapidly; this is called an ice-fall and is equivalent to a waterfall in a river. Some of the crevasses below Gillock Island, formed where the glacier is forced to flow around the island as it enters the Amery Ice Shelf, are more than 440 yards (402 m) wide and up to 25 miles (40 km) long – larger, indeed, than some Alpine glaciers.

These enormous crevasses or rifts are bridged by snow and present a daunting prospect to a traveller whose route lies across them. Yet despite their size they are relatively safe to cross, because the additional weight of a tractor is infinitesimally small compared to the weight of snow supported in the bridge. Sir Vivian Fuchs' Trans-Antarctic Expedition (1955–8) encountered similar crevasses after leaving the South Pole, and reported driving down a slope onto the bridge and then up a slope on the far side. The main danger was from small crevasses in the edge of the bridge itself. Elsewhere on the glacier travel can be relatively straightforward provided care is taken to avoid known crevassed areas. Like the rivers of Africa for the early explorers of that continent, the glaciers of Antarctica frequently provide the obvious routes to the interior. Shackleton discovered the Beardmore Glacier that provided a direct route south from the Ross Ice Shelf onto the polar plateau; Scott and his four companions took the same route on their ill-fated trek to the Pole.

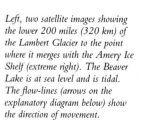

Left, two satellite images showing the lower 200 miles (320 km) of the Lambert Glacier to the point where it merges with the Amery Ice Shelf (extreme right). The Beaver Lake is at sea level and is tidal. The flow-lines (arrows on the explanatory diagram below) show the direction of movement.

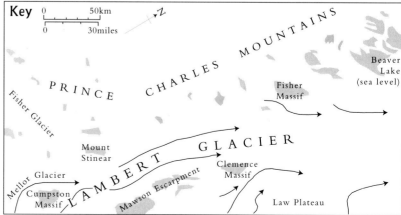

Antarctica
MOUNT EREBUS

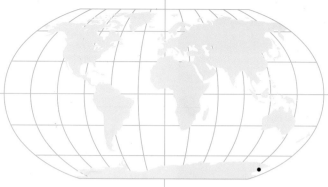

Volcanic sentinel of the pathway to the South Pole.

Mount Erebus lies towards the north of Ross Island at the head of the Ross Sea. Supply ships and aircraft *en route* for the American McMurdo Station, and vessels visiting the historic huts of Scott and Shackleton, will have spectacular views of the mountain in good weather.

O N 9 January 1841 James Clark Ross and Francis Crozier, in their ships H.M.S. *Erebus* and H.M.S. *Terror*, emerged from the pack ice into the open water of the Ross Sea. Three days later they saw a magnificent

mountain range with peaks rising to 8,000 feet (2,438 m), that Ross called the Admiralty Range. The ships continued south following the mountains, and on 28 January 1841 were astonished to see, according to the *Erebus*

Right, a whisp of steam marks the top of one of Antarctica's most famous landmarks, viewed across broken sea-ice.

Facing page, the great Antarctic explorer Shackleton built his hut in view of Mount Erebus.

surgeon Robert McCormick, "a stupendous volcanic mountain in a state of high activity". The volcano was named Mount Erebus, and a smaller extinct cone to the east was called Mount Terror.

In those early days when the science of geology was in its infancy, an active volcano amid the ice and snow of a frozen continent seemed extremely enigmatic. Today's geologists are no longer surprised by such phenomena and can readily explain the presence of volcanoes wherever they occur; the climate is merely incidental. Volcanic rocks are actually common in Antarctica, although most of them are geologically very old and represent activity at times when the continent was not in its present polar position. Volcanic rocks are important indicators of continental movements and can be a useful aid to plotting the ancient wanderings of the continents over the surface

of the globe. The geologically young McMurdo Volcanic Province in the Ross Sea region and the related volcanoes of Marie Byrd Land are simply indicative of recent continental movement in Antarctica.

Mount Erebus on Ross Island forms a beacon for anyone travelling to the area. Inevitably, ascent of the mountain was also a target for the early explorers and mountaineers. During Ernest Shackleton's 1907–9 *Nimrod* expedition a party of six men, led by the 50-year-old Professor Edgeworth David, made the first ascent of the mountain. They reached the 12,448 foot (3,794 m) summit on 10 March 1908. There they found a crater 2,640 feet (805 m) across and 900 feet (274 m) deep, at the bottom of which was a small lake of molten lava. This lake is still present today, and Erebus is one of only three volcanoes in the world that has a long-lived lava lake. During the 1974–5 season a New Zealand geological party descended into the main crater and established a camp there, but the violence of an eruption prevented a further descent into the inner crater. On 17 September 1984 the volcano erupted again, throwing volcanic bombs outside the main crater. It is still the subject of intense geological research.

But it is not only geologists who are drawn to Mount Erebus. Modern explorers cannot resist the temptation to photograph the mountain in all its moods, and the early explorers were compelled to commit its beauty to paper in watercolours. Some of the best of these were the work of Edward Wilson, the doctor and naturalist on both of Captain Scott's expeditions. Botanists too have a special interest in Tramway Ridge, high on the flanks of the mountain, where an area of fumaroles supports a rich vegetation on the warm ground.

Antarctic Volcanoes

THERE are many volcanoes in Antarctica and some of these, particularly the island volcanoes of the Southern Ocean, have been active during the last 200 years. Many eruptions have gone unwitnessed, to be recorded towards the end of activity or after the event, simply because the region is so sparsely populated. Only on Deception Island are there stations within the damage radius of the volcano. Mount Melbourne, just across McMurdo Sound from Ross Island, has fumarole activity on its summit. The combination of steam and sub-zero temperatures has formed many delicate ice pillars, and despite the altitude there is a unique bacterial flora living around the fumaroles. In 1893 the Norwegian C. A. Larsen, making a rare voyage south into the Weddell Sea along the east coast of the Antarctic Peninsula, reported seeing volcanic activity at Seal Nunataks. For many years this distant observation was regarded with scepticism by many geologists, arguing that it was probably a cloud that he had seen, but recent work has found evidence of fumarole activity in the area, so perhaps Larsen was right after all. To witness a volcanic eruption is always an exciting experience, but the stark contrast of molten rock and freezing snow makes an Antarctic eruption all the more spectacular.

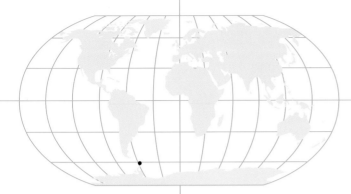

DECEPTION
ISLAND

A natural harbour inside an active volcano.

Deception Island lies off the south coast of Livingston Island in Bransfield Strait. It is one of the South Shetland Islands and is a regular port of call for tour ships and private yachts visiting the Antarctic Peninsula region during the southern summer.

AMONG the South Shetland Islands, Deception Island is shaped like a horseshoe, a roughly circular ridge open to the sea on its southern side. It is an ancient volcano whose central cone has collapsed to form a caldera, now occupied by a crater lake breached by the sea. Many minor vents and centres have since been active around the rim of the caldera and reinforced the shape of the island. The South Shetland Islands are largely volcanic, formed in response to the consumption of oceanic crust along their north-western margin; Bransfield Strait is also volcanic in origin, but formed by sea-floor spreading behind the volcanic arc of the islands. Penguin and Bridgeman islands are also young volcanoes but, unlike Deception Island, they are no longer active.

In 1819 news of the discovery of the South Shetland Islands soon reached the sealers working in South Georgia, and they were quick to exploit the new, more profitable beaches farther south. In the two seasons 1819–20 and 1820–1, the slaughter was so great that the fur seals were virtually extinguished, making further voyages unprofitable. However, Deception Island and its unique situation had been discovered, and the scene was set for its future role in Antarctic exploration and exploitation.

Whalers had been operating in the Southern Ocean in the 18th century, but it was not until 1912 that a shore station, Aktieselskabet Hektor, was established at Whalers Bay on Deception Island. A Stipendiary Magistrate had been appointed by the Falkland Islands government for the 1911–12 and 1912–13 whaling season, who was resident on Deception Island during the seasons until the station closed; whaling from the island ceased in April 1931. During this time a post office operated, and the first stamp was cancelled on 6 March 1913. Deception Island was the site of the first powered flight in the Antarctic on 16 November 1928. Sir Hubert Wilkins made several flights over the Antarctic Peninsula but

did not achieve his goal to fly westward along the coast to the Ross Sea.

A British base was built at Deception Island in 1944, followed by Argentine and Chilean

Right, the curve of the volcano rim at Deception made a perfect, sheltered inner harbour for whaling vessels.

stations in January 1948 and February 1955. On 4 December 1967 a sudden eruption in the north-west corner of Port Foster showered ash and pumice over the Argentine station, and everyone was quickly evacuated onto the nearby Chilean vessel *Piloto Pardo*. Subsequent visits revealed that a new island had been formed by the eruption. Some personnel returned to Deception Island the following season to assess the damage, and the bases were partly re-occupied. Then, in 1969 and again in 1970 there were more eruptions and activity on Mount Pond, near the British and Chilean bases; there were heavy falls of ash over the buildings, and the entire Chilean station collapsed except for the brick-built entrance arch. A lahar, a river of mud, ash, blocks of ice and slurry, triggered by the heat of the eruption, flowed through the British base,

knocking down one wall as it went in and creating a picture window with a fine view of the bay as it went out again. Earthquakes shook the ground and tilted some of the oil storage tanks. Once again it was the *Piloto Pardo* that came to the rescue. Evacuees were grateful that the volcano had chosen to erupt during the summer season while ships were about; if the eruptions had occurred during the winter the story might have been quite different.

Deception is a popular visit for tour ships. Not only is there the spectacular volcano, but swimming is a viable option in the waters of Port Foster, where volcanic activity warms the waters. When the fumaroles are particularly active, the water can be very warm indeed, and krill that swim too close to steam vents on the sea floor can sometimes be found washed ashore, ready cooked.

A party of tourists makes the most of Deception's natural hot springs.

Discovery of Deception Island and the Antarctic Mainland

DECEPTION Island is one of the South Shetland Islands, so-called because they lie in the same latitude south as the Scottish Shetland Islands in the north. The islands were discovered in February 1819 when William Smith in the brig *Williams* was blown off course to the south while rounding Cape Horn, on its way from Buenos Aires to Valparaíso. It is possible that Dirck Gherritz, a Dutchman, may have sighted the islands in 1599, and it is also conceivable that American sealers had known about them for some years but had kept their discoveries secret for commercial reasons. The Admiralty chartered the *Williams* and placed her under the command of Edward Bransfield, with Smith as pilot; they were charged with charting the South Shetland Islands in the 1819–20 Antarctic summer.

They sighted Deception Island on 29 January 1820, and the following day, after crossing Bransfield Strait, they sighted "Trinity Land" (now known as Trinity Peninsula) and became, arguably, the first men to sight the Antarctic mainland. The doubt arises because on 27 January 1820 the Russian Captain Thaddeus von Bellingshausen recorded in the log of the *Vostok* his position as 69 degrees 21 minutes South, 2 degrees 14 minutes West, and described continuous hillocks of ice. He had almost certainly sighted the mainland coast of Dronning Maud Land, but he never described it as land and did not follow the coast.

BOUVETØYA

Bouvetøya can only be reached by sea after a long and frequently stormy voyage. Some private yachts as well as ancient and modern expedition ships have made the voyage, but landing on the island is not always possible.

The world's remotest island lies in the Southern Ocean.

Right, capped with ice and scoured by the strongest winds, Bouvetøya is one of the most inhospitable as well as remotest islands on earth.

Facing page, the brown specks visible along the rough shoreline of the island are seals.

THE most remote island on the face of the globe is Bouvetøya in the Southern Ocean. The thrill of discovery for any explorer is likely to be short-lived, for this is a forbidding place. The island is an active volcano surrounded by steep cliffs, the whole capped by a sheet of ice. The weather is frequently poor, and attempts to land are rarely successful. Anyone marooned on Bouvetøya will feel very lonely indeed; the nearest point of land is the uninhabited Antarctic coast of Dronning Maud Land, 1,050 miles (1,689 km) to the south;

Cape Town, South Africa, lies 1,590 miles (2,558 km) to the north-east.

The island was discovered by the French navigator Jean-Baptiste Charles Bouvet de Lozier on 1 January 1739, while he was searching for a mythical tropical paradise described by another Frenchman, Paulmyer de Gonneville, in the early 16th century. Bouvet was unable to land because of persistent fogs and an ailing crew, and he was forced to retreat. He named his discovery the Cape of Circumcision, believing that he had found the tip of the southern continent. However, he recorded the latitude and longitude of the island and, on his return to France, was able to report that his discovery was not a tropical paradise. Several other explorers, notably renowned navigators such as Captain James Cook and James Clark Ross, subsequently searched for the island, but without success. The main reason for their failure was that they were looking in the wrong place, because Bouvet, like other mariners of his time, had no means of accurately determining longitude. A reliable chronometer, the instrument essential for measuring longitude, had not

was discovered yet again by George Norris on a British sealing expedition. He renamed it Liverpool Island and took possession for King George IV. Norris also named nearby Thompson Island and described it as volcanic in origin. This island has never been seen since and is considered non-existent, but modern opinion suggests that it was destroyed by eruption in 1895 or 1896. Successive visitors redefined Bouvetøya's position, but it was not until 1898–99 that its position was reliably fixed by the German Deep Sea Expedition, at 54 degrees 26 minutes South, 3 degrees 24 minutes East, a very different longitude

Bouvetøya in the 20th Century

THE early history of Bouvetøya was one of discovery, rediscovery and sealing activities; the 20th century history is somewhat different. In 1926 the British Colonial Office sold a whaling lease over Bouvetøya to a Norwegian company, and on 1 December 1927 the Norwegian (Christensen) Antarctic Expedition claimed the island for Norway. The members of this sealing expedition erected a hut, carried out a survey and scientific investigation of the island and also made oceanographic observations in the surrounding waters.

On 23 January 1928 Bouvetøya was formally annexed by Norwegian Royal Proclamation, and on 19 November that year it was announced in the British Parliament that Britain renounced all claim to the island in favour of Norway. In 1928–9 the second Norwegian (Christensen) Antarctic Expedition attempted to establish a meteorological station on the island, but no suitable site could be found and the hut built in 1927 had been destroyed by gales. A third expedition in 1929–30 succeeded in erecting another hut and also photographed the island from the air. In 1955 a South African naval voyage also attempted to establish a meteorological station, but abandoned the project. Several expeditions visited the island and made scientific investigations, but it was not until the 1978–9 season that a small research station was established and occupied for about ten weeks.

been developed and accurate navigation is the first requirement to find this tiny island, just 22 square miles (57 sq km) in area and only 3,068 feet (935 m) high.

For many years after Bouvet's discovery the existence of the island was doubted, but after almost 70 years it was re-discovered in 1808 by two English whalers, James Lindsay and Thomas Hopper. In 1822 the American Benjamin Morrell made the first landing and named it Bouvet's Island in honour of its discoverer. On 16 December 1825 the island

from Bouvet's determination at 28 degrees 30 minutes East.

The wildlife of Bouvetøya is typical of the Southern Ocean but, with so little exposed ground, there are few plants. Penguins and seals are found on and around the island, and in the 19th and early 20th centuries sealing expeditions took fur seal skins and elephant seal oil. Otherwise, human visitors have been relatively few, and nobody has ever wintered on the island. The remotest piece of land on earth seems destined to remain the loneliest as well.

INDEX

ACKNOWLEDGEMENTS

The Automobile Association would like to thank the following photographers, libraries and associations for their assistance in the preparation of this book:

ARDEA LONDON 37 European bison (J P Ferrero), 39 White pelicans, 54/5 El Torcal de Antequera (J Mason), 55 Serrania de Ronda (J Mason), 57 Bajkal seals, 59 Sable (M Iijima), 64 Panda habitat (K & L Laidler), 65 Giant panda (K & L Laidler), 150/1 Meteor Crater (J Mason), 151 Meteor Crater (F Gohier), 154 Mexican free-tail bats (J Mason), 188/9 Duck-billed platypus (P Morris), 192 Waiotapu Champagne Lake (J P Ferrero), 202/3 Mt Erebus (J P Ferrero); **AA PHOTO LIBRARY** 16/17, 17 (E Ellington), 50/1 (R Surman), 63 (P Aithie); **BRITSOCK-IFA LTD** 193 Geyser, Rotorua; **BRUCE COLEMAN LTD** Front cover: Kilamea-Iki Volcano, Back cover: Giant tortoise, 12/3 Strokkur (E Pott), 13 Namaskard (A Price), 18/9 Giant's Causeway (J Murray), 19 Staffa (A G Potts), 20 Mountain aven (J Murray), 21 The Burren (P Clement), 24/5 Waders, Waddensee (J Van de Kam), 25 Sea lavender (J Van de Kam), 32/3 Grand Canyon du Verdon (J Fry), 41 Pasterze Glacier, 42/3 Matterhorn (H Merten), 43 The Alps (H Reinhard), 48/9 Earth pyramids erosion (H Reinhard), 61 Hot springs deposits, Pamukkale (S Prato), 70 Sunderbans Tiger Reserve (G Cubitt), 71 Tiger, Kanha Reserve (G Cubitt), 74/5 Himalayan Range, 75 Everest & Naptse (D & M Plage), 78/9, 79 Mt Fuji, 80/1, 81 Japanese macaque (F Bruemmer), 82/3 Keli Mutu, three crater lakes (A Compost), 84/5 Anak Krakatau (A Compost), 85 Javan rhino (A Compost), 90/1 Great Rift Valley (C Fredriksson), 97 Mt Kenya (M P Kahl), 103a Fairy Tern (F Lanting), 103b Girl, Seychelles (H P Merten), 104 Soalala fishing boat (O Langrand), 106/7 Betsiboka River

(K Wothe), 107b Ring-tailed lemur (C Zuber), 110/1 Namib Desert (G Cubitt), 111 Beetle (C Hughes), 112 Okavango Swamps, 113 Lechwe, Okavango (P Davey), 114/5 Table Mountain (G Cubitt), 115 Table Mountain & Lion's Head (G Cubitt), 116/7 'Big Hole', Kimberley (G Cubitt), 119 Trapper's hut, Myggbukta Bay (O Langrand), 130/1 Niagara Falls, 131b Niagara Falls (J Langsbury), 136/7 Devil's Tower NM (M P L Fogden), 137 Mitten Rocks, Monument Valley (J Cowan), 139 Dinosaur NM (J Foot Productions), 140/1 Yosemite NP (H Reinhard), 141 Yosemite NP (K Gunnar), 142/3 Checkerboard Mesa (B & C Calhoun), 148a Zabrisk Point, Death Valley (B & C Calhoun), 148/9 Poppies, Mojave (B & C Calhoun), 152/3 Petrified log, Blue Mesa (M Freeman), 162/3 Napali coast, 170/1 Amazon rainforest (L C Marigo), 171 Red Piranha (J Burton), 174 Giant tortoise (U Hirsch), 184/5 Ayers Rock (P R Wilkinson), 185 The Olgas (D Austen), 191 Tasmanian devil (J Cancalosi), 201 Glacier, Elephant Island (E Pott); **ROBERT ESTALL PHOTOGRAPHS** 132/3 Moncton Tidal Bore, 133 Hopewells Rocks; **MARY EVANS PICTURE LIBRARY** 131a Bob Leech, Niagara Falls; **DR J E FRANCIS** 120/1 Evening hills, 121a Leaves & cones, 121b Cone-shaped tree; **L GOULD/OXFORD SCIENTIFIC FILMS** 159a Sargasso weed; **ROBERT HARDING PICTURE LIBRARY** 49 S Tyrol Dolomites, 66/7 Yangshuo limestone towers, 69 Yellow River, 76 Nomads' tent, yak & mountains, Tibet; 83 Keli Mutu crater lakes, 144/5 Grand Canyon; **HEDGEHOG HOUSE NEW ZEALAND** 194/5 Franz Josef Glacier, 196/7, 197a Blue Whale (Tui de Roy); **HUTCHINSON LIBRARY** 68/9 Quinghai, Upper Yellow River, 73 Demra Bustee, Bangladesh, 100/1 R Zaire, 101 Huts, R Zaire, 164/5, 165 Pitch Lake, Trinidad; **BAERBEL LUCCHITTA, US GEOLOGICAL SURVEY, FLAGSTAFF, AZ** 200/201 Lambert Glacier;

NATURAL HISTORY PHOTOGRAPHIC AGENCY 9 Northern Lights (B & C Alexander), 26 Crowberry (M Garwood), 27a Spider's web (L Campbell), 27b Bog asphodel, 34 Tengmalm's owl (R Sorensen & J B Olsen), 35 Sumava NP (A Nardi), 36/7 Forest, Bialowieza NP (D Woodfall), 44 Mt Vesuvius crater (A Nardi), 52 Apollo butterfly (W Zepf), 91 Oldonyo Lengai (C Ratier), 92/3 Lesser flamingos (M Harvey), 93 Lesser flamingos (R Tidman), 99 Black rhino (J Shaw), 107a Panther chameleon (K Schafer), 109 Victoria Falls (P Pickford), 117a Diamonds (P Johnson), 117b Diamond miners (A Bannister), 122/3 Collared lemming (A Williams), 123 Grey/timber wolf (S Krasemann), 143 Bryce Canyon NP (J Shaw), 146 Giant sequoia (D Middleton), 156 Manatee (Norbert Wu), 166 Canaima NP (K Schafer), 167 Angel Falls (K Schafer), 169 Capybaras (K Schafer), 172 , 173 Iguaza Falls (M Wendler), 175 Marine iguana (W Paton), 178/9 Tierra del Fuego NP (T Mead), 179 Tierra del Fuego, Lago Alto (G Dixon), 182/3 Boulder opal (O Rogge), 186 Coral/Red grouper (B Wood), 187 Great Barrier Reef (R & D Keller), 189 Short-tailed echidna (K Griffiths), 190/1 Cushion plants (ANT), 198/9 Ross ice-shelf (P Johnson); **NATURE PHOTOGRAPHERS LTD** 31 Salin de Girund (R O Bush), 96/7 Elephants & Mt Kilimanjaro (M E Gore), 98/9 Burchell's zebra (H Van Lawick), 102/3 Aldabra (P Roberts); **T OLIVER** 28/9 Cevennes NP, 29 Orchids; **S OSOLINSKI/OXFORD SCIENTIFIC FILMS** 138/9 Dinosaur NM; **R PACKWOOD/OXFORD SCIENTIFIC FILMS** 94/5 Ruwenzori Mountains; **PICTURES COLOUR LIBRARY LTD** 22/3 , 23 Dover, White Cliffs, 67 Reed Flute Cave, 108/9 Livinstone, Victoria Falls, 118/9 Angmasalik, 145 Grand Canyon, Colorado River, 147 Grants Grove, Sequoia NP, 157 Everglades, 176/7, 177 Llamas, Atcama Desert; **PLANET EARTH PICTURES** 14/5 Fair Isle, 15 Puffins, 105 Coelacanth, 158 Common freshwater eel, 159b Elvers, 180/1 Marianas Trench, 181 Deep sea Pseudoscopelus, 197b Krill, 199 Ice cliffs, 204/5 Deception Island; **E ROBINSON/ OXFORD SCIENTIFIC FILMS** 135 Horseshoe crabs; **ROYAL ONTARIO MUSEUM** 128/9 The Burgess Shale Quarry (D Collins), 129 Anomalocaris Canadensis fossil (B Boyle); **ROYAL TYRRELL MUSEUM /ALBERTA COMMUNITY DEV** 126/7 Dinosaur PP, 127 Dinosaur fossils; **SPECTRUM COLOUR LIBRARY** 40/1 The Grossglockner, 60/1 Pamukkale, 153 Petrified Forest, Arizona; **FRANK SPOONER PICTURES** 72/3 Cyclone disaster, Bangladesh; **B STONEHOUSE** 203 Shackleton's hut, 205 Hot springs, Deception, 206/7, 207 Bouvetøya; **TONY STONE IMAGES** Back cover: Iguaçu Falls; **S TURNER /OXFORD SCIENTIFIC FILMS** 95 Mountain gorilla; **T ULRICH/ OXFORD SCIENTIFIC FILMS** 134/5 Horseshoe crabs; **WORLD PICTURES** 86/7 Aswan, R Nile; **ZEFA PICTURES** Back Cover: Canyonland NP, Utah, 8 Indian Ocean, 10/1 Fjord, Norway, 11 Naeroyfjord, Norway, 30/1 Horses, Camargue, 33 Verdon Gorge, 38/9 Danube Delta, hay pyramid, 45 Mt Etna, 46/7, 47 Castellna Grotto, 51 Thessalien Metéora, 52/3 Picos de Europe, 56/7 Bajkal Sea, 58/9 Taynir Tundra, 62/3 Dead Sea, 77 Tibet, Kula Kangri, 80 Hot springs, Beppu, 88/9 Algeria, dunes, 124/5 Caribou, 124 Migrating caribou, 155 Carlsbad Caverns, 160/1, 161 Hawaii, lava flow, 163 Surfer, 183 Mine worker & opal, 195 Fox Glacier.

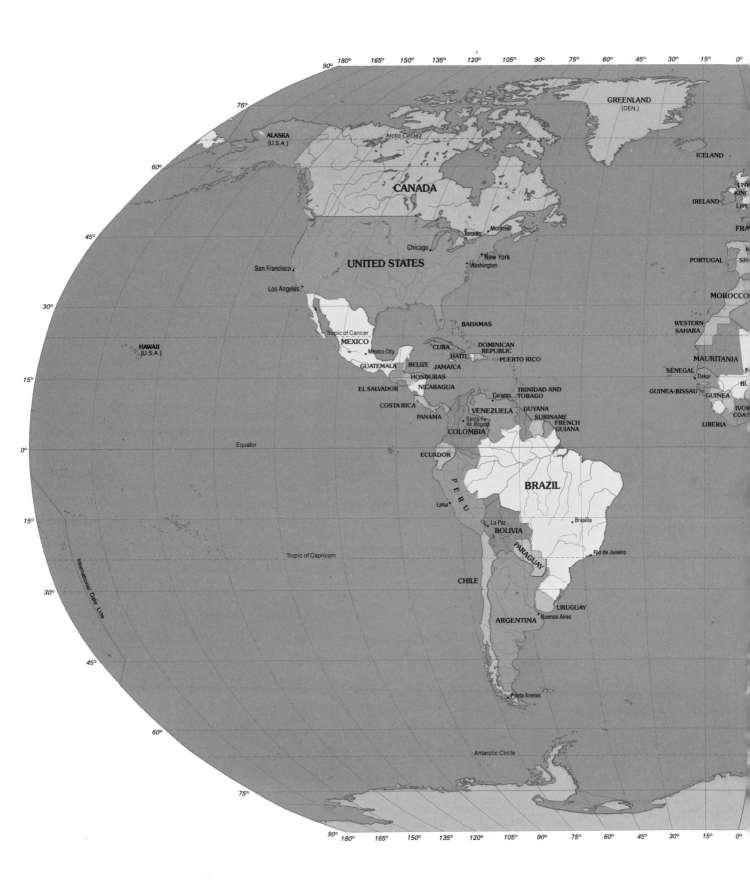

90°　180°　165°　150°　135°　120°　105°　90°　75°　60°　45°　30°　15°　0°

75°

GREENLAND
(DEN.)

ALASKA
(U.S.A.)

Arctic Circle

ICELAND

60°

UN
KIN

IRELAND

CANADA

Lon

FRA

45°

Montreal
Toronto

PORTUGAL　SP

Chicago

UNITED STATES

New York
Washington

MOROCCO

San Francisco

30°

Los Angeles

WESTERN
SAHARA

Tropic of Cancer

BAHAMAS

HAWAII
(U.S.A.)

MEXICO

CUBA

DOMINICAN
REPUBLIC

MAURITANIA

Mexico City

15°

HAITI

PUERTO RICO

SENEGAL

GUATEMALA　BELIZE　JAMAICA

Dakar

BU

HONDURAS

GUINEA-BISSAU　GUINEA

EL SALVADOR　NICARAGUA

TRINIDAD AND
TOBAGO

IVOR
COAS

Caracas

COSTA RICA

LIBERIA

0°

PANAMA

VENEZUELA　GUYANA

Santa Fe
de Bogotá

SURINAME
FRENCH
GUIANA

Equator

COLOMBIA

ECUADOR

P
E
R
U

BRAZIL

15°

Lima

Brasília

La Paz

Tropic of Capricorn

BOLIVIA

International Date Line

PARAGUAY

Rio de Janeiro

30°

CHILE

URUGUAY

Buenos Aires

ARGENTINA

45°

60°

Punta Arenas

Antarctic Circle

75°

90°　180°　165°　150°　135°　120°　105°　90°　75°　60°　45°　30°　15°　0°